A GOOD DEATH?

To family and friends for their ongoing support

A Good Death?
Law and Ethics in Practice

Edited by

LYNN HAGGER
University of Sheffield, UK

SIMON WOODS
University of Newcastle, UK

ASHGATE

Published by
Ashgate Publishing Limited
Wey Court East
Union Road
Farnham
Surrey, GU9 7PT
England

Ashgate Publishing Company
110 Cherry Street
Suite 3-1
Burlington, VT 05401-3818
USA

www.ashgate.com

British Library Cataloguing in Publication Data
A good death? : law and ethics in practice. -- (Medical law and ethics)
1. Right to die. 2. Right to die--Law and legislation.
3. Terminal care. 4. Terminal care--Law and legislation.
5. Palliative treatment--Moral and ethical aspects.
I. Series II. Hagger, Lynn. III. Woods, Simon, 1961-
344'.04197-dc23

Library of Congress Cataloging-in-Publication Data
Hagger, Lynn.
  A good death? : law and ethics in practice / By Lynn Hagger and Simon Woods.
      p. cm.
  Includes bibliographical references and index.
  ISBN 978-1-4094-2089-7 (hardback) -- ISBN 978-1-4094-2090-3 (ebook) 1. Terminal care--Law and legislation--Great Britain. 2. Palliative treatment--Great Britain. 3. Terminal care--Moral and ethical aspects. 4. Medical ethics--Great Britain. I. Woods, Simon, 1961- II. Title.
  KD3410.E88H34 2012
  344.4104'197--dc23

                                                                    2012022044

ISBN 9781409420897 (hbk)
ISBN 9781409420903 (ebk – PDF)
ISBN 9781409472551 (ebk – ePUB)

Printed and bound in Great Britain by the
MPG Books Group, UK.

Contents

Notes on Contributors

Daniele Bryden qualified in medicine from the University of Manchester. Her postgraduate training was in intensive care medicine and anaesthesia, during which she was an Intensive Care Society Travelling Fellow, undertaking research at the North West Injury Research Centre. In 2001, she moved to Sheffield Teaching NHS Foundation Trust where she works as a Consultant in Intensive Care Medicine and Anaesthesia. Daniele sits on a NICE Technology Appraisal Committee, is the national Critical Care Tutor (Anaesthetics) for the Royal College of Surgeons of England and is an editorial board member of the British Journal of Anaesthesia. In 2004 she completed a qualifying LLB (Hons) from the Open University fulfilling a long-term interest in the law and its operation within medicine. She completed a Master's in Medical Law and Ethics at the University of Glasgow in 2008, and concentrates her non-clinical time on areas where her legal and ethical knowledge is utilized such as doctors in training, resource utilization within the NHS and providing education and support regarding end of life care to anaesthetic and intensive care unit professionals. Daniele also teaches legal aspects of medical practice to undergraduate medical and law students at the University of Sheffield.

Lynn Hagger became a legal academic with lectureships at the Universities of Manchester, Liverpool and currently Sheffield after careers in social work and legal practice. She has taught administrative/public law, contract, environmental and European law but now teaches torts and specializes in medical law and ethics. In parallel with her academic career, she has been involved in the NHS for over 20 years, mostly as a non-executive director of acute hospital boards. She was Chairperson of Sheffield Children's NHS Foundation Trust for nine years and currently serves as a Non-executive Director at Leeds Teaching NHS Trust. This has provided opportunities to focus her research on how the law might strengthen the rights of the individual citizen in the field of health care law and policy. She is part of a network of multidisciplinary research collaborators in the national and international context.

Vincent Kirkbride qualified in 1988 and was trained in paediatrics in London, Canada and Australia. He was a Medical Research Council lecturer with the Perinatal Brain Research Group at University College Hospital in London, a Perinatal Fellow at the Hospital for Sick Children in Toronto, and a Senior Neonatal Fellow at Monash Medical Centre, affiliated to the University of Monash, in Melbourne. He was appointed as a Consultant in Neonatal Medicine at Royal Hallamshire Hospital in Sheffield (now the Sheffield Teaching NHS

Foundation Trust) in 1997. He has postgraduate qualifications in epidemiology, business management and health care ethics and law. He has been a member of the Appraisals Committee of the National Institute for Health and Clinical Excellence since 2007. He is also Chair of the Sheffield Teaching Hospitals NHS Foundation Trust's Clinical Ethics Committee. He is interested in the ethics and economics of intensive care, and also neonatal transplantation and end of life care.

James Munby was called to the Bar in 1971 and made a Queen's Counsel in 1988. In 2000 he was appointed a Judge of the High Court, sitting in both the Family Division and the Administrative Court. In 2009 he was appointed Chairman of the Law Commission and a Lord Justice of Appeal.

Jeff Perring is a Director of the Paediatric Critical Care Unit and a consultant paediatric intensivist at the Sheffield Children's NHS Foundation Trust. Following his medical qualification at the University of Liverpool, Jeff trained in anaesthesia within Merseyside and the North-East of England. He took time out during this training to focus on neonatology, researching into the metabolism of premature infants before specializing in paediatric intensive care. He became a consultant at Sheffield Children's Hospital in 2002. In 2007, he completed an MA in Healthcare Ethics and Law at the University of Manchester with a dissertation entitled 'Gross negligence manslaughter and understanding medical disasters'.

Christoph Rehmann-Sutter is Professor of Theory and Ethics in the Biosciences at the University of Lübeck in Germany and Visiting Professor at the BIOS Centre (a centre for the study of bioscience, biomedicine, biotechnology and society) at the London School of Economics. After training in molecular biology at the Biozentrum Basel, he studied philosophy and sociology in Basel, Freiburg i.Brsg. and Darmstadt, where he obtained his PhD in 1995. Between 1996 and 2009, Christoph was Head of the Unit of Ethics in the Biosciences at the University of Basel in Switzerland, first as Assistant Professor from 2000 and then as Professor of Philosophy from 2007. He was appointed by the Swiss government as Chair of the Swiss National Advisory Commission on Biomedical Ethics in 2001 and served until 2009. His research focuses on phenomenological and hermeneutic methodology for bioethics, genomics, synthetic biology, hematopoietic stem cell donation by children to siblings and end of life issues.

John Erik Troyer is the Deputy Director and Research Council's United Kingdom Academic Fellow in the Centre for Death and Society at the University of Bath. He received his doctorate from the University of Minnesota in Comparative Studies in Discourse and Society and began working at the University of Bath's Centre for Death and Society in 2008. He is a co-founder of the Death Reference Desk website (www.deathreferencedesk.org) and his first book, *Technologies of the Human Corpse*, will be published by the University of North Carolina Press in spring 2012.

Sabine Vanacker is a lecturer in English at the University of Hull. Her research and teaching interests centre on twentieth-century literature, with a particular interest in crime fiction, the literature of migration and women's writing. She has published on Agatha Christie, Sara Paretsky, Patricia Cornwell and Sue Grafton, and is currently preparing *The Crime Fiction of P.D. James: Death and the Melancholic Detective*, for Palgrave. With Dr Catherine Wynne she is co-editing a critical collection, *The Cultural Afterlives of Arthur Conan Doyle and Sherlock Holmes: Representations Across the Media*, also for Palgrave. She is married to David Kelly, an IT professional; their daughter Isabel Vanacker-Kelly suffered from Tay-Sachs Disease and died in 2004, aged four.

Simon Woods is a senior lecturer and Co-Director at the Policy, Ethics and Life Sciences Research Centre (PEALS), University of Newcastle (UK). PEALS is an ethics 'think tank' involved in research, teaching and public engagement on the ethical and social implications of the life sciences and medical ethics. Simon spent ten years as a clinical cancer nurse and holds Bachelor and Doctoral degrees in philosophy. He is a member of several national and international ethics committees and provides training to members of such committees. Simon is involved in empirical and conceptual research in bioethics and publishes on a range of issues including those concerning the end of life.

Foreword

Lynn Hagger and Simon Woods, in producing this impressive collection of essays, offer a book that will be of enduring value. The volume, constructed around discussions of 'the good death', demonstrates not just the emotional, ethical and legal difficulties, but also the levels of complexity and nuance faced by patients, patients' families, practitioners, policy-makers and scholars when considering questions concerning the end, and ending, of life. Of particular importance is the careful focus the contributors give to the subtlety and vastness of pertinent problems, to practical difficulties implicated in discussions of the good death, and to the peculiarly human and social uncertainties that make many of these debates so intractable. The range of perspectives, expertise and experience that the following ten chapters draws together is remarkable. And the great variety of matters unified around attempts to understand and explain what the good death might imply shows quite what a broad and complex area end of life law and ethics have become.

It almost goes without saying that the questions explored in this book are of considerable concern, both socially and as areas of study. Citizens and scholars alike keep a keen eye on practical developments and possibilities, both within this jurisdiction and overseas. High profile 'right-to-live' and 'right-to-die' cases constantly hit the headlines. The effects of globalization and international travel, be it to receive treatments or to practise 'death tourism', are a source of ongoing scrutiny, comparison and controversy. Understanding what constitutes good palliative care and how its provision is assured remains a central concern, and raises further questions of how such care should be funded. And continuing philosophical disputes about when life begins and ends add greater complications.

It is clear that the exploration of such problems cannot usefully be considered by isolated academics, especially those who would shelter themselves and their inquiry within the comfortable bounds of individual disciplines. Rather, expertise afforded by distinct disciplines – most obviously in this volume law and philosophy – must be brought into a much wider, cross-disciplinary discourse that is open, too, to those who work formulating, implementing and challenging policy, to practitioners in a variety of fields, and, of course, to the people who are at the heart of the matters – patients and those close to them. Although our views and experience will differ, the question of the good death has obvious relevance to all of us. Exploration requires continued, mutually informative dialogue between groups such as those represented in this volume, with a careful awareness of developments in policy and practice.

Whilst, therefore, arguments on end of life law and ethics can be, and often are, based more on abstracted concepts than on concrete situations, practical questions and experience must assume their rightful place. This book is rich in conceptual and principled analysis, but is the richer still for including contributions from authors who practise in law and health care. Their experience affords crucial insights into the possible roles and limits of the state in relation to the good death, both in assuring and delimiting people's enforceable rights, and in the practical possibilities and problems in a socially funded health care system. And, perhaps most importantly, the final chapter of the book, by Sabine Vanacker, demonstrates the depth and complexity involved in understanding what is meant by the good death.

The editors of this book are to be congratulated for compiling an excellent collection of chapters. The theme of the good death draws them all together, whilst simultaneously demonstrating the immensity of the challenge that we, as a society and as individuals, face. Whether their final resolution is found to be a private or a public matter, the distinct questions explored below are all intensely personal, and it is their intensity that underwrites the debates' importance. The book makes clear how fragile choice can be, how distant certainty often is, and thus how difficult it is to establish what would be the right course of action even with the benefit of hindsight. The collection says a lot about end of life, but it also says a good deal about bioethical debate and discourse at its best: the mix of contributors and the accessibility of the markedly different contributions is a great credit to contemporary scholarship.

John Coggon
Reader in Law
University of Southampton

Preface

This book was born out of a successful UK Clinical Ethics Network Conference, 'The Value of Life, the Value of Death', held at Sheffield Hallam University in May 2008. A key factor in its success was the multi-disciplinarity of the speakers and the participants. Scholars of law, philosophy and other disciplines came together with clinicians and families to listen and debate end of life issues. The theoretical frameworks of law and ethics are important in these discussions, but how these are reflected in practice, nuanced to particular and often complex circumstances, is equally significant.

During the Conference, the story of a child's life and death, given by her parents, was particularly compelling. They described the care Isabel received towards the end of her life. Hearing the family's voice had a powerful effect upon those in attendance. Isabel's story will be no less moving and instructive to academics, students and health professionals; to all readers of this collection. It was this contribution especially that made us think that a book drawing on this experience, and others, would offer invaluable insight into the examination of the 'good death'. Although the 'good death' is a well-worn phrase, there is nevertheless value in an ongoing reflection upon this ideal from a variety of perspectives. The editors, an academic lawyer and a philosopher, have also drawn upon their experiences as professionals within health care, as members of ethics committees and as educators of health professionals, to steer their own and others' contributions towards some of the key issues within debates about end of life care.

There are many people to whom we are very grateful for their support as we wrote this book. Particular thanks are owed to the organizers of the conference and contributors to the book. None of this would have been possible without the emotional and practical support from our family and friends.

Chapter 1

Introduction

Lynn Hagger and Simon Woods

Health professionals and lay people alike will easily recognize that virtually all clinical practice engages with ethical issues and that decisions at the end of life have a poignancy and significance of their own. While medicine endeavours to cure and ameliorate disease, its powers are finite and the same level of skill and concern must also apply to those it cannot save. Clinical judgment, policy and practice must be mindful of public interest but must also conform to the law and professional ethical guidance. The latter, however, often presents a potentially bewildering array of sources for the health professional and at times such guidance may stand at odds with public opinion and sit uncomfortably with the intuitions of the clinician in the workplace. Health care law rarely provides a definitive guide to good clinical practice but it does stipulate certain boundaries: for example, in most jurisdictions, one may never directly take a life even at the request of the person whose life it is, although hastening death as a foreseen but not directly intended consequence of a clinical decision is permitted.[1] While some law does provide very detailed and thoughtful reflections,[2] much is left to clinical judgment.

Health professionals are keen to ensure that they are engaged in the highest possible standards of clinical practice because, in addition to their professional codes, most are also driven by strong personal ethical beliefs. It might be suggested that a health professional's intuition will suffice when a difficult ethical dilemma is presented. However, the role of intuition might rightly be questioned not least because some people may be moved to justify abhorrent actions on this basis. Intuition can constitute a significant obstacle for proper debate but opened to reasoned scrutiny it can be an important starting point for reflection and can form the basis of principles to guide action. Health professionals do want guidance that

---

1   *R v Bodkin Adams* [1957] CLR 365, 375 per Devlin J and affirmed in *Airedale NHS Trust v Bland* [1993] AC 789, 867. Since Devlin J's ruling, palliative care specialists have emphasized that shortening life is not a routine consequence of properly managed analgesia and sedation as there has been significant advance in the use of opiates and sedatives such that the routine and titrated use of these substances does not have a lethal 'double effect': see Hanks, G., Cherny, N.I., Christakis, N.A., Fallon, M., Kaasa, S. and Portenoy, R.K. (eds). 2011. *The Oxford Textbook of Palliative Medicine*. 4th edn. Oxford: Oxford University Press.

2   See e.g. the Mental Capacity Act 2005 and its accompanying Code of Practice on the steps to be taken to enable decision-making and *R (Axon) v Secretary of State for Health (Family Planning Association intervening)* [2006] EWHC 37 (Admin).

has an intuitive 'feel' and accords with their manner of dealing with problems in everyday practice, some of which may require speedy resolution. It is highly likely that intuitions form out of the experience of moral encounters throughout life and contribute to the development of a personal moral code whether this has involved an explicit discussion of philosophical perspectives or not.

Understandably, there may be resistance to examining closely one's belief system, which may be thought adequate for the task of effecting clinical decision-making. Close examination is challenging both intellectually and emotionally but, arguably, 'an unexamined reason is no reason at all'.[3] As Woods argues,[4] in considering ethical dilemmas, it is necessary to adopt a reflexive and deliberative approach to the morally relevant features that ought to be taken into account. Reflective deliberation enables the individual to map the moral domain, establish the 'givens' of moral action and provide skills that help to make them habitually sensitive to the interests of others. This is a process that can be carried out individually, or collectively, on an ongoing basis to improve moral understanding. The hope is that these chapters, each taking a different view of what constitutes a 'good death', will contribute to this reflective process and contribute theoretically and practically to its diverse aspects.

The scope of the book is not exhaustive. A single text could not hope to address comprehensively this complex topic and the coverage of relevant law, ethics and other theory is more than adequately dealt with elsewhere.[5] The topics and themes of this book are not novel but there is value in having ongoing discourse and reflection on the nature of the good death from a wide range of perspectives. The collection brings together legal scholars, philosophers, social scientists, practitioners and parents to present aspects of the multifaceted story of the good death, often drawing from personal experience, but certainly offering different accounts from within policy, practice and academic analysis.

The order of the chapters follows a natural structure though there are connections and cross-references, debates and leitmotifs across many of them.[6] A key theme visited in several of the chapters is the vexed question of patients'

---

3   See Pattinson, S.D. 2006. *Medical Law and Ethics*. London: Sweet and Maxwell, at p. 3.

4   See e.g. Woods, S. 2007. *Death's Dominion: Ethics at the End of Life*. Berkshire: Open University Press: McGraw-Hill Education.

5   See e.g. McLean, S.A.M. 2007. *Assisted Dying: Reflections on the Need for Law Reform*. Abingdon: Routledge; Mason, K. and Laurie, G. 2010. *Mason & McCall Smith's Law and Medical Ethics*. 8th edn. Oxford: Oxford University Press; Jackson, E. 2009. *Medical Law: Texts, Cases and Materials*. 2nd edn. Oxford: Oxford University Press; Gillon, R. 1986. *Philosophical Medical Ethics*. Chichester: Wiley Medical Publications; and Hope, T., Savulescu, J. and Hendrick, J. 2008. *Medical Ethics and Law: The Core Curriculum*. 2nd edn. Oxford: Churchill Livingstone Elsevier.

6   The house style of using non-specific pronouns should be noted apart from Chapter 2, which is based upon a keynote presentation, and chapters 9 and 10, which address specific individuals.

rights to shape and determine their own good death, the challenge of determining a patient's best interests when they lack the capacity to express them, and the role and responsibility of health professionals within this domain.

The legal framework that circumscribes patients' rights and professionals' duties in general and, specifically, in relation to end of life matters, is set out by Lord Justice Munby in Chapter 2. Munby LJ provides an invaluable context for the discussion in the following chapters of what constitutes a good death. The chapter explores the limited rights patients have in relation to their health care whether from the private or public law perspective and how this can be at odds with what patients want for themselves, what ethical argument may support and what professional values may deny. As far as end of life matters are concerned, the main focus of the discussion is on treatment decisions and how these are reached with respect to incompetent and competent individuals. What emerges is that patients may refuse treatment but cannot, apparently, demand it, which the Court of Appeal's instructive ruling in Burke[7] seems to make clear. In this case, Leslie Burke, diagnosed with a progressive degenerative condition, cerebella ataxia, sought a court declaration that he should be given clinically assisted nutrition and hydration (CANH) when he reached the 'locked-in' stage of his degenerative condition. At this phase, he would be aware of his surroundings but unable to communicate. Inter alia, he did not want his doctors to decide whether to give him CANH on the basis of his best interests at that time, but for this to be agreed in advance. It is worth reminding ourselves of the eloquent exposition of Leslie Burke's human rights vis-à-vis those of the medical profession given by Munby J (as he then was) in the High Court ruling: '[…] his willingness to use the law as a forum for discussing and determining controversial ethical issues; the use of human rights discourse to stress fundamental moral values and principles, such as human dignity'.[8] His reasoning was more in accordance with the aspirations many academic medical lawyers have for the law. However, the Court of Appeal did not agree and advocated restricting the role of the judiciary to using traditional common law approaches.

The Burke decision was in relation to CANH but Munby LJ's view appears to be that this would extend to other forms of treatment, including routine interventions. He believes that, in practice, patients' wishes and those of the doctors caring for them will coincide and offers practical solutions where they do not. Beyond these propositions, Munby LJ suggests that lawyers are not best placed to resolve the issue. This is not surprising given the resource implications of allowing patients to demand treatment but if this could be restricted to routine interventions at the end of patients' lives the resource implications might well be self-limiting. Given the

---

7   *R (Burke) v General Medical Council (Official Solicitor and others intervening)* [2005] EWCA Civ 1003, [2006] QB 273.

8   Veitch, K. 2007. *The Jurisdiction of Medical Law.* Aldershot: Ashgate.

government's apparent commitment to improving end of life care,[9] the economic aspects of such choices should be specifically addressed as part of the debate, a point that Vincent Kirkbride's Chapter 6 begins to address.

In discussing the good death, it may be implied that the issues under scrutiny have their origin in the certainty of death. Though death is unconquered and thus remains inevitable for us all, the point at which we enter '[t]he undiscover'd country, from whose bourn no traveller returns'[10] has become a matter of more and not less uncertainty. Though we are beyond the Victorian anxiety that burial may precede death we are nevertheless faced with new concerns and related anxieties that death may go unrecognized. In Chapter 3, Daniele Bryden questions whether the determination of death has been given serious enough consideration as it has often been delegated to the most junior member of the medical team. This is not to cast radical doubt on whether death can be easily established in routine cases but rather to show that dying, in some contexts, has become so medicalized through technology that the point of death becomes less determinate, more constructed and thus more open to dispute. The common intuition that death entails a lifeless body is challenged by the sight of the pink and ventilated body of a 'brain-dead' person. In such circumstances the person may be judged either living or dead by fiat of law, regarded as good as dead in the eyes of loved ones, yet still viewed as theologically alive. Many are agreed that death is a process in which breathing, cardiac function and brain activity gradually decline to a point of irreversible cessation. However, medical technology has, to a degree, made each of these functions separable, and, in the case of heart and lung function, individually sustainable and increasingly reversible. The result of such interventions has been that some individuals exist in an ambiguous state between life and death, seemingly alive yet not meaningfully alive. This has very significant implications for medical practice and the public interest there is in facilitating the good death. In some instances, the deployment of life-sustaining technologies has had quite profound implications for the quality and viability of donor organs to the extent that there is seen to be a conflict between the best interests of the patient and the best interests of others who might benefit from the death of the patient. Bryden argues that there is a role for the law in this context through legal recognition of the status of the 'pre-dead' individual together with clarification and guidance on the appropriate measures that may be taken, including the withdrawal and withholding of treatment and the possible active preparation for organ retrieval before the person becomes a corpse.

There is certainly some overlap with the concerns raised by Bryden and Munby LJ's contention that there ought to be greater recognition of the rights of patients to demand active intervention in terms of treatment and care and perhaps especially in advance of terminal care when a person may have lost the capacity to decide for themselves. For Bryden this would mean that a person might anticipate their

---

9   Department of Health. 2008. *End of Life Care Strategy: Promoting High Quality Care for All Adults at the End of Life*. London: Department of Health.

10   Shakespeare, W. *Hamlet*, Act 3, Scene 1, 55–87. London: Penguin Classics.

'managed' death and provide consent for the active management of their body in order to maximize the success of organ donation. Any such changes to legal frameworks would have to include an expanded concept of 'best interests' perhaps most usefully in the light of ethical debates around autonomy.

For some, the question of whether the person is alive or dead is seen to take precedence over whether the body is alive or not. One kind of personhood essentialism has led those who favour the close alliance of cognitive capacity and personal autonomy to regard these as the essential criteria as to whether others have moral responsibilities to the breathing body. Such considerations have led to arguments that the person to whom we have moral obligations should be considered as distinct from the human body. There is no doubt that there is a moral tension, so difficult to resolve, when we are confronted with a breathing patient who shows no other sign that there is a life being lived 'from the inside'. Many of the authors in this volume make direct or implicit reference to this dilemma but often with particular reference to Bland[11] and Schiavo[12] whose ambiguous state of existence tested judicial wisdom, familial love and public concern. In Chapter 4, John Troyer describes the attempts to define away the dilemmas embedded within such cases through the efforts of the Personhood Movement in the USA who are coordinating a state-by-state effort to define the 'person' in law.

A central goal of the Personhood Movement is to protect the earliest forms of human life and thus prevent the destruction of, in their view, the human person when first formed. However, the definitions of the person proposed in revisions to state legislation also have profound implications for the end of life. The 'person' is thus a living human being irrespective of 'heartbeat or brain activity', prompting Troyer to ask: 'how does a person die?'[13] The idea that a good and dignified death may be achieved by the well-judged removal of life-sustaining treatment in order to allow nature to takes its course is regarded by the Christian fundamentalists behind the Personhood Movement as a secular interference in a divine domain. Troyer leaves readers with the chilling thought that should attempts to change the law in the US be successful then the 'good death' may become unconstitutional.

The strength of feeling that underpins those who take a faith inspired stance on end of life matters is bolstered by the no less sincere secular concerns regarding end of life care and the diagnosis of death. If, as Troyer argues, changes to law as proposed by the Personhood Movement would prove too stringent for medicine, then Bryden's proposals face the opposite but no less significant problem of allowing medicine too much discretion in determining who is alive and who is dead. Any major change to the laws regarding end of life decisions are likely to face opposition from the diversity of opinion within society.

---

11   *Supra* n. 1.

12   See e.g. *Robert Schindler et ux v Schiavo et al.* [2005] Supreme Court of Florida, Case SC05-497. Available at: http://www6.miami.edu/ethics/schiavo/pdf_files/032605_ Fla_S_Ct_Order.pdf [accessed 29 August 2011].

13   Chapter 4 of this volume.

The challenges of making end of life decisions for the living but non-autonomous individual stand in stark contrast to the claims made for assistance in dying by autonomous individuals seeking a version of their own good death. In Chapter 5, Christoph Rehmann-Sutter and Lynn Hagger turn to individual rights of autonomy in end of life matters and consider the contrasting approaches taken to assisted suicide by two different jurisdictions, England and Wales (hereafter England for expediency) on the one hand and Switzerland on the other. The issue of suicide tourism from the UK to Switzerland has achieved considerable attention through a number of high-profile cases. In these, the potential application of the Suicide Act 1961 to relatives of English residents who have helped their loved ones to travel to Switzerland in order to utilize the services of Dignitas, one of the organizations established there to assist the suicides of both nationals and visitors from abroad, has caused concern.

Assisted suicide is unlawful under section 2(1) of the Suicide Act 1961 but the Director of Public Prosecutions (DPP) has considerable discretion as to whether a prosecution should be commenced once the evidential test is met under public interest considerations. Although the current guidelines promulgated by the DPP provide greater clarity for those who help their loved ones to commit suicide, complete certainty remains elusive. The chapter sets out the case for a more permissive regime in England and Wales and considers whether this should extend as far as the proposal for suicide centres. In a comparative analysis of the Swiss and domestic legislation, Rehmann-Sutter and Hagger make the case for a cautious and considered adoption of the Swiss approach into English law.

From a consideration of the potential for a legally recognized right to the deliberate foreshortening of life, Chapter 6 turns to a consideration of the mechanisms through which policy and law impose quite different controls on the means by which people achieve a good death. Vincent Kirkbride observes that, though a common consensus allows for a degree of individual choice in the manner of one's passing, many are exercising their choice by insisting upon every potential means to extend life. The question posed in this chapter is whether the cost of life-extending treatment should be immune to considerations of cost? Kirkbride's answer is a resounding 'no' but, on his own admission, it is a position that is difficult to sustain in territory that has become infused with an inflammable mixture of political debate and public opinion. There are several strands to his analysis, not the least of which is the role that public faith in new medical technologies is playing in creating inflated expectations for cure and life extension. Spending in the last years and months of life is rising exponentially with little of this spend going to palliative care. For most patients such an investment returns a meagre life extension with little regard to the quality of that life; on this account the good death becomes a prolonged dying.

Kirkbride also decries the inadequacy of the economic evaluations that are used to inform policy. There seems no escaping from the fact that economic evaluations result in the pricing and commodification of life rather than providing a source of evidence in an informed policy debate. What policy debate there is also seems mired by political machinations. For example, the government's proposed cancer drug policy seems to offer a counter-intuitive form of economic exceptionalism for those with life-limiting conditions, a strategy that defies the austerity being applied in all other domains of public spending. Kirkbride is also concerned about the inequities between disease groups with a disproportionate attention given to cancer rather than other chronic, life-limiting diseases. There is no shying away from the hard choices but Kirkbride concludes with an appeal to the public's sense of fairness calling for an informed and inclusive public consultation on these profound issues.

In Chapter 7, Simon Woods takes a philosophical approach from which to explore some of the key questions implicit in the other contributions to this volume. What do we mean by a good death? Can such a historically and culturally relative concept be rendered meaningful in the context of contemporary health care? What is permissible in order to secure a good death for oneself? Woods' analysis begins with an account of the emergence and evolution of palliative care setting out the aspirations for achieving the good death as envisaged within the philosophy of palliative care. In the second part of the chapter, he explores some of the candidate 'good-making' parameters, of not only the good death but also the 'good life'. Woods argues that talk of such parameters or qualities is meaningful and that there is a significant consensus that underpins their validity as components of a good death. Where there is disagreement this is usually in terms of what may be directly 'engineered' in order to achieve a good death as opposed to what may only be achieved indirectly as side effects or unintended consequences of actions instigated with other goals in mind, but that may also steer a person to the least worst death.

The final trio of chapters turns our attention to the sad but necessary truth that death is no respecter of age or innocence. In Chapter 8, Lynn Hagger provides an analysis of the law as it pertains to end of life decisions for children. The law should determine how parental responsibility should be exercised in relation to the end of life treatment of younger children where there is disagreement with health professionals. It may not be appropriate to accede to parents' wishes that their child is kept alive at all costs, understandable though that is. To do so may inflict on these children an unnecessary level of suffering that only delays their inevitable demise. Conversely, there may be circumstances where health professionals are not in the best position to judge what is truly in some children's best interests.[14] In discussing some of the cases that have explored children's best interests in end of life situations, Hagger argues that health professionals and the courts must listen very carefully to the views of parents in the manner exemplified in the final two chapters.

Where children are competent, or should be seen to be, it may be legitimate to allow them to refuse life-saving interventions when these are perceived by that child to be unduly burdensome or against their deep and long-held beliefs. This

---

14 Baines, P. 2008. Death and *best* interests. *Clinical Ethics*, 3(4), 171–5.

can mean that, for them, they can have the good death that they want. It is when a consensus about this position cannot be achieved that the law has a clear role. The key message from Hagger is that if there is scope for individuals to shape their own end then the same rights of autonomy should apply to the child whose burgeoning capacity for self-determination demands to be heard.

In Chapter 9, Jeff Perring provides the experienced clinician's perspective on managing the end of life care of the child with severe disability or progressive disease. Using two fictionalized case studies, Perring draws together an amalgam of cases from his clinical experience to paint a picture of the journey that many families and their health carers have travelled together. He explores potential models for decision-making in a context that seems to invite disagreement and where the possibility for bitter dispute hangs in the air. However, Perring manages to distil an approach to caring for children in such extreme circumstances that is compassionate, professional and caring. It allows the family the support and dignity to feel that they have preserved something of their power to pursue the best interests of their child to the very end.

The final chapter of the collection is Isabel's story. Written by her parents, it gives the testimony of a brave individual, born with Tay-Sach's disease, a rare genetic condition that would diminish her capacities and foreshorten her life. There are many important messages in this short piece and not the least of these is the sense one is given of Isabel as a person in her own right, living her own life and, through the power of relational causality, influencing the lives of others who encounter her. Even though she was eventually profoundly impaired, Isabel never lost her humanity or the human ability to reciprocate love and affection. The reader is offered another account of caring for the terminally ill child from a parent's perspective. Isabel's parents talk of their experiences with different health professionals, in hospital and in their own home. They combined professionalism, compassion, and basic human care to enable Isabel to live the best possible life in the midst of her family. The idea of the good death is of course complex but nobody can read this account and continue to believe that the good death is but a fiction.

What is clear from this book is that there is no single conception of the good death but rather there are many commonly shared and cross-cutting concerns regarding the possible and permissible means of achieving it. The expertise and know-how that has grown alongside the palliative care specialism has meant that symptoms of refractory disease can often be well controlled without fear of foreshortening life. However, there is no doubt that there is a strong and consistent desire to advance the personal autonomy of patients and to limit the restrictions of the state in terms of the active management of the dying process. This includes determining the place of death and the form of care. The latter may be active treatment or the proactive bringing about of death. Realizing such aspirations enhances the possibility that an optimal number of us will be able to experience a good death.

Chapter 2

The Right to Demand Treatment or Death[1]

James Munby

Introduction

My purpose here is to look at the legal landscape for health care decision-making in England and Wales with particular reference to decisions made at the end of life. The chapter commences with private law, which sets out doctors' duties and the limits to patients' expectations. This is followed by an exploration of the effects of the Human Rights Act 1998 on the rights of patients. The final discussion turns to particular cases where end of life matters have been subject to the scrutiny of the courts. It is within this context that the variety of perspectives on what constitutes a 'good death' discussed in the following chapters must be considered.

I refer to the *legal* landscape. I am by training and profession a lawyer, and whatever competence I may have in that regard I certainly have no competence in the many other fields – ethics, morality, philosophy, theology, medicine and public administration – that in this context also have such important roles to play.

Let me start with what lawyers call private law – the body of law that regulates relations between private individuals.

Private Law

Private law traditionally draws a fundamental distinction between acts and omissions: penalizing or providing financial remedies against those who commit wrongful *acts* but, generally speaking, providing no remedy for omissions, however wrongful or even immoral. It follows that there is, generally speaking, no duty to go to the help of someone who is in trouble, that is, no duty to rescue. As a great judge once expressed it,[2] the Biblical parable of the Good Samaritan translates, in law, into no more than the duty not to injure one's neighbour. Some legal systems have what are sometimes called 'Good Samaritan laws', though ours does not. The law is stark. As another great judge expressed it: I may see a baby drowning in a pond only 6 inches deep, who I could rescue at no greater risk to

---

1   This chapter is drawn from a paper given at the UK Clinical Ethics Network National Conference, 'The Value of Life, the Value of Death', in 2008. References have been added but the paper is otherwise unrevised apart from minor editorial changes.

2   Lord Atkin in *Donoghue v Stevenson* [1932] AC 562, 580.

myself than getting my shoes wet, yet if I pass by and the baby drowns I commit no actionable legal wrong. Morality and ethics may rightly have some damningly stringent things to say about me, but the law says nothing.[3]

What goes for the layman goes also for the doctor. I talk, of course, about the law; the General Medical Council, which regulates the practice of doctors, might have something rather different to say as a matter of professional ethics. A doctor who passes a road traffic accident and carries on, not stopping to provide medical assistance to those whom he can see so obviously need it, commits no wrong in the eyes of the law.[4] So far as the law is concerned, he has no duty. His only duty, derived from the Hippocratic Oath, is ethical or professional.[5]

Positive duties to care for someone (duties that give rise to liability for omissions as well as acts) arise only if one has assumed the burden of caring for them. There need be no contract; indeed typically there is not. Thus parents owe a positive duty of care to their helpless children, just as someone does if they take an elderly and helpless relative into their home to look after them. If someone allows their baby or bedridden grandmother to starve to death in their house, they commit a very serious wrong. Indeed, they commit a criminal offence: manslaughter if they were merely feckless or incompetent;[6] murder if they intended death or really serious harm.[7]

Exactly the same principle applies to doctors. A doctor who has assumed care for someone as their patient thereby assumes, in the eyes of the law, a duty to take positive steps where these are appropriate: the doctor becomes liable not merely for acts that injure but also for injurious omissions. The lawyers have some puzzling questions to resolve in determining at precisely what point a doctor does assume the care of someone as their patient. The Good Samaritan doctor who stops to tend the injured at the roadside does not, it would seem, assume such care and is therefore liable only if he makes matters worse, but it is not necessary to ponder that matter further here. Proceed on the basis, then, that the doctor has assumed the care of someone as their patient. What then? In particular, to what extent can the patient then tell the doctor what to do?

Traditionally, the law has tended to limit the right of patient choice. In the first place, the predilection of the law – uncontroversial in an earlier age when laymen tended to defer to professional expertise but more controversial today when such deference has in large part gone – is to assume that, because the professional person knows best, they must be left to decide matters by reference to professional skill and, perhaps more controversially, by reference to professional judgment. This is

---

3   Stephen, J.F. 1883. *A History of the Criminal Law of England.* Vol. 3. London: Macmillan, p. 10; see also Stephen, J.F. 1883. *A Digest of the Criminal Law: Crimes and Punishments.* London: Macmillan, at p. 147.

4   *Capital and Counties plc v Hampshire County Council* [1997] QB 1004, 1035.

5   *Re F (Mental Patient: Sterilisation)* [1990] 2 AC 1, 77–78.

6   *R v Stone* [1977] QB 354.

7   *R v Gibbins and Proctor* (1919) 13 Cr App R 134.

because medicine, like the law, involves not merely technical knowledge and skill, the manual dexterity of the surgeon, for example, but also judgment. Medicine, like law, is as much a matter of art as of science. The tenderness that in this regard the law extends to doctors is not unique to their profession. Barristers, for example, are required by their professional code of conduct to decide themselves which witnesses to call on behalf of their clients and what questions to ask them: they are forbidden to delegate that responsibility to their client. However much the client may want a particular line of questioning to be followed, in the final analysis the barrister must decide in accordance with their professional judgment what questions to ask and must not follow a line of questioning that they think to be inappropriate even if the client insists.

Secondly, the law traditionally tests professional performance by reference to the law of negligence: a professional person is not negligent if they adopt an approach acceptable to a respectable body of professional opinion (even if it is not in accordance with majority professional opinion) and exhibit the standard of care and skill to be expected of an averagely competent practitioner (even if it falls short of the standards of the leaders of the profession). This is the principle enshrined in the *Bolam* test.[8]

Thirdly, the law does not compel doctors to act in a manner contrary to personal conscience. There is, therefore, a gap between what the law permits a doctor to do and what the law requires a doctor to do (performing an abortion is an obvious example),[9] although the gap is probably quite narrow. Just as a barrister cannot refuse to act for a racist or a rapist because of who or what they are, the doctor in an Accident and Emergency department cannot refuse to treat the racist or the rapist injured by their enraged or terrified victim.

Finally, the law recognizes the reality that mutual trust and confidence are usually central to any effective relationship between a professional person – doctor or lawyer – and their patient or client. Where there is a breakdown in that mutual trust and confidence, or where conscience properly intervenes, the time has come for the parting of the ways. But this does not mean that the doctor can simply abandon their patient, least of all where treatment has started and the patient is dependent upon continuing professional care. Then, surely, the doctor's obligation is to do their best to assist their patient in finding another doctor who will be able to work together with the patient.

I will consider in due course where all this leaves the patient, particularly in the kind of situation envisaged in the questions posed at the beginning, but next I must turn to deal with what lawyers call public law – the body of law that regulates relations between private individuals and the state or public bodies.

---

8 *Bolam v Friern Hospital Management Committee* [1957] 1 WLR 582.
9 S. 4, Abortion Act 1967.

Public Law

Until the Human Rights Act 1998 came into force in October 2000, there were, generally speaking, few rights as against the state or public bodies, at least if one uses the word 'right' in its correct legal sense as the correlative of 'duty'.[10] There were many freedoms and liberties, most fundamentally the freedom to say and do whatever one wanted unless someone could point to some specific statute or other law prohibiting it, but the state owed people few legally enforceable duties. Indeed, at common law, the state owed no or virtually no legally enforceable duties at all. In a looser sense, the state owed people many duties, not least the duty to protect them from foreign invasion and the duty to enforce the law and the Queen's Peace, but most such duties were enforceable only politically through the ballot box, though individuals holding public office and under specific duties could in appropriate circumstances be compelled to perform their duty by what was known as an order of mandamus and might even in limited circumstances be held liable in damages if it could be shown that they had been guilty of misfeasance in public office. These, however, are details. The state was under few duties; certainly the state was under no duty to provide medical care or treatment.

Before October 2000, if it was to be said that the state owed some duty it was usually to be found, if at all, in statute. Now the welfare state, and the National Health Service in particular, were created by statutes which, on casual reading, might be thought to create all kinds of duties enforceable, in the case of the NHS, by patients. Ever since the earliest days of the NHS the governing legislation has contained a provision imposing on the relevant Minister the obligation to maintain an NHS whose functions are then described in positive, if very general, terms. But these obligations barely transmit through to the individual patient in terms of any specific duty or obligation enforceable by the patient. There are four reasons for this.

In the first place, the most general and aspirational provisions in the legislation have been held not to be justiciable at all. Their enforcement has been held to be a matter not for judges but rather through political means: censure of the Minister in the House of Commons or, ultimately, by the electorate through the ballot box.

Secondly, and prior to the coming into force of the Human Rights Act, the public law remedies available to a disgruntled patient for alleged breaches of the statutes regulating the NHS were few and usually, at least from the patient's perspective, unsatisfactory. Assuming that the Minister or other decision-maker had acted in a manner falling within the letter of the statute, a decision could be successfully challenged only if the patient could establish that it was what the

---

10   See Hohfeld, W.N. 1943. *Fundamental Legal Conceptions as Applied in Judicial Reasoning by Wesley Newcomb Hohfeld*, ed. by D. Campbell and P. Thomas. Newhaven, CT: Yale University Press.

lawyers call *Wednesbury* unreasonable,[11] that is, a decision so unreasonable that no competent and conscientious decision-maker could have arrived at it. That, as will be appreciated, is a very high test to have to satisfy, and it rarely is.

Thirdly, the courts were, and are, particularly reluctant to intervene to investigate, let alone overturn, policy decisions, especially those having to do with the allocation and prioritization of resources, whether financial or human, which are, almost inevitably, always in short supply. There are, I think, two reasons for this judicial reticence. One is that the courts simply lack the relevant expertise and, even more pertinently, lack the relevant information. The point is, at root, a very simple one. A judge, whether he is sitting to hear cases in the Family Division about children in the care of the local authority, or sitting in the Administrative Court to hear cases where patients challenge decisions denying them particular forms of medical treatment, is necessarily concerned with and focusing upon that child or that patient. The judge knows nothing about the scores, perhaps hundreds, of other children in the care of the local authority, or the hundreds, perhaps thousands, of other patients under the care of the bodies who commission health care services on their behalf. How, then, can the judge fairly and justly, that is, fairly and justly to all who may be affected directly or indirectly by his decision, decide how resources are to be allocated? The other reason is that, since there will always be priorities to be assessed and evaluated, and, at the sharp end, excruciatingly difficult decisions to be made, there are powerful arguments for saying that these are, in the final analysis, matters to be decided by public officials who are democratically accountable and not by unelected and, in that sense, unaccountable judges.

Fourthly, and finally, the courts have tended to hold that even where the relevant legislation does contain justiciable duties and obligations, they are enforceable by public law remedies and give no private law remedy. The practical effect of this is that the patient cannot obtain an order requiring the NHS to provide a specific form of treatment for him, nor damages if it fails to do so. At best, and then only if he can show that the relevant decision was irrational, all that the court is likely to be able to give the patient is an order quashing the earlier decision and requiring the decision-maker to come to a fresh and lawful decision. What the court cannot do, except in the very rare case where there is literally only one possible lawful decision, is to take the decision itself or to tell the original decision-maker what his new decision is to be. These are matters that Parliament has left to those whom it has identified as the relevant decision-makers in the legislation in question. They are not matters for the judges. In public law cases the duty of the judge is to ensure that those who have to take these decisions act lawfully and rationally; it is no part of the judge's function to take the decision himself.

Thus one can appreciate the difficulties in the way of a patient who, before the coming into force of the Human Rights Act, demanded some particular form

---

11   *Associated Provincial Picture Houses Ltd v Wednesbury Corporation* [1948] 1 KB 223.

of treatment. If the doctor was willing to provide it, and if, where the patient was being treated by the NHS, the relevant NHS body was willing to allow the doctor to give the treatment, then there was no problem. But if either the doctor was professionally unwilling to give the treatment or the NHS was unwilling to fund the treatment, the patient was unlikely to have any ultimately very effective judicial remedy.

There were many examples of this in the books. But perhaps the most open and obvious manifestations of the consequences of the legal framework described here were, first, the existence of waiting lists that were for all practical purposes immune to judicial scrutiny and that, in the long run, were addressed only when the political pressures became too strong for politicians to ignore, and, secondly, the not infrequent refusal of the NHS to provide forms of treatment that were said to be either experimental or lacking in cost effectiveness or that were treated for other reasons as having a lower priority than other forms of treatment.[12]

That is not to say that these are matters that necessarily ought to have been decided by judges. On the contrary, there are very powerful arguments for saying that they should not be. For it must be for democratically elected politicians, and in the final analysis for the electorate, to decide whether the NHS budget is to be X or Y, X per cent or Y per cent of government spending, just as it must be for democratically accountable public officials to say, for example, whether limited resources are more appropriately spent on hip replacements, heart surgery or gender reassignment procedures, on drugs that are tried, tested, comparatively cheap and can help the many, or on drugs that are still experimental, very expensive and likely to help only the few.

How has the Human Rights Act 1998 affected matters? On one level its impact has been revolutionary, for, as its name might suggest, it has for the first time imposed on the state and on public bodies (of which, of course, the NHS is one) legally enforceable duties, including in some circumstances legally enforceable duties to act, to take positive steps. Although much of the European Convention for the Protection of Human Rights and Fundamental Freedoms to which the Human Rights Act now gives effect in our domestic law consists of negative prohibitions of what the state may not do it also imposes a number of positive obligations on the state and on public bodies. Where the Human Rights Act applies, therefore, a claimant may be able to bring legal proceedings to compel some state body to act and, where it has failed to act, to obtain damages for its omission to act.

On the other hand, the Human Rights Act is not a panacea for disgruntled patients. In the first place, perhaps unsurprisingly given the Convention's age and provenance (it dates from 1950 and marked the determination of the European family of nations that never again would we suffer the monstrosities of the Nazi regime), it focuses on political rather than on social or economic rights. Secondly,

---

12   See e.g. *R v Cambridge Health Authority ex p B* [1995] 1 WLR 898; and *R v North West Lancashire Health Authority ex p A* [2000] 1 WLR 977.

as an eminent judge has pointed out,[13] it is accordingly not concerned with distributive justice, that is with the allocation of social or economic resources. Thirdly, the extent of the positive duties imposed on the state by the Convention is limited. As another judge has commented,[14] although the Convention may protect the pursuit of happiness it does not confer a right to happiness. In all these respects the Convention is to be contrasted with other and more recent constitutional documents, the Constitution of South Africa, for example.

In the context of medical treatment there are three provisions of particular relevance in the Convention. Article 2, which protects the right to life, Article 3 which protects the right not to be subjected to inhuman or degrading treatment, and Article 8, which enjoins respect for private and family life, can each, in principle, be engaged in cases where access to medical treatment is in issue. But in day-to-day practice they are all of rather limited impact.

Let me give two examples. In a case called *D*,[15] it was held by the European Court of Human Rights in Strasbourg that the United Kingdom would be in breach of Article 3 if it returned a terminally ill man suffering from HIV-AIDS to a developing country where he would not be able to receive in his final days the treatment that he was receiving from the NHS. Implicit in this, it might be thought, is the proposition that the NHS would have been acting in breach of Article 3 if, having begun such treatment, it then decided to withdraw it from D without good reason. On the other hand, *D* was an extreme case where D was very close to death. Later cases show that Article 3 provides no protection for HIV-AIDS sufferers not as close to death as D was, even if it is clear that their prospects, and in the fairly near future, will be fatally prejudiced by removal to a country without the facilities provided by the NHS.

The other case is *Watts*,[16] where an elderly lady was, in the view of her consultant, suffering considerably by being placed on an unduly long waiting list for hip replacement surgery. Neither domestic law nor the Convention gave her any remedy. So far as domestic law was concerned, the issue was one of the prioritization and allocation of resources, and thus a matter for those administering the NHS, not for the courts. So far as the Convention was concerned, her life was not in peril, so Article 2 was not engaged; her treatment – or, rather, her lack of treatment – by the NHS was not inhuman or degrading, although her condition was painful, so Article 3 was not engaged; and Article 8 gave her no remedy, because it does not provide a remedy where the issue is the allocation and prioritization of resources. The Convention, remember, is not really concerned with problems of

---

13   Lord Hoffmann in *Matthews v Ministry of Defence* [2003] UKHL 4, [2003] 1 AC 1163, para 26.

14   Lord Walker of Gestingthorpe in *R (Razgar) v Secretary of State for the Home Department* [2004] UKHL 27, [2004] 2 AC 368, para 34.

15   *D v United Kingdom* (1997) 24 EHRR 423.

16   *R (Watts) v Bedford Primary Care Trust* [2003] EWHC 2228 (Admin), on appeal [2004] EWCA Civ 166, (2004) 77 BMLR 26.

distributive justice. In fact, Mrs Watts had a remedy, but not in domestic law or under the Convention; rather under the law of the European Union (EU).

What she wanted was to have her hip replacement carried out in another member state but at the expense of the NHS. Ultimately she succeeded, following a hearing in the European Court of Justice,[17] on the ground that the United Kingdom's refusal to pay for the cost of her treatment abroad involved a breach of the provision in the European Treaty protecting the right of those who provide services in a member state to provide those services throughout the Union. So Mrs Watts succeeded, though only because the United Kingdom was acting in breach not so much of her rights as in breach of the rights of the French doctors who were prepared to treat her! Now *Watts* is, of course, a very important decision in relation to EU law, but it is equally revealing in illustrating the limited impact the Convention has had in relation to medical law, except, that is, as *Burke*[18] demonstrates, where it is Article 2 that is in play.

It is against this background that we have to consider the extent to which patients can demand what is to happen to them at the end of their lives.

Can Patients Demand What is to Happen?

It might be thought that the answer is fairly simple, at least where the patient has been accepted as such by the treating doctor. It might be said that, having assumed responsibility for the care of his patient, the doctor is obliged to provide appropriate treatment. After all, if it becomes apparent to a parent that their baby is seriously ill and seemingly in need of medical attention, and they nonetheless fail to call for medical assistance and their baby dies, they may find themselves prosecuted for manslaughter. Can the doctor be in any better position?

There are, of course, no simple or easy answers. If a terminally ill patient contracts some independently life-threatening condition that is in principle amenable to medical (or surgical) intervention, is the doctor to intervene in order to gain for his patient a few more days, weeks or months of life? It all depends. A principle common to theological analysis and American jurisprudence is that there is no obligation on the doctor to resort to what are called heroic or extraordinary measures; but that raises almost as many questions as it answers. And what if the treatment is experimental, or very expensive, or has only a relatively modest prospect of being successful? And what part is to be paid in all this by the patient's wishes and feelings, particularly if the patient is competent and demanding the treatment in question?

---

17   *R (Watts) v Bedford Primary Care Trust and another (Case C-372/04)* [2006] Q.B. 667.

18   *R (Burke) v General Medical Council (Official Solicitor and others intervening)* [2005] EWCA Civ 1003, [2006] QB 273.

These are very wide and difficult questions, to which the law at present does not provide any very clear or compelling answers. But let us narrow the focus somewhat to consider measures of a 'routine' nature. Leaving aside the obvious lawyer's quibble, 'what is a routine measure?', and recognizing, as we must, that many surgical measures that would nowadays be considered routine can be very expensive, sometimes very expensive, problems still remain.

It may be helpful at this point to consider the patient whose life depends upon artificial ventilation or upon artificial hydration and nutrition. It might be thought that the case is simple. The techniques are fairly straightforward, and once in place do not necessarily involve ongoing medical involvement. They also address what some might think are the basic necessities of life, air, water and food, and not really medical treatment at all.

But in *Bland*[19] the House of Lords told us that they are nonetheless to be treated, as a matter of law, as medical procedures to which the ordinary principles of medical law apply. Moreover, it is clear as a matter of law that there can be circumstances where it is lawful to withdraw, or not to put in place in the first instance, both artificial ventilation and artificial hydration and nutrition. *Bland* is clear authority in the case of artificial hydration and nutrition and an earlier decision of the Court of Appeal in *J*[20] is equally clear authority in the case of artificial ventilation.

What, then, are the principles that apply in such a case and what role, in particular, does the patient's own decision play?

Now *Bland* and *J* were both cases of patients who lacked capacity not merely to decide what should happen to them but even to express their own wishes and feelings: Anthony Bland was in a persistent vegetative state (PVS) and had made no advance declaration. J was a baby. The law's answer is that the decision should be taken by reference to their best interests. That has always been the test in relation to children, in respect of medical as in respect of all other decisions taken on their behalf. And that is now the test in relation to adults, for although in *Bland*, as earlier in *Re F*,[21] the House of Lords had espoused the principle that an adult patient's best interests were to be assessed in accordance with the *Bolam* test, that view was rejected by the Court of Appeal in *Re S*[22] in 2000. *Bolam* may mark out the boundaries of what is capable of being in the patient's best interests (though even that limitation has not been applied rigorously in subsequent cases), but, in the final analysis, 'best means best', and what is best is to be determined by the judge and not by the doctor.

Now this is all very well, but it produces both a puzzle and a difficulty. The puzzle is to identify what part resource issues play in evaluating best interests, or, putting the point perhaps more accurately, what the proper solution is, and

---

19   *Airedale NHS Trust v Bland* [1993] AC 789.
20   Re *J (A Minor) (Wardship: Medical Treatment)* [1991] Fam 33.
21   Re *F (Mental Patient: Sterilisation)* [1990] 2 AC 1.
22   Re *S (Adult Patient: Sterilisation)* [2001] Fam 15.

who decides, when the treatment identified as being in the patient's best interests carries with it severe, or perhaps very severe, resource implications.

The traditional answer that the law provides is clear, but not particularly reassuring for the patient. The judge sitting in the Family Division (or now in the new Court of Protection) and exercising the best interests jurisdiction has the right and the responsibility of deciding and declaring what the patient's best interests require, but he lacks jurisdiction to compel either the doctor or the NHS to implement his decision.[23] Compulsion can be applied only in public law proceedings in the Administrative Court and even there only against the NHS, as a public body (which a doctor is not), and only if grounds for compulsion exist either under domestic public law (which is rarely the case) or where the Convention and the Human Rights Act provide a remedy. If a judge cannot compel the doctors to act, neither can the patient.

The difficulty is that the courts have traditionally, and not merely in the medical context, been reluctant to conceptualize and analyse what is meant by a person's best interests. Best interests are something that can be identified once a particular forensic process has been gone through, a process that importantly involves drawing up a 'balance sheet' comparing and contrasting the benefits and advantages of what is proposed as against the disbenefits and disadvantages,[24] but they are not to be defined or categorized in the abstract.

In *Bland* the House of Lords identified the futility of what was being done as the justification for holding its discontinuance to be lawful. *Bland* was in truth a comparatively simple case from this point of view. Once it had been held that there could be circumstances in which it was lawful to discontinue artificial hydration and nutrition (and that was the fundamentally important ruling in *Bland*), then the rest followed quite easily, for if ever there is a case where such a decision can be justified it must be a case of PVS. But, PVS apart, there may be comparatively few cases where such treatment can properly be categorized as futile. In what other categories of case can life-preserving treatment be withheld or withdrawn? Earlier authorities[25] had suggested, for example, that artificial ventilation could be withheld where to resort to it would impose an intolerable burden on the patient. But in *Burke* intolerability was rejected as a test or criterion for the withholding of treatment.[26] What, then, is the test? The answer appears to be best interests pure and simple.

The one thing that is clear (and it might be thought to carry with it some very important implications) is that a patient's best interests are not to be determined having regard only to medical matters. Best interests are not the same as medical

---

23   *A v A Health Authority* [2002] EWHC 18 (Fam/Admin), [2002] Fam 213.

24   *Re A (Male Sterilisation)* [2000] 1 FLR 549, 560.

25   *Re J supra* n. 19, 55.

26   *Burke supra* n. 17, paras 62–63.

best interests; they embrace a much wider range of personal, social and general welfare considerations.[27]

Now this is not perhaps very helpful to the doctor, who, although he can evaluate his patient's best medical interests (for that, after all, is his expertise and his calling), may be in no particularly advantaged position to assess his patient's best non-medical interests. And it is this that in part, no doubt, underlies the rejection of the *Bolam* test as being determinative in such cases and why it is, in the final analysis, the judge rather than the doctor who determines what is in truth in the patient's best interests, having regard both to his best medical interests and his best non-medical interests.

Thus far this chapter has been considering the patient who lacks the capacity to make decisions or to express their wishes and feelings. What of the capable patient?

Traditionally, and at least rhetorically, it is to the principles of patient autonomy and self-determination that one turns at this point. First given classical form in 1914 by Cardozo J, one of the greatest of all American judges,[28] and repeated and emphasized in this country in the 1980s by one of its greatest judges, the late Lord Scarman,[29] this is a principle of the very first importance. In the first place it enunciates a moral, ethical, social and legal principle of the very greatest magnitude, implicating directly, and in the most personal and intimate contexts, the principle, now enshrined in the Convention as in almost all other human rights instruments, of the essential dignity of all human beings. As the Strasbourg court made plain in *Pretty*,[30] dignity and autonomy are core values permeating the Convention.

Secondly, it reflects one of the abiding realities of the human condition, that different people placed in the same situation may have very different views as to what they would want and as to where their best interests truly lie. How can a doctor, however experienced and humane, know what is truly in his patients' interests? He knows better than a layman can ever do what is medically good (or not) for them, and having advised and treated many patients in a situation that may be novel for them, but with which he is familiar, he can no doubt give them much practical advice as to how patients tend to think before, during and after the treatment he has in mind for them, but that is really the limit of his professional abilities. In the final analysis only the patient can know what is best, not for patients generally but for themselves individually.

Thirdly, it protects us, at least negatively, against paternalism, whether professional paternalism or paternalism at the hands of the state. A competent adult patient, or a patient who although now incapable expressed his decision whilst

---

27 *Re A supra* n. 23, 555.

28 *Schloendorff v Society of New York Hospital* (1914) 105 NE 92.

29 *Sidaway v Board of Governors of the Bethlem Royal Hospital and the Maudsley Hospital* [1985] AC 871, 882.

30 *Pretty v United Kingdom* (2002) 35 EHRR 1, para 65.

competent in a valid advance directive, has an absolute right to refuse treatment, for reasons that are good or bad or for no reason at all, and even at the price of his own life.[31] To this principle there are, in our law, no exceptions whatever. So, allowing a juxtaposition, a competent prisoner can starve himself to death in prison[32] rather than serve his sentence and a competent adult woman in labour can refuse to submit to a Caesarean section,[33] even if the probable or even inevitable consequence will be both her own death and the death of her child.[34] Thus, when it comes to consenting to medical treatment it is the patient, if adult and having capacity, rather than the doctor (or indeed the judge) who has the last word. This, surely, is as it should be.

It is at this point that we are confronted with the fundamental question: are there circumstances in which the competent adult patient can demand to be treated or to be given a particular form of treatment? Does the principle of patient autonomy, of patient self-determination, entitle the patient not merely to refuse consent to treatment X being offered by the doctor or to choose between treatments X and Y, both of which are being offered by the doctor; does it entitle him to demand treatment Z, which is not being offered by the doctor?

Expressed in these wide terms the answer can only be no, for a variety of reasons that should by now be apparent. But are there circumstances where the answer might be yes? There may be, though the circumstances in which the point might arise in theory are probably sufficiently narrow as to make it unlikely that they would in fact arise in practice.

Let us at this point return to *Burke*. The Court of Appeal stated that:

> [...] where a competent patient indicates his or her wish to be kept alive by the provision of ANH any doctor who deliberately brings that patient's life to an end by discontinuing the supply of ANH will not merely be in breach of duty but guilty of murder. Where life depends upon the continued provision of ANH there can be no question of the supply of ANH not being clinically indicated unless a clinical decision has been taken that the life in question should come to an end. That is not a decision that can lawfully be taken in the case of a competent patient who expresses the wish to remain alive.[35]

Now that seems clear enough, which is why, it might be thought, Mr Burke in fact achieved by the proceedings much the greater part of what he had wanted. And in practical terms it is not much affected by what the Court of Appeal then added:

---

31   *Re MB (Medical Treatment)* [1997] 2 FLR 426, 432.

32   *Secretary of State for the Home Department v Robb* [1995] Fam 127.

33   *St George's Healthcare NHS Trust v S* [1999] Fam 26.

34   As an aside, it may be noted that many jurisdictions in the US adopt a less absolutist approach, recognizing that there may be narrow circumstances in which the refusal of a competent patient to submit to medical treatment can be overridden.

35   *Burke supra* n. 17, para. 53.

There is one situation where the provision of ANH will not be clinically indicated that is not relevant to Mr Burke's concern but which received a disproportionate amount of attention in this case. In the last stage of life the provision of ANH not only may not prolong life, but may even hasten death. Unchallenged evidence from Professor Higginson illustrated the latter proposition. At this stage, whether to administer ANH will be a clinical decision which is likely to turn on whether or not it has a palliative effect or is likely to produce adverse reactions. It is only in this situation that, assuming the patient remains competent, a patient's expressed wish that ANH be continued might conflict with the doctor's view that this is not clinically indicated.

As we understand Munby J's judgment, he considered that in this situation the patient's wish to receive ANH must be determinative. We do not agree. Clearly the doctor would need to have regard to any distress that might be caused as a result of overriding the expressed wish of the patient. Ultimately, however, a patient cannot demand that a doctor administer a treatment which the doctor considers is adverse to the patient's clinical needs. This said, we consider that the scenario that we have just described is extremely unlikely to arise in practice.[36]

So the patient's wishes are not determinative in the limiting case.

Explicit in the Court of Appeal's reasoning is the protection afforded to a patient in Mr Burke's situation by Article 2 of the Convention, although the Court of Appeal were also clear that this would in any event have been the position at common law:

So far as ANH is concerned, there is no need to look far for the duty to provide this. Once a patient is accepted into a hospital, the medical staff come under a positive duty at common law to care for the patient [...] A fundamental aspect of this positive duty of care is a duty to take such steps as are reasonable to keep the patient alive. Where ANH is necessary to keep the patient alive, the duty of care will normally require the doctors to supply ANH.[37]

So at the end of the day, at least where artificial hydration and nutrition is concerned, the question would seem to come back to the question of whether the doctor has assumed the responsibility of caring for his patient.

The Court of Appeal, it may be noted, did not much analyse the issues that might arise in relation to resources. In *Burke*, as previously in *Bland*, the analysis focused more on the treating doctor's obligations, and the treating doctor's clinical judgment, than on the resource implications for the NHS. Perhaps there are in reality no major resource implications in the provision of artificial hydration and nutrition to someone in Mr Burke's situation, though the same can hardly be said

---

36 *Ibid.* paras. 54–55.
37 *Ibid.* para. 32.

of the potential resource implications of keeping Anthony Bland alive for what the medical evidence indicated might have been many years.

How far can one extrapolate, as it were, from the Court of Appeal's analysis in relation to artificial hydration and nutrition to other forms of treatment in end of life cases? Here we enter very difficult territory. For reasons already indicated, it is suggested that it is indeed the patient, and not the doctor, who is in the best position to decide where his best interests lie and to decide what medical treatment is in his best interests, and doctors and judges must have the humility to recognize this and must not seek to impose their own views, however seemingly reasonable, on the competent patient. But it does not follow from this that, as a matter of law, the patient is entitled to demand that he receives the treatment he thinks is best suited to his interests.

Often, as the Court of Appeal has explained, the problem will not arise in practice, particularly where one is concerned with medical treatment at the end of life, because up to a point the resource implications may be, at least comparatively speaking, limited, if only in time, and more particularly where one is concerned with routine treatments. In such cases the patient's wishes are likely to coincide with clinical judgment and are unlikely to run up against major resource issues.

But the fact remains that there will be cases where the patient's wishes, even in the case of seemingly routine treatment, will come into conflict with either the treating doctor's clinical assessment or the administrator's budget. Does the patient in that situation hold the trump card? The answer, almost certainly, is that he does not. His remedy then lies not in a court of law. If the issue is one of clinical assessment, his remedy is to find another doctor who is prepared to give him the treatment he wants. If the issue is one of resources, his remedy, at least in theory, is to fund the treatment himself or find a health care provider whose budget will run to it.

Is this desirable? The issues engaged are surely such that they cannot be resolved, in the final analysis, by mere lawyers.

Chapter 3
Redefining Death?

Daniele Bryden

Introduction

There was a time when death was a certainty that no one doubted, but the medical technologies of resuscitation and ventilation have robbed us of that certainty. There is therefore an ambiguity that now surrounds the diagnosis of death and this has implications for end of life planning, for organ donation and retrieval, and for the concept of the 'good death'.

The fact that medicine has become more adept at interrupting the dying process, of sustaining the near-dead and of successfully utilizing the bodily resources of the dead to sustain the living has created a need to be more precise in the diagnosis of death. Accuracy in the diagnosis of death is important for social, medical and legal purposes so as to maintain public trust and to justify the legitimacy of certain medical interventions that might otherwise be open to charges of neglect or euthanasia.

Cardiorespiratory criteria for diagnosing death run parallel to the brain stem definition of death. However, some groups of patients have a physical status that does not satisfy the criteria for either of these definitions of death. There is no UK legislation supporting euthanasia, but cases have utilized notions such as consciousness, best interests and quality of life in determining whether to continue the provision of life support to some individuals.[1] This chapter argues that a category of 'pre-dead' persons is being created by default and that the ethical implications of some judicial decisions, and disquiet that such persons may not be experiencing a good death, suggest that statutory intervention is necessary and overdue. This is most clearly illustrated in concerns around the linkage of the diagnosis of death to organ donation. As Pernick has argued: 'Can I ever be certain that doctors would do everything possible to save my life [...] that they would not be influenced by what I could contribute to another person?'[2] Recent professional concerns from the Intensive Care Society have also highlighted the problems of

---

1 E.g. *Airedale NHS Trust v Bland* [1993] AC 789.

2 Pernick, M.S. 1999. Brain death in a cultural context, in *The Definition of Death: Contemporary Controversies*, ed. by S.J. Younger, R.M. Arnold and R. Schapiro. Baltimore: Johns Hopkins University Press, pp. 3–33, at p. 14.

linking death to organ donation in a presumed consent system.[3] Worries centre on the relatives' perception of a potential conflict of interest and the damage this may do to the relationship of trust between intensive care doctors and relatives. A re-examination is therefore needed of what we understand by death in legal and ethical terms in order to ensure that medical practitioners, patients and the public are clear about the motives and intentions of health care practitioners involved in caring for those who are dying. An improved legislative definition of death and what constitutes the dying process would provide this clarity and would help to provide reassurance that a good death is compatible with a body being maintained in a state where individuals are not dead in the currently recognized sense.

This chapter begins by setting out the history and contemporary context of the diagnosis of death as a springboard to the discussion of how its ambiguities present difficulties in clinical practice, the problematic current legal position, what alternatives should be considered and whether these should be enshrined in law to provide public confidence that all patients are provided with the optimal good death even if they do not satisfy traditional and lay notions of clinical death.

Diagnosing Death

Professional determination of death was historically left to the newest and least qualified members of the medical team. The necessary routine of bodily examination and documentation of death was an oral tradition handed down to newly qualified doctors, as it was not required to be taught or tested at medical school.[4] Since 2005, newly qualified doctors in the UK undergo a two year foundation programme of training providing a framework of core competencies. This includes understanding of the legal and ethical requirements in death certification and also the responsibilities regarding sudden or suspicious deaths, but it does not actually require doctors to understand or demonstrate competence in the diagnosis of death.[5] As Charlton has identified, '[m]aking a clinical diagnosis of death is rarely mentioned in modern textbooks [... and] there is often considerable doubt about the actual moment of death, particularly for those witnessing the process of dying'.[6]

---

3   Jeffreys, B. Doctors split on organ donation. BBC News [Online, 3 September]. Available at: http://news.bbc.co.uk/1/hi/health/7596810.stm [accessed 14 September 2011].

4   Jellinek, S. 1947. *Inspection of the Dead, Dying, Apparent Death and Resuscitation*. London: Balliere Tindall and Cox.

5   The Foundation Programme. 2011. Foundation Programme Curriculum and Reference Guide [Online: The Foundation Programme]. Available at: http://www.foundationprogramme. nhs.uk/index.asp?page=home/keydocs#c&rg [accessed 28 September 2011].

6   Charlton, R. 1996. Diagnosing death. *British Medical Journal*, 313, 956–7.

Traditional cardiorespiratory criteria are the commonest form of medical diagnosis of death, and are based on the diagnosis of three elements of cardiovascular collapse: unresponsiveness, apnoea (no breathing) and the absence of central circulation.[7] These have been developed by the Academy of Medical Royal Colleges' guidance on the diagnosis of death to try to cover many of the situations frequently seen in clinical practice as medicine has advanced.[8] The UK Resuscitation Council also considers these to be the criteria to decide whether to establish cardiopulmonary resuscitation and offer a patient advanced life support after cardiac arrest.[9] However, the meeting of these criteria alone cannot be sufficient to diagnose death, since there is the possibility of recovering these functions following resuscitation. Therefore there is an additional requirement for death to be determined that these changes are 'simultaneous' and 'irreversible'.[10] However 'irreversibility' is not defined. Cole argues that without a clear epistemological definition there is an inevitable clinical ambiguity.[11] 'Irreversible' could mean: (1) no logical possibility of restoring function at any current or future point; (2) with current skills and technology function cannot be restored; and (3) even though restoration of function is a technical possibility, a decision has been made not to restore function. Irreversibility is therefore the defining point by which the traditional criteria of death are determined, but it is not a fixed point. It is as much determined by extraneous social factors, for example the morality of the decisions and 'overall benefit',[12] as by the biological mechanisms.[13] For these reasons, it may be reasonable to remove the criterion of irreversibility from the definition of death because it is unhelpful. However, although reversibility may be a possibility, establishing how plausible this is seems a sensible additional requirement.[14] The finality of death is an important and necessary boundary albeit vulnerable to conceptual challenge; while it is true that '[m]ost doctors when asked to sign a death certificate for a putrefying corpse [...] are satisfied with empirical criteria for irreversibility and lose no sleep over the possibility of misdiagnosis,

---

7   Ethics Committee, American College of Critical Care Medicine, Society of Critical Care Medicine. 2001. Recommendations for non-heartbeating donation. A position paper by the Ethics Committee, American College of Critical Care Medicine, Society of Critical Care Medicine. *Critical Care Medicine*, 29(9), 1826–31.

8   Academy of Medical Royal Colleges. 2008. *A Code of Practice for the Diagnosis of Death*. London: Academy of Medical Royal Colleges.

9   Resuscitation Council (UK). 2006. In-hospital resuscitation, in *Advanced Life Support*, ed. by J. Nolan. London: Resuscitation Council (UK).

10   *Ibid.* at p. 7.

11   Cole, J.D. 1992. The reversibility of death. *Journal of Medical Ethics*, 18, 26–30.

12   As suggested by the General Medical Council. 2010. *Treatment and Care towards the End of Life*. London: General Medical Council.

13   Youngner, S.J. and Arnold, R.M. 2001. Philosophical debates about the definition of death: who cares? *Journal of Medicine and Philosophy*, 26(5), 527–37.

14   Lamb, D. 1992. Reversibility and death: A reply to David J. Cole. *Journal of Medical Ethics*, 18, 31–3.

even if it is not ruled out by logic'.[15] However, when there is lack of certainty or clarity over empirical criteria about the moment of death, there is a need for further guidance.

The drive to utilize organs for transplantation purposes from non-heartbeating cadaver donors has led to debate about the point after cessation of the heartbeat at which irreversibility occurs and viable organs can be removed from a corpse.[16] The challenges of diagnosing death in this context contrast markedly with that of the putrefying corpse.

Further complexity arises because traditional cardiorespiratory criteria cannot be applied to all patients because these functions may be maintained artificially. As medicine inevitably progresses and affects the means by which individuals die as well as the timing of their deaths, new definitions are needed to accommodate these compounding factors and maintain consistency with ethical principles. The most radical development away from the use of cardiorespiratory criteria was the introduction of a definition of death based on the absence of brain stem function, that is, brain stem death (BSD). Intensive care medicine is often able to maintain cardiorespiratory functioning artificially with the purpose of treating underlying reversible illnesses, for example, following an accident causing a head injury. On occasion, these illnesses become untreatable and irreversible damage to the brain stem may then ensue.

An ad hoc committee of Harvard Medical School initially examined the viability of using brain death criteria as a proxy definition for 'death' and in 1981 the President's Commission for the Study of Ethical Problems in Medicine and Biomedical and Behavioural Research standardized this with a uniform model death law.[17] UK criteria from the Conference of Medical Royal Colleges modified this, concentrating on death of the brain stem.[18] Other countries have since developed their own guidelines, although some, such as Japan, have been slow to adopt the concept owing to some unwillingness to equate a brain-based definition of death as equivalent to a cardiorespiratory one.[19]

The motive for developing the definition was a pragmatic attempt to reconcile the need to stop intensive care treatment and ventilation in patients whose brain stems were irrecoverably damaged, and allow for the parallel growth of a transplant programme in which organs fit for transplantation could be removed at the earliest opportunity, for example, removal of the kidneys before the heart has

---

15   *Ibid.* at p. 31.

16   Gardiner, D. and Riley, B. 2007. Non-heart-beating organ donation: Solution or a step too far? *Anaesthesia*, 62, 431–3.

17   President's Commission for the Study of Ethical Problems in Medicine and Biomedical and Behavioral Research. 1981. Defining Death: Medical, Legal and Ethical Issues in the Definition of Death. Washington DC: US Government Printing Office.

18   Mohandas, A. 1971. Brain death: A clinical and pathological study. *Journal of Neurosurgery*, 35, 211–18.

19   Bagheri, A. 2006. Individual choice in the definition of death. *Journal of Medical Ethics*, 33, 146–9.

stopped beating rather than after. An additional definition of death, which allowed death to occur before the heart stopped beating, was a neat way of tying up these two 'loose ends'. Though some authors have disputed this,[20] correspondence from Henry Beecher, who became the Harvard committee chairman, suggested that this linkage was very much at the forefront of his thinking: 'The time has come for a further consideration of the definition of death. Every major hospital has patients stacked up waiting for suitable donor[s].'[21]

Unlike the US, UK criteria concentrate purely on brain stem functioning and do not consider the presence or absence of brainstem neurohormonal activity within that diagnosis, preferring instead to examine for the absence of cranial nerve and respiratory centre activity to make a diagnosis. Similarly, there is no requirement for electroencephalogram examination or brain stem evoked potentials (indicating potential brain cell activity in other parts of the brain), which are a necessary test in some other countries.[22]

There are differences in practices but there remains a common problem of interpretation: do such tests show that a person is dead or are they merely an indication that death is imminent? Pallis argues that 'the satisfaction of the clinical tests means that the stem has ceased functioning [...] and that asystole will occur within days';[23] but just because asystole will occur within days means only that the patient will be dead within days – it says nothing about the patient's current status. As Holland[24] argues: 'We're supposed to base the way we treat patients on their being alive or dead, not decide whether they are alive or dead on the basis of how we want to treat them.'[25]

Youngner showed that US doctors accepted brain death tests for patients because they '[...] would confidently never recover consciousness and would soon die traditional deaths [...] and were quickly and irreversibly approaching cardiac arrest'.[26] Moreover, Pernick suggests that brain death was portrayed to the public as a way of stopping physicians 'from using futile machinery that

---

20   Machado, C., Kerein, J., Ferrer, Y., Portela, L., de la C Garcia, M. and Manero, J.M. 2007. The concept of brain death did not evolve to benefit organ transplants. *Journal of Medical Ethics*, 33, 197–200.

21   Pernick, M.S. 1999. Brain death in a cultural context, in *The Definition of Death: Contemporary Controversies, supra* n. 2, at p. 9.

22   Halevy, A. and Brody, B. 1993. Brain death: Reconciling definitions, criteria and tests. *Annals of Internal Medicine*, 1119(6), 519–25.

23   Pallis, C. 1983. ABC of brain stem death: The arguments about the EEG. *British Medical Journal*, 286, 284–7.

24   Holland, S. 2003. *Bioethics: A Philosophical Introduction*. Oxford: Blackwell, at p. 72.

25   Youngner, S.J., Seth Landfeld, C., Coulton, C.J., Juknialis, B.W. and Leary, M. 1989. Brain death and organ retrieval: A cross-sectional survey of the knowledge and concepts among health professionals. *Journal of the American Medical Association*, 261, 2205–10.

26   *Supra* n. 25.

prolonged and intruded upon a good death'.[27] These comments clearly indicate the confusion apparent in this redefinition of death and almost suggest brain death as a form of 'precursor death' to that which has been conventionally understood as death. However, whether precursor death is death as properly understood has profound implications. For example, the Chief Rabbi and London Beth Din indicated in 2011 that carrying donor cards is incompatible with Jewish law as '[l]ive people (irrespective of how close to death) may not donate organs to save another person's life if in doing so it will hasten their own demise. [... In Jewish Law] cardiorespiratory death is definitive'.[28]

Evidence from US and Swedish studies has demonstrated that, because of 'uncertainty as to the concept of death', people fear that they will be treated as dead when they are not.[29] De Yong showed that only 80 per cent of family members of organ donors believed that a brain-dead patient could not recover and the figure was only 48 per cent amongst relatives of those who did not go on to become donors.[30] Even medical authors are unable to agree as to the meaning of brain stem death criteria: 'One should remember that the consensus brainstem death criteria are arbitrary, and lack prospective validation. It is probable that the UK brainstem death criteria have a specificity of 100 per cent for loss of consciousness.'[31] The use of the word 'probable' has been interpreted by some anaesthetists as indicative of a need to administer anaesthesia to organ donors. Although there are valid physiological arguments that provision of some forms of anaesthesia reduces the damage to organs before removal and improves their success post transplant,[32] there is also an element of doubt within some members of the medical profession as to whether consciousness remains in those who satisfy the current brain stem death criteria thus adding to the confusion as to whether a person in such a state is really dead.

Relatives have also influenced the determination of death by sometimes insisting upon the continued ventilation of a patient deemed BSD. For example, Swinburn[33] reported in one case that ventilation of a legally dead person continued for 48 hours based on 'advice from the management of the hospital, the hospital's

27   *Supra* n. 21, at p. 18.

28   Wise J. 2011. Rabbi says brain stem death is not enough for organ donation. *British Medical Journal*, 342. DOI: 10.1136/bmj.d275.

29   Sanner, M. 1994. A comparison of public attitudes towards autopsy, organ donation and anatomic dissection. *Journal of the American Medical Association*, 271, 284–8.

30   DeJong, W., Franz, H.G., Wolfe, S.M., Nathan, H., Payne, D., Reitsma, W. and Beasley, C. 1998. Requesting organ donation: An interview study of donor and nondonor families. *American Journal of Critical Care*, 7, 13–23.

31   Young, P. and Matta, B.F. 2000. Anaesthesia for organ donation in the brainstem dead: Why bother? *Anaesthesia*, 54, 105–6.

32   Shann, F. 1995. A personal comment: Whole brain versus cortical death. *Anaesthesia and Intensive Care*, 23, 14–15.

33   Swinburn, J.M., Ali, S.M., Banerjee, D.J. and Khan, Z.P. 1999. Discontinuation of ventilation after brain stem death. *British Medical Journal*, 318, 1753–5.

legal advisers, and a medical defence union'.[34] The implications of adopting such an approach are manifold. For example, there is a strong legal consensus that there is no right to demand treatment[35] and to require treatment for BSD individuals would also raise issues of distributive justice: individuals with a real chance of recovery may have this jeopardized because intensive care beds are 'blocked' by the ventilated dead. If a death certificate is not issued because a diagnosis of BSD contravenes a religious law such as a Jewish rabbinical canon,[36] this quite clearly runs counter to the current established case law of *Re A*[37] in terms of determining death. The Archbishop of Canterbury recently became embroiled in just such a dispute based on comments he made at the Royal Courts of Justice about a desire to consider 'exploring ways in which reasonable accommodation might be made within existing [legal] arrangements for religious conscience'.[38]

The following section illustrates how the problems highlighted in the preceding discussion affect clinical practice.

Treatment Withdrawal in Critical Care

Within a critical care environment, active medical treatment may involve support of the respiratory system with artificial ventilation and support of the cardiovascular system with drugs. These therapies are provided in the hope that the underlying disease process can be arrested and treated. However, continuation of active treatment may not always be in the patient's best interests, and on occasion it is recognized that discontinuation of active treatment leading to the patient's death is warranted. There are guidelines detailing withdrawal of treatment in such circumstances, such as those produced by the Intensive Care Society.[39] Accepted practice is to discontinue drug infusions and continue artificial ventilation on the equivalent of room air, until there is no detectable circulation or cardiac activity. At this point, death is determined and artificial ventilation discontinued. However,

---

34 *Ibid.*

35 *R (on the application of Burke) v General Medical Council and Others* [2005] EWCA Civ 1003, CA. See also the discussion in Chapter 2 of this volume.

36 Inwald, D., Jakobovits, I. and Petros, A. 2000. Brain stem death: Managing care when accepted guidelines and religious beliefs are in conflict. *British Medical Journal*, 320, 1266–8.

37 *Re A* [1992] 3 Med LR 303.

38 Archbishop of Canterbury. 2008. Civil and Religious Law in England: A Religious Perspective [Online: Archbishop of Canterbury]. Available at: http://www.archbishopof Canterbury.org/1581 [accessed 28 September 2011].

39 Cohen, S.L., Bewley, J.S., Ridley, S., Goldhill, D. and Members of the ICS Standards Committee. 2003. Guidelines for limitation of treatment for adults requiring intensive care [Online: Intensive Care Society]. Available at: http://faculty.ksu.edu.sa/Wisam/Documents/ Critical%20Care/Intensive%20Care%20Unit/LimitTreatGuidelines2003.pdf [accessed 16 September 2011].

the situation can be complicated by patients who have an artificial pacemaker in place that may stimulate the heart electrically for minutes or even hours. In these cases, the detection of a palpable pulse alone, an otherwise 'sure' sign of life, would need to be accommodated in the determination of death.

The Ethicus study[40] conducted in intensive care units across 17 European countries demonstrated that, whilst there is considered to be no moral distinction between withholding and withdrawing therapy, such activities varied widely in incidence depending on the country and religious beliefs of physicians. Moreover, in those centres that took part in the study, 2.4 per cent of patients were subjected to what was termed 'an active shortening of the dying process' though the doses and drugs used were similar to those used for symptom relief, which would be lawful under the doctrine of double effect. This doctrine allows doctors to administer palliative treatment that incidentally hastens death even though this is an inevitable consequence of the intervention, providing the primary aim is to relieve pain or suffering.[41] In Ethicus, therefore, the only real difference between active shortening of the dying process and 'symptom palliation' was in the intentions or beliefs of those administering treatment.

Rather than attempt to define intentions and beliefs it would be better to clarify whether these forms of treatment, withdrawal or administration, are occurring ante-, peri- or post-mortem and to define circumstances when the courts would infer intent. In current medical practice it is not always easy to make a clear distinction between allowing a death to occur 'naturally' and one where the death has been 'hastened'. The nature of medical treatment is frequently to delay the point of death beyond a 'natural' death. To acknowledge that treatment will be administered, withheld or withdrawn appropriately without any desire to bring death about is a complex notion to explain when it must also be acknowledged that treatment, withholding and withdrawal may still influence the dying process. The Ethicus study showed that doctors continue to find such distinctions problematic. Some of these difficulties might plausibly be addressed if a consensus could be agreed on the definition of a person in a peri-mortem state. The peri-mortem state might plausibly be defined as one of deep irreversible unconsciousness in a status of dependency that can only deteriorate unless artificially maintained by life-sustaining technology without which cardiorespiratory arrest would eventually occur.

However, the justifications for medical intervention, its withholding or withdrawal are particularly challenging in several of the candidate scenarios in which patients are commonly managed. Two such scenarios are now considered.

---

40   Sprung, C.L., Cohen, S.L., Sjokvist, P., Baras, M., Bulow, H.H., Hovilehto, S., Ledoux, D., Lippert, A., Maia, P., Phelan, D., Schobersberger, W., Wennberg, E. and Woodcock, T. 2003. End-of-life practices in European intensive care units: The Ethicus study. *Journal of the American Medical Association*, 290(6), 790–97.

41   *Supra* n. 1, at 867 per Lord Goff.

Persistent Vegetative State

A persistent vegetative state (PVS) is the particular state of brain damage where a patient has a functioning brain stem but is otherwise incapable of consciousness. Anthony Bland was in PVS as a result of the injuries he suffered in the Hillsborough disaster. A case was brought to clarify the legality of withdrawing his artificial nutrition and hydration (ANH – as it was then called) that also considered the implications of such a withdrawal on the cause of his death. To withdraw ANH lawfully and prevent a possible charge of murder required ANH to be defined as a medical treatment, and its withdrawal as a legally permissible omission. Despite his profound injuries it was acknowledged: 'Anthony's brain stem is still alive and functioning and it follows that, in the present state of medical science, he is still alive and should be so regarded as a matter of law.'[42] The inference from this is that medical knowledge determines life and death, and that the law plays a regulatory rather than a deterministic role. In order to make a diagnosis of PVS the original Official Solicitor's Note required changes in functioning to be permanent and stipulated a requisite time interval before diagnosis, reflecting the uncertainties of the condition.[43] However, this timescale is one of months not the hours or days that would be needed to enable the law to identify a period that could be termed the 'dying process'. The logic of the diagnosis of PVS is that once the diagnosis is made, despite a person being alive, the law would consider their subsequent death from withdrawal of ANH as owing to the initial insult, that is, the process of dying had started and with the implication that '[t]he physical state known as death has changed. In many cases the time and manner of death is no longer dictated by nature but can be determined by human decision.'[44]

Non-heartbeating Organ Donation

Non-heartbeating organ donation (NHBOD) also presents particular difficulties. Despite the introduction of protocols to guide practice, controversy still surrounds NHBOD programmes.[45] After a period of observation following circulatory arrest and apnoea, the unresponsiveness of the patient is used to confirm death, before organs are removed. The initial inconsistency in this observational time period led the US National Academy of Sciences to attempt to unify practice and endorse a five minute period after cessation of activity as a point at which loss

---

42 *Supra* n. 1, at 866.

43 Practice Note (Official Solicitor) Vegetative State [1996] 4 All ER 766.

44 *Supra* n. 1, at 879 per Browne-Wilkinson LJ.

45 Devita, M. and Snyder, J. 1993. Development of the University of Pittsburgh Medical Center policy for the care of terminally ill patients who may become organ donors after death following the removal of life support. *Kennedy Institute Ethics Journal*, 3, 131–44.

of cardiac function could be considered to be irreversible.[46] However, debate has continued about several aspects of this procedure, the minimum period of observation required to diagnose death before proceeding to organ removal,[47] the observation method (as clinical assessment of circulation is not as accurate as mechanical measurement), the non-correlation of electrical activity of the heart with effective contraction, and the exact time course or ruling out of the potential spontaneous (albeit rare) transient recovery of these functions. A person may satisfy these criteria yet could potentially be resuscitated, so the defining factor is the decision whether or not to attempt resuscitation.[48] NHBOD moves the pronouncement of death (and by inference its 'certification' time) from the moment of cardiorespiratory arrest to a later artificially determined point. This converts a weaker diagnosis of death to a stronger one, based on ensuring that the potential for reversibility and restoration of cardiac function is irretrievably lost. There is no requirement for the diagnosis of an irrecoverable condition, but rather an understanding that the people who go on to become donors are having treatment withdrawn on the grounds of futility. As a consequence of such withdrawals of, for example, artificial ventilation, these people sustain similar brain damage as those diagnosed as brain stem dead, though they never satisfied those criteria to begin with. The subjective nature of futility judgments has, however, been a source of major criticism of the programme.[49]

Controversy has been fuelled further in the US by the use of procedures to reduce the damage to organs. The patient is prepared before actual death in order to retain greater organ quality.[50] This is not considered ethically acceptable in the UK as it is of no benefit to the patient, the required justification for medical interventions for those who lack capacity. In the US the practice is arguably an acceptance that death is imminent and inevitable and thus patient benefit is irrelevant. More controversially, this could be interpreted as evidence of a shift in thinking to suggest that, whilst life no longer has a value to the individual, it does have one for wider society.[51] It has been argued that an individual who is unconscious, imminently dying and a registered organ donor has an autonomy-related interest in having their organs removed in the best condition possible,

---

46   National Academy of Sciences Institute of Medicine. 1997. *Non-heartbeating Organ Transplantation: Medical and Ethical Issues in Procurement.* Washington, DC: National Academy of Sciences Institute of Medicine.

47   *Supra* n. 7.

48   Youngner, S., Arnold, R. and DeVita, M.A. 1999. When is dead? *Hastings Center Report*, 29, 14–21.

49   *Supra* n. 14.

50   *Supra* n. 46, at p. 52.

51   Harris, J. 2003. Organ procurement: Dead interests, living needs. *Journal of Medical Ethics*, 29, 130–34.

an interest that is comparable to other post-mortem interests such as bequests or funeral arrangements.[52] However, this has yet to receive judicial support.

The principle of pre-mortem bodily preparation was put to the test in the 'Exeter Protocol', where patients dying from irrecoverable neurological conditions on hospital wards were removed to intensive care units for elective ventilation in order for brain death to supervene and their organs to be subsequently removed for transplantation purposes. This was abandoned because the act of subjecting a person to invasive treatment that is of no direct benefit to them was deemed unethical, and so invasive procedures preparing organs pre-mortem may be rejected for similar reasons.[53] However, that protocol differed in several ways from NHBOD protocols as patients were moved away from their point of care, potentially altering their mode of dying, whereas for NHBOD 'patients' are only moved to an operating theatre once cardiac arrest has occurred. Proponents of the NHBOD programme assert that the mode of dying is not altered. Some UK hospitals are engaging in this practice,[54] and the programme receives endorsement from the Department of Health,[55] but others are reluctant to follow suit as some clinicians remain unconvinced about the ethics of the practice.[56]

That practices differ even within a single jurisdiction suggests that the law has yet to provide clear and appropriate guidance on an acceptable definition of death, as the following section outlines.

The Law and Determining Death

Although registration of death is legally required, there is no legal requirement to confirm that a person has died and to record the time and the circumstances, unless a body is to be cremated when a documented examination must be performed by a medical practitioner.[57] Many NHS Trusts have written guidelines based on the traditional cardiorespiratory criteria for the determination of death. This was partly in response to concerns raised by the Shipman Enquiry about the laxity of

---

52   Cave, R. 2009. Who decides who owns your body? Law in action. BBC News [Online, 23 June]. Available at: http://news.bbc.co.uk/1/hi/health/8115399.stm [accessed 16 September 2011].

53   Feest, T.G., Riad, H.N., Collins, C.H., Golby, M.G.S., Nicholls, A.J. and Hamad, S.N. 1990. Protocol for increasing organ donation after cerebrovascular deaths in a district general hospital. *Lancet*, 335(8698), 1133–5.

54   This is the case at Sheffield Teaching Hospitals NHS Foundation Trust, June 2011.

55   Department of Health. 2009. Legal Issues Relevant to Non-heartbeating Organ Donation. London: Department of Health.

56   *Supra* n. 46, at p. 52.

57   The nearest that exists to a legal requirement is found in s. 1(4) of the Human Tissue Act 1961, which still applies in Scotland, and requires a surgeon undertaking organ removal from a beating heart donor that he has '[satisfied] himself by personal examination of the body that life is extinct'.

a system whereby medical practitioners could determine death with very little scrutiny of their actions.[58]

Legal commentators also struggle with a workable definition of death. For example, Mason and McCall Smith describe 'the brain, the heart and the lungs as forming a "cycle of life" which can be broken at any point; […] different criteria, and different tests, can be used for identifying that the cycle has been broken'.[59] Case law supports the Medical Royal Colleges' concept of BSD[60] but problems with the timing of death remain. Johnson J, in *Re A*[61] identified the first set of tests as marking the diagnosis of death whereas the guidelines produced by the working parties identified death as diagnosable after two sets of tests had been performed. When these tests may be separated by 24 hours, this could lead to confusion as to the date and time of death for registration purposes, and may also be confusing and distressing for relatives. Greater legal clarity is required.[62]

There are limited statutory and common law protections for the corpse[63] but there is a need for a legal definition of death that goes beyond the mere biological. Mason and McCall Smith state that '[t]he major purpose of [BSD] is to establish a consensus by which patients who can no longer benefit can be removed from ventilator support [,… which is] essential if the patient is to die with dignity'.[64] This is the confused language of the cardiorespiratory definition of death. However, the claim that a BSD person is no more than a ventilated corpse is contradicted by the intuitions aroused by a body that is pink, warm and with a palpable pulse. The law could go some way towards ameliorating the confusion by providing explicit criteria by which to judge when a state of peri-mortem is reached and specifying what interventions may be lawfully applied or withdrawn because these might not be in a patient's best interests as traditionally understood.[65]

For patients such as Bland, the principle of double effect cannot be applied as a lawful means of shortening life as such patients are unable to feel pain or to suffer and thus the interventions would be robbed of their justification to 'do all that is proper and necessary to relieve pain and suffering, even if the measures [taken] may incidentally shorten life'.[66] It is ethically and legally permissible to

58   Smith, J. 2002. *The Shipman Inquiry, First Report, Death Disguised* (Volume 1). Norwich: HMSO, at pp. 49–61.

59   Mason, J.K. and Laurie, G.T. 2006. *Law and Medical Ethics*. Oxford: Oxford University Press, at p. 466.

60   Conference of Medical Royal Colleges and their Faculties in the United Kingdom. 1979. Diagnosis of death. *British Medical Journal*, 332, 1187–8.

61   *Supra* n. 37.

62   Price, D.P.T. 1997. Organ transplant initiatives: The twilight zone. *Journal of Medical Ethics*, 23,170–75.

63   E.g. Human Tissue Act 2004.

64   *Supra* n. 59, at p. 44.

65   Notwithstanding the broad interpretations of these in cases such as *Re A (Male Sterilisation)* [2000] 1 FLR 549 and *Re Y* [1997] 2 WLR 556.

66   *R v Bodkin Adams* [1957] CLR 365.

withdraw treatment that maintains life by, for example, stopping artificial support of the heart and circulation with drugs if the underlying condition is untreatable as in the case of multiple organ failures. The case of *Bland* illustrates how this might be seen as being in the patient's best interests.[67] It is particularly interesting that, in determining the cause of death under such circumstances as ANH withdrawal, the predominant legal view was that the doctors are 'allowing [the] patient to die of his pre-existing condition and his death would be regarded in law as exclusively caused by the injury or disease to which his condition was attributable'.[68] This is an astonishing attribution of the cause of death, as Bland had sustained his anoxic injury over three years previously and his death was only brought about by judicial creativity in classifying ANH as a treatment that could be legitimately withdrawn. Whilst it is important to ensure that there is no medical attribution of criminal liability in such cases, the long timescale between injury and death suggests that it is a conceptually untidy solution.

Legal reasoning distanced the cause of Bland's death from the withdrawal of feeding because it was important to show that the management of his dying was not a direct, and unlawful, killing. It is also arguable that the reasoning used in the *Bland* case also described a form of dying. There is some logic to this approach, with implications for death certification, as, had Bland died of an intercurrent condition in the interim, it is likely that PVS would be indicated as merely a contributory cause and not the cause, whereas in the event PVS was identified as the proximate cause of death.

Whilst the judgment confirmed that any active measures to bring about Bland's demise would be classed as euthanasia, there is an implicit recognition of a category of persons in a peri-mortem state for whom dying and death can be legally and ethically 'managed'. Based upon this approach, the case for the explicit statutory recognition of the peri-mortem state and its medical management will be explored.

Redefining Death

Do brain-related definitions of death focus on the right qualities? Arguably, it is meaningful life that matters and not merely being alive. However, this intuitive view has long been disputed in debates about the relationship between the holistic characteristics that make human life meaningful and valued, and the biological activity of the body and of the brain in particular. Using a faith perspective, Pope Pius XII's view was that '[i]t remains for the doctors [...] to give a clear and precise definition of "death" and "the moment of death" of a patient who passes away in a state of unconsciousness'.[69] However, if death

---

67 *Supra* n. 1.

68 *Ibid.* at 823.

69 Pius XII to an International Congress of Anesthesiologists, Nov. 24, 1957, *The Pope Speaks*, Vol. 4. No. 4 (Spring 1958). 393–8, at 396.

becomes synonymous with brain death this is potentially problematic, not only for Catholics and people of other faiths, but for others who harbour concerns for the vulnerable who wish to be reassured that death can be diagnosed with certainty. For Catholics the issue is captured in Pope Pius XII's address to Anesthesiologists in which he states that '[...] human life continues for as long as its vital functions – distinguished from the simple life of organs – manifest themselves spontaneously or even with help of artificial processes [...]' and '[... i]n case of insoluble doubt, one must resort to presumptions of law and of fact. In general, it will be necessary to presume that life remains, because there is involved here a fundamental right received from the Creator, and it is necessary to prove with certainty that it has been lost.'[70]

Shewmon[71] has noted that, despite the eloquent arguments that have advocated for loss of personhood, or loss of social membership, in terms of criteria of death it is the biological criterion that remains the cornerstone of the standard orthodox definition of death; but this has never been validated. In his critique of the brain death concept, he goes on to argue that BSD does not equate to the death of the organism as a whole because it has not been shown that the brain has a uniquely integrating function for the whole organism. For him, the brain may be dead but the organism may well be alive. Although Shewmon is only concerned to show the inadequacy of brain death as a biological concept, his criticisms must leave room for doubt in the minds of those seeking the reassurance of certainty that brain death does indeed equal death proper. Morison[72] also argues that there is no 'infallible physiological index to what we value about human personality'[73] and thus no threshold for showing when these are absent and meaningful life ended.

Some Catholic theologians have argued that it is the presence or absence of the soul that represents the threshold of meaningful life and that the loss of the soul is the loss of capacity for a relationship with that person such as in a case of BSD:[74] it is this that is key evidence of a meaningful life. Yet the problem of circularity remains: on this view, death is the point at which the soul leaves the body so it is still necessary to show that the person is dead in order to establish that the soul has left. However, the potential slippage from talk of life and death to meaningful/ meaningless life might be perceived as a dangerous move on to a slippery slope. For example, a person with advanced dementia is clearly alive but may have no capacity for a relationship with others and in some opinions may have no qualities

---

70   *Ibid.*

71   Shewmon, D.A. 2001. The brain and somatic integration: Insights into the standard biological rationale for equating 'brain death' with death. *Journal of Medicine and Philosophy*, 25, 457–78.

72   Morison, R.S. 1971. Death: process or event? *Science*, 173, 694–8.

73   *Ibid.*

74   Singer, P. 1994. *Rethinking Life and Death: The Collapse of Our Traditional Ethics.* Oxford: Oxford University Press, at p. 15.

of meaningful life; yet few would argue that such a person was dead or that it was right to bring about their death in order to use such a person's organs for transplantation

A secular turn in this debate has focused with some force on the concept of personhood. Shewmon notes the potential for this approach[75] and Glover[76] argues that the value of life is only as a vehicle for consciousness: '[t]herefore in a subjective respect, death concerns only consciousness'.[77] McMahon[78] argues that we are 'embodied minds'[79] and that we cease to exist in any meaningful sense when we lose the capacity for consciousness despite the continuing function of the organism. Brain death testing is not therefore a test for death (although it has come to equate to that), but is rather a test for the irreversible loss of the capacity for consciousness, the very foundation of personhood. To use the criterion of loss of personhood (based upon the irreversible loss of consciousness) for the diagnosis of death would render those in a PVS as dead even though aspects of the organism remain temporarily alive. In order for this to become a routine diagnosis, the current law would need to change so that there would no longer be any need to apply to the courts to withdraw clinically assisted nutrition and hydration (as it is now called).

The idea that a person may be dead before their whole body is dead coheres with the view in medicine that 'death [...] is a process and not an instantaneous event'.[80] However, as Beecher[81] observes, 'whatever level we choose to call death, it is an arbitrary decision [...] The need is to choose an irreversible state where the brain no longer functions'.[82] Youngner asserts that the time has come for greater honesty and to 'admit that death is both a biologically based and socially constructed notion about which there is little prospect for social consensus in the near future'.[83]

Although complete consensus may be hard to establish, there has been a growing body of opinion that the concepts of BSD and the irreversible loss of personhood provide a useful threshold between meaningful life and death. The Declaration of Sydney, produced contemporaneously with the Harvard criteria for BSD in 1968, took a far more conceptual approach in recognizing that the interests

---

75   *Supra* n. 71.

76   Glover, J. 1990. *Causing Death and Saving Lives*. London: Penguin Books.

77   *Ibid.* at p. 46.

78   McMahon, J. 2002. *The Ethics of Killing: Problems at the Margins of Life*. Oxford: Oxford University Press, chapter 5.

79   *Ibid.* at p. 423.

80   *Supra* n. 12.

81   Beecher, H. 1971. The new definition of death, some opposing viewpoints. *International Journal of Clinical Pharmacology*, 5, 120–21.

82   *Ibid.*

83   *Supra* n. 13.

of an individual are not vested in the fate of their cells, but in their personhood.[84] This approach is perhaps more useful to end of life care than the more mechanistic one adopted by the Harvard group.

What, then, are the implications of this approach for redefining death? Singer's book-length reflection on rethinking death reports the dilemma faced by Dr Shann, a clinician working with anencephalic children. Singer reports Shann's words: 'If the cortex is dead, there is permanent loss of consciousness and there can be no person, no personality even though the organism may still be alive.'[85] In presenting the case of anencephlic infants, Singer draws the same conclusions as Beecher in his discussion of BSD:[86] where BSD marks the end of a person's meaningful life, the anencephalic is a living organism incapable of achieving personhood. For Singer the conclusions are the same for the 'no longer conscious' as for the 'never to be conscious': both are lives lacking in value because the individual is incapable of valuing it. The acceptance that mere biological life without awareness is of no benefit to the individual supports the claim that the peri-mortem practices of NHBOD are ethically acceptable but this would also require recognition in law that death is compatible with 'organic' life. Adopting this nuanced approach to death coheres with the view that life may reach such a state that there is no longer an ethical imperative to preserve it and in turn accords with lawful withdrawal of life-sustaining interventions: 'Life has a natural end [and] the point may come in the progression of a patient's condition where death is drawing near. In these circumstances doctors should not strive to prolong the dying process.'[87] Such decisions are not receptive to objective, scientific examination because '[i]f there is no infallible physiological index to what we value about human personality, are we ultimately forced to make judgments about the intactness and value of the complex interactions themselves?'[88] Clinicians are engaging in just such an activity when they withdraw treatment from individuals whom they judge to be damaged to such an extent that their personhood is lost as is the case when they have suffered severe irreversible brain damage. As noted earlier, the General Medical Council guidance on end of life care recognizes the difficulty but advises professionals to consider their actions within the context of overall benefit to the patient.[89]

---

84   Machado, C., Korein, J., Ferrer, Y., Portela, L., de la C García, M., Chinchilla, M., Machado, Y. and Manero, J.M. 2007. The Declaration of Sydney on human death. *Journal of Medical Ethics*, 33(12), 699–703.

85   Singer, P. 1994. *Rethinking Life and Death: The Collapse of Our Traditional Ethics*. Oxford: Oxford University Press, at p. 42

86   *Ibid.* at p. 26.

87   General Medical Council. 2006. *Withholding and Withdrawing Life-Prolonging Treatments: Good Practice in Decision-Making*. London: General Medical Council, para. 12.

88   *Supra* n. 72.

89   *Supra* n. 12, at p. 79.

The implication of the debates reviewed here suggests that a category of death premised upon the irreversible loss of consciousness and loss of personhood might take its place alongside the cardiorespiratory and brain stem forms. Such a move might go some way towards alleviating the concerns about the management of the 'breathing dead', though not the concerns of those with a religious faith or the cautious agnostic. Glover[90] acknowledges the potential concern that attitudes of indifference or worse towards killing in less justifiable circumstances may be fostered by adopting such changes. However, he goes on to argue that historical experience and fear that some will act for ideological or political reasons is insufficient justification for acting in a way that preserves biological life beyond the point at which it ceases to have any meaning for the individual or family members.[91]

There is evidence that the law is capable of accommodating broad and seemingly contradictory approaches. With the advent of the Mental Capacity Act 2005 and the Adults with Incapacity (Scotland) Act 2000, there is a greater legal recognition of the utility and legality of advance directives giving legal force to the recognition of personal wishes for withholding and withdrawing treatment. Japan has been able to adopt both a cardiac definition of death alongside the generally less culturally acceptable brain stem death approach by allowing individuals to choose the criteria by which their death will be determined. If new legal considerations regarding treatment of the pre-dead are introduced, then the provisions ought to allow individuals to express prior wishes as to their preferences for how they wish to be cared for in pre-dead states, or even to allow for a 'conscience clause' such that they or their advocates could reject such a notion whilst retaining no right of veto over the existing cardiorespiratory and brain stem considerations of death. In the absence of such directives, it is important to consider both when a person ceases to exist and when the organism can be considered to be dead along the lines discussed earlier.[92]

The de facto creation of a new category of 'pre-dead' individual requires a proper examination within the law. Mason and Mulligan[93] have proposed that the withdrawal of treatment should not be considered unlawful if medical opinion was such that 'a patient has sustained such damage to the central nervous system that: (1) he cannot exist in the absence of continuous care; (2) he is permanently unable to participate in human relationships or experiences; (3) continued treatment cannot improve this condition and is [...] futile; and (4) the patient's

---

90   Glover, J. 1990. *Euthanasia without Request in Causing Death and Saving Lives: The Moral Problems of Abortion, Infanticide, Suicide, Euthanasia, Capital Punishment, War and Other Life-or-death Choices.* London: Penguin.

91   *Ibid.* at p. 200.

92   Rachels, J. 1986. *The End of Life: Euthanasia and Morality.* Oxford: Oxford University Press, at p 55. This ties in with Rachels' view of the life occurring in both a biological 'being alive' and a biographical 'having a life' sense.

93   Mason, J.K. and Mulligan, D. 1996. Euthanasia by stages. *The Lancet*, 347, 810–11.

nearest relatives or carers have been consulted'.[94] It might be possible to consider cohorts of patients who, regardless of medical interventions, will die imminently as being in a peri-mortem state that justifies certain interventions or their absence. Statutory recognition of this could provide regulation that offers clarity as to what is permissible practice. This would lend coherence to what is currently fragmented and afford reassurance to those close to the patient in this peri-mortem state that the withdrawal of treatment or removal of organs does not preclude the possibility of a good death.

Conclusion

The intuitive linkage between death of the organism and death of the person remains a powerful one but the countervailing intuition that some bodies are alive, sustained by medical technologies but lacking the characteristics of personhood, is equally powerful. The fact that there is a growing cohort of living non-persons means that here is a growing need for a clear legal framework for the medical management and care of those individuals. This chapter has argued that a category of pre-dead persons is being created by default and has argued that a statutory approach is both possible and required. Clarity is needed so that the death of an organism may be legitimately brought about through the withholding or withdrawal of medical technology following the established death of the person as Brock suggests.[95] This would allow for mourning and funerals to take place without being delayed by the prolonged dying of the human organism. Legal clarity might also allow for the extension of, and greater respect for, the autonomous wishes of the living who anticipate and plan for measures that will maximize the benefit from their death: through the preparation of their body for organ transplantation after their death as a person but before the death of their organic body. Any such changes will need to be mindful of the plurality of societal values,[96] facilitating respect for previously expressed wishes and allowing for conscientious objections to organ retrieval procedure. The changes advocated in this chapter would lend coherence to the law, provide clarity for practitioners and reassure the public that their loved ones are able to have, wherever possible, a good death.

---

94   *Ibid.*

95   Brock, D.W. 1999. The role of the public in public policy on the definition of death, in *The Definition of Death: Contemporary Controversies, supra* n. 2, at p. 296.

96   Coggon, J. 2010. Assisted dying and the context of debate: 'medical law' versus 'end-of-life law'. *Medical Law Review*, 18(4), 541–63.

Chapter 4
Defining Personhood to Death

John Erik Troyer

Introduction

With its very enunciation, the post-mortem term 'a good death' implies a person who has lived a long, full life. This question of lifespan is somewhat different, however, than other possible criteria for evaluating an individual's death. The good death can be quantified as quick, qualitatively described as painless, and/or ethically evaluated on how the death conformed to the dying person's wishes. If the dying person has lived a long life, then these kinds of criteria are useful and can make the death potentially easier to accept. But what if that lived life has only existed for a few seconds, minutes, or days after biological conception? What kind of death, good or otherwise, emerges when the death of a person can occur in the moments after a human sperm and egg meet? In this essay on personhood and the good death, I explore how some American anti-abortion groups are pursuing a new legal strategy for the definition of human life that would radically alter the legal definition of death more generally. The strategy's planners refer to themselves as the Personhood Movement and a whole series of these groups is now working across America to alter the state-by-state legal definition of a person.[1]

The goal of the Personhood groups is to change either individual state constitutions via popular vote or to have sympathetic legislators introduce new statutory language. My interests in both the Personhood groups and the Personhood Movement are not with abortion. Instead, I am interested in how these changes to the statutory definition and concept of personhood alter the legal definition of human death, let alone a good death. The oft-stated goal of the Personhood groups is to defend human life at its earliest stages, but I am curious as to how that goal necessarily involves challenges to contemporary definitions of death. Indeed, many Personhood groups extend their arguments

---

1   See the Personhood USA's Mission Statement at http://www.personhoodusa.com: 'Personhood USA desires to glorify Jesus Christ in a way that creates a culture of life so that all innocent human lives are protected by love and by law. Personhood USA serves the pro-life community by assisting local groups to initiate citizen, legislative, and political action focusing on the ultimate goal of the pro-life movement: personhood rights for all innocent humans. We intend to build the support of at least two thirds of the states in an effort to reaffirm personhood within the U.S. Constitution. Personhood USA opposes vigilante violence.'

beyond the origins of human life to include the ends of human life. Colorado for Equal Rights, one of the first formalized groups in the movement, consistently uses the phrase 'until natural death' to describe how a person should die.[2] The embrace of what pro-life, anti-abortion groups consider a good death, that is, a *natural* one, is a common trope for the Personhood Movement and that language hints at a central political tenet for all these groups: the legislative adoption of absolute, conservative Christian legal definitions for the beginnings and ends of human life. In the broadest of terms, this legal strategy is about more than just abortion; the proponents of early cellular personhood clearly see dying as part of their campaign. It is a strategy that enables the sovereign power of the modern state, as Michel Foucault suggested in his 1975–76 lectures at the Collège de France, to absolutely control, 'the right to make live and to let die'.[3] What the Personhood groups do not consider, however, is another argument also made in the same lectures. Foucault points out that:

> [p]ower [i.e. the state] has no control over death, but it can control mortality. And to that extent, it is only natural that death should now be privatized, and should become the most private thing of all [...] Power no longer recognizes death. Power literally ignores death.[4]

How death is ignored is a point developed towards the end of the chapter.

The focus of the proposed laws, then, is the absolute control of human life, so much so that any and all things will be done to keep a person alive; death will be fought until the limit of human mortality is reached. This limit becomes difficult to define, however, when the very moment at which a 'person' begins living means that the definition of death has also been radically altered. In this sense, the *natural death* becomes a tightly defined legal category that makes the *good death* more about juridical definitions than, say, palliative care. This absolutist language creates a paradox, however, when the already extant laws regarding death have to incorporate human persons that seemingly escape well-established post-mortem definitions. In the middle of that paradox is an intriguing question about the limits of sovereign control over a politics of life (bios) and a politics of death (thanatos). The use of these two political concepts, the bio and the thanato, is an aggregate of work done by Agamben[5] and Foucault.[6] These two concepts are important because the Personhood Movement is attempting to exercise total control over the origin of human life *and* the finality of human death. Yet the Personhood groups cannot

---

2   See Colorado for Equal Rights: http://www.coloradoforequalrights.com.

3   Foucault, M. 2003. *Society Must Be Defended*, trans. by D. Macey. New York: Picador, at p. 241.

4   *Ibid.* at p. 248.

5   Agamben, G. 2000. *Means Without End*, trans. by V. Binetti and C. Casarino. Minneapolis: University of Minnesota Press.

6   Foucault, *supra* n. 3.

fully accomplish this feat without radically altering the concept of the dying and/ or dead body. In this sense, it is on the dead and dying body that the Personhood Movement has its greatest potential effect. But the dead body is also the most difficult body to control. While it is true that the dying body can experience a good death (however that is defined), the dead body has no use for any kind of death. Dead bodies defy absolute external control by remaining that one human state of existence that always defies the social order, namely, dead.

Colorado: The Personhood Movement's Origins

In November 2008, the citizens of Colorado went to the voting booth to elect a new American President; they also voted on Amendment Question 48, a petition driven initiative that asked:

> Shall there be an amendment to the Colorado constitution defining the term "person" to include any human being from the moment of fertilization as "person" is used in those provisions of the Colorado constitution relating to inalienable rights, equality of justice, and due process of the law?[7]

Approval of the amendment by a majority of voters would have changed the Colorado state constitution to read:

> Section 31. Person defined. As used in sections 3, 6, and 25 of Article II of the state constitution, the terms "person" or "persons" shall include any human being from the moment of fertilization.[8]

Despite this constitutional addendum's legal significance, Amendment Question 48's language was so vague that it was difficult to fully comprehend what exactly the change entailed. How *exactly* did Colorado's definition of a person change by including '[...] any human being from the moment of fertilization'? Here, then, are how those sections of the Colorado constitution would read and/or be legally understood:

> Article II, Section 3. Inalienable Rights. All persons, including any human beings from the moment of fertilization, have certain natural, essential and inalienable rights, among which may be reckoned the right of enjoying and defending their lives and liberties; of acquiring, possessing and protecting property; and of seeking and obtaining their safety and happiness.

---

7 Norris, W. 2007. *Colorado Supreme Court Affirms 'Egg-As-Person'* [Online, 13 November]. Available at: http://www.rhrealitycheck.org [accessed 3 August 2011].

8 *Supra* n. 2.

Article II, Section 6. Equality of Justice. Courts of justice shall be open to every person, including any human being from the moment of fertilization, and a speedy remedy afforded for every injury to person, including any human being from the moment of fertilization, property or character; and right and justice should be administered without sale, denial or delay.

Article II, Section 25. Due Process of Law. No person, including any human being from the moment of fertilization, shall be deprived of life, liberty or property, without due process of law.[9]

This was not a minor change to the Colorado state constitution. By legally defining personhood as beginning at the moment of fertilization, early human zygotes were afforded full constitutional protections. The Colorado state constitution would literally guarantee inalienable rights, equality of justice and due process of law to human forms-of-life that consisted of only a few cells. The vagueness of the ballot language notwithstanding, the voters of Colorado ultimately rejected Amendment Question 48 by a 73 per cent majority. That defeat, however, was hardly the end to this juridical proposition. Indeed, it was only the beginning.

Personhood Groups

When Colorado for Equal Rights sponsored Amendment 48, the organization provided the following rationale for it:

[E]very human being deserves equal rights under our laws, regardless of the stage of life he or she is in. Colorado for Equal Rights will stand up for the protection of every innocent human life [...] from the very beginning until natural death.[10]

Colorado for Equal Rights, along with most other Personhood groups, is engaged in a battle, as they see it, between the modern world's simultaneous rejection of life and its embrace of death. This is especially true in contemporary American culture and politics. All of the groups are unabashedly affiliated with evangelical, fundamentalist Christian groups. Burton, who founded Colorado for Equal Rights,

---

9   See NARAL Pro-Choice Colorado. Available at: http://www.prochoicecolorado.org [accessed 3 August 2011].

10   *Supra* n. 2.

was quite open about stating that: 'I honestly feel that this is what God called me to do.'[11] Campbell explains the origins of the life/death battle this way:

> One cannot speak of a politically mobilized and socially active fundamentalist movement until after the Roe v. Wade decision legalizing abortion in 1973 [...] Nor was euthanasia a realistic end of life option for patients until recently. Thus, current moves to redefine death are understood with a quite different social context [... I]indeed, the current social ethos reflects, according to many religious conservatives, an embrace of a "culture of death".[12]

The reference Campbell makes to *Roe v. Wade* is crucial. Personhood Movement thinking hinges on a particular interpretation (however tenuous) of section IX of the majority decision in the *Roe v. Wade* case:

> The appellee and certain amici argue that the fetus is a "person" within the language and meaning of the Fourteenth Amendment. In support of this, they outline at length and in detail the well-known facts of fetal development. If this suggestion of personhood is established, the appellant's case, of course, collapses, [410 U.S. 113, 157] for the fetus' right to life would then be guaranteed specifically by the Amendment. The appellant conceded as much on reargument. On the other hand, the appellee conceded on reargument that no case could be cited that holds that a fetus is a person within the meaning of the Fourteenth Amendment.[13]

As a result of their interpretation, the logic employed by the groups is simple enough: change the definition of personhood to the moment of conception and abortion is illegal in the United States. Yet, by defining personhood for a human form-of-life as beginning at the time of conception (a complicated task on its own), the assignation of legal individuality starts at a moment of 'life' without a heartbeat or brain activity. If persons can exist and be legally recognized as citizens without a heartbeat or brain activity, then the question to really ask is this: how does a person die? Not the human body, the *person* legally attached to that body. What does the good death become in those situations? All US states, and

---

11   Sealover, E. 2008. A woman fights to ban abortion with new definition of a person. *Denver Gazette*, 3 May, 1.

12   Campbell, C.S. 1999. Fundamentals of life and death: Christian fundamentalism and medical science, in *The Definition of Death: Contemporary Controversies*, ed. by S.J. Youngner, R.M. Arnold and R. Schapiro. Baltimore: Johns Hopkins University Press, pp. 194–209, at p. 199.

13   *Roe v Wade* 410 US 113 (1973), section IX.

Colorado is no exception, use the absence of neurological and/or cardiac activity to define when an individual is dead. According to Colorado statute 12-36-136:

Determination of Death

(1) An individual is dead if:

    (a) He has sustained irreversible cessation of circulatory and respiratory functions; or
    (b) He has sustained irreversible cessation of all functions of the entire brain, including the brain stem.

(2) A determination of death under this section shall be in accordance with accepted medical standards.[14]

If personhood can simultaneously exist outside the cardio-neurological legal framework for death and still be guaranteed concrete constitutional rights, then what juridical power decides the moment of death? In this conundrum, the human body might actually be dead but the person could very well remain alive in perpetuity, or at least as long as legal battles ensued over rights of inheritance, property ownership, and removal of life-support machinery. Indeed, all of the proposed personhood laws share this legal uncertainty and in ways that suggest it is hardly coincidental. In fact, it seems that this ambiguity over when a person dies is precisely the point for groups defending human life until a 'natural death'.

The pro-life Personhood Movement's use of the term natural death is clear enough in its meaning: a death that does not interfere with God's decision over when a person lives and when a person dies. Natural death, in this context, is not a total rejection of human life-support technology; rather it is a rejection of a secularized dying process. Life-support machinery, such as ventilators and feeding tubes, can be part of God's 'plan' but the human decision to remove these devices often means assuming 'godlike' powers. Ironically, this is the very same secularized dying process that might otherwise be considered a model of a good death.

Campbell argues that 'the concept of *personhood* is from the fundamentalist perspective considered a secular reduction of the image of God'.[15] So in order to re-inscribe modern personhood with Christian ideals, the laws being proposed embrace the moment of conception as both God's creation *and* the time at which personhood begins. Since only God (in the oldest tradition of the sovereign king) can decide when a person lives and when a person dies, there is no longer a problem. The larger problem for any American state passing one of the personhood laws, however, is that it uses a theocratically based concept about lifespan for a secular

---

14   See http://www.colorado.gov.
15   *Supra* n. 12, at p. 198.

social code. Personhood law proposals across the American states use this same theological foundation, and they also create a potential life/death paradox. Here is a sampling of some proposed personhood laws, each with its own particular slant on the legal recognition of persons. None of these proposals has become law.

Mississippi:

Be it Enacted by the People of the State of Mississippi: SECTION 1. Article III of the constitution of the state of Mississippi is hereby amended BY THE ADDITION OF A NEW SECTION TO READ: Section 33. Person defined. As used in this Article III of the state constitution, "The term 'person' or 'persons' shall include every human being from the moment of fertilization, cloning or the functional equivalent thereof."[16]

Montana (where a Senate bill was used):

[Senate Bill] 406, which defines person for the purposes of application of inalienable rights, states, "All persons are born free and have certain inalienable rights. Person means a human being at all stages of human development of life, including the state of fertilization or conception, regardless of age, health, level of functioning, or condition of dependency."[17]

North Dakota (where a House of Representatives bill was used):

SECTION 1. References to individual, person, or human being [...] For purposes of interpretation of the constitution and laws of North Dakota, it is the intent of the legislative assembly that an individual, a person, when the context indicates that a reference to an individual is intended, or a human being includes any organism with the genome of homo sapiens. SECTION 2. STATE TO DEFEND CHALLENGE. The legislative assembly, by concurrent resolution, may appoint one or more of its members, as a matter of right and in the legislative member's official capacity, to intervene to defend this Act in any case in which this Act's constitutionality is challenged.[18]

While it is fairly clear that these proposed laws, if passed, would make situations that involved IVF treatments, birth control and abortion more difficult (if not outright illegal), it is less clear what happens to the 'living person' in a dead body. The Mississippi language follows the same path as the Colorado amendment and stresses the moment of fertilization as the beginning of both life and personhood. This would again mean that using either neurological or

---

16 See http://www.personhoodmississippi.com.
17 See http://www.personhoodmontana.com.
18 See http://www.personhoodnorthdakota.com.

cardiopulmonary criteria to determine the moment of death could be in conflict with the current legal understandings.

The inclusion of 'cloning' in the Mississippi bill is another layer of legal change advocated by Personhood groups. Its placement in the proposed law is an attempt to prevent scientists from producing human-animal hybrids. A similar way of thinking is also present in the North Dakota bill, in the section that uses this phrase: 'organisms with the genome Homo sapiens'. The Personhood groups' concerns about cloning raise a kind of speculative point about the definition of the human but also a 'human' whose DNA might explicitly include non-human genetic sequences. It is unclear how concerned the Personhood groups are with guaranteeing a dignified end of life for human-animal hybrids but the promise of personhood status to those individuals would follow the same legal guidelines. Suffice it to say that the cloning/hybrid issue is largely viewed by anti-abortion, conservative Christian groups as challenging the sanctity of human life and a further secular incursion into God's unquestionable power.

This sanctity of human life concern also raises an interesting end of life issue in the Montana bill. Similar to Colorado's and Mississippi's, the Montana bill includes 'fertilization' and 'conception' but it also contains the phrase 'condition of dependency'. This final clause in the Montana bill is a gesture towards including any person attached to life-support machines and whose 'level of functioning' (to quote the bill) might necessitate artificial support. The point of these clauses is to prevent other individuals, such as next-of-kin or medical staff, from removing life-support technology while the attached person is still minimally alive. This is another potentially problematic situation, when one group wants to cease treatment and a second group does not. In short, each of the proposed laws alters the beginning of personhood to such an extent that a person's *end of life* could be exponentially drawn out. The very idea of a good death, where life support is removed in order to allow a person to die, could itself become potentially illegal, even if the next-of-kin requests it.

Herein lies the key issue with these proposed laws and the definition of death: an incapacitated, dying person can no longer be the legal responsibility of a spouse or parent. The state would, in theory, have to defend the rights of the dying person as a matter of Constitutional urgency until that person died, whenever that natural death took place. The Montana bill goes the furthest in this direction but all the laws share this common trait. An end of life care directive that is written down (and legally recognized) might mediate some of these legal issues but there is no guarantee, especially when family members disagree over how a dying person should die. Even without any of the personhood bills becoming law, there are examples of how these changes to the legal landscape might function. Since the 1980s, numerous cases have occurred in which individual's bodies were kept alive by a combination of both machines and legal decisions. These cases are important to contemplate when applying any of the proposed personhood laws to a good death.[19] One particular American right-to-die case, Terri Schiavo's in Florida, offers an important insight into how the bio–thanato relations discussed in the introduction can intrude into the end of human life and the possibility of a good death.[20]

Terri Schiavo was a 41-year-old woman in a persistent vegetative state who could breathe on her own but required a feeding tube for sustenance. Her end of life story began on 25 February 1990 when Schiavo collapsed at home and her heart stopped beating long enough to cause permanent brain damage.[21] Terri Schiavo was eventually placed in a Florida medical facility for what would become many years of long-term care. Schiavo's husband, Michael, went to court with her parents in 1998 to have the feeding tube removed. As Terri Schiavo's husband and lawful guardian by writ of marriage, Michael had the legal right to remove the tube under Florida law. He repeatedly explained that Terri would not want to continue living in her current state. Seven years later, a few weeks after the feeding tube had finally been removed, Terri Schiavo died on 31 March 2005 in a Florida hospice but only after unprecedented court battles between Michael Schiavo and Terri's parents.[22] The legal fight's culmination came on 21 March 2005 when President George W. Bush signed a bill into law that was specifically written by the United States Congress for Terri Schiavo. The Federal Courts ultimately overturned the law, *For the Relief of the parents of Theresa Marie Schiavo*, before it was ever used.[23]

---

19   For an international comparison, the 2009 case involving an Italian woman in a persistent vegetative state, Eluana Englaro, is instructive. The case captured European attention as it pitted her father, Beppino, against Prime Minister Silvio Berlusconi and the Vatican. Eluana's father wanted her feeding tube removed after 17 years of care and the Italian courts eventually sided with him. Both Berlusconi and Vatican officials criticized the legal ruling as defiling the sanctity of human life. For the Catholic Church, the legal decision meant that Eluana would not die a natural death. For Beppino Englaro, it meant that his daughter would finally stop living in a manner that the courts agreed she would not have wanted. The feeding tube was removed, as requested by Eluana's next-of-kin, and she died a few days later.

20   The entire Terri Schiavo case is a long and complicated story that went in political, bioethical, and medical directions no one person seemed to ever anticipate. For a complete and extremely thorough discussion of the Schiavo case, see the website run by the University of Miami Ethics Programs and the Shepard Broad Law Center at Nova Southeastern University: http://www.miami.edu/ethics/schiavo/timeline.htm.

21   Newman, M. 2005. Justices set back Florida's right-to-die case. *New York Times*, 24 January, 1.

22   See Caplan, A., McCartney, J. and Sisti, D.A. 2006. *The Case of Terri Schiavo: Ethics at the End of Life*. New York: Prometheus Books.

23   For a reprint of the law see Babington, C. and Allen, M. 2005. Congress passes Schiavo measure; Bush signs bill giving U.S. courts jurisdiction in case of fla. woman. *Washington Post*, 21 March, A08. Available at: http://www.washingtonpost.com/wp-dyn/articles/A51402-2005Mar20.html [accessed 4 September 2012].

A Good Death?

The Schiavo case is compelling for several legal and historical reasons that directly involve how Personhood groups view the concept of a good death. Terri Schiavo's end of life legal battles became (and remain) a persistent political cause amongst conservative Christian Personhood groups. Most of the groups believe, for example, that removing Schiavo's feeding tube was an act against the sanctity of life. More importantly, many Personhood activists argued that Terri Schiavo was only suffering from a severe functional disability and was not in a persistent vegetative state. Aspects of that argument appear in Montana's personhood bill. Furthermore, the rhetoric and political tactics used by social and conservative Christian groups during the Schiavo case remain an indicator of future conflicts over the concept of death if personhood begins at conception.[24] *The Washington Post* newspaper published a story in February 2005, highlighting the work of the anti-abortion group Operation Rescue in those efforts:

> [...] groups more commonly associated with antiabortion demonstrations urged their followers to hold prayer vigils and protests at Pinellas Park, where Schiavo lives at a hospice, and at neighboring communities. Activists with the antiabortion group Operation Rescue led demonstrations and promised "to pull out all the stops" to prevent Michael Schiavo from ending his wife's tube-feeding.
>
> "We're not going to stand idly by while she is starved to death," said Troy Newman, an Operation Rescue spokesman. "This wouldn't happen to a dog; you wouldn't do it to your pet."[25]

The argument made by Newman about human pets is a telling one because it focuses attention on the ethical limits placed by humans on the sanctity of human life and death. If a pet is terminally ill, most people will have the animal euthanized. The goal with these actions is to prevent the animal from feeling pain and, perhaps most importantly, to keep the pet owners from watching a non-human companion suffer. Euphemistic language surrounds this form of euthanasia and it is often rephrased as putting the animal 'to sleep'. This constitutes an *unnatural* but acceptably good death for the non-human animal. So Newman is correct when he says a dog would not be treated like Terri Schiavo: the dog would be euthanized as a humane, ethical act. Painful as losing a pet can be, the dog would

---

24   The Christian Communication Network, a clearinghouse for press releases from conservative Christian groups, sent out dozens of email press releases to 'Save Terri' and 'Fight for Terri' in the weeks leading up to her death. Examples of some of the groups involved were Operation Rescue, the Concerned Women for America, the Christian Defense Fund, the Family Research Council, and the Liberty Defense Counsel. For an archive of the Schiavo press releases go to http://www.ChristianWireService.com.

25   Roig-Franzia, M. 2005. Another hearing in right-to-die case. *Washington* Post, 23 February, A02.

have experienced a good death. Terri Schiavo simply became death in motion but dying without terminus. She could choose neither life nor death, and her husband's legal right to make those decisions fell into conflict with multiple levels of groups all acting as advocates for life by denying death. Terri Schiavo was/is the paradox of a living dead body, around and through which the law is in conflict over when personhood ends (if ever) and death begins.

Bio–Thanato Relations and the Good Death[26]

One way of thinking through this supposed paradox is that, even though life can be controlled by external power, the persistence of death forces sovereign authorities to seek control of all biological forces. This exertion of control most certainly includes dying. Michel Foucault's explication of the limits placed on state power by death during his *Society Must Be Defended* lectures[27] foreshadowed current right-to-die legal fights. If life must be brought under control, then logically so should death. Control of death by sovereign authorities then becomes the focus of thanatopolitical relations, or the politics of death, between the citizen and the state.

A problem quickly arises, however, because sovereign power can attempt to control death but in only the most superficial of ways. As a result of the impossibility of permanently stopping or reversing death, the state (as an example) is forced to manage a citizen's life via biopolitics, or the politics of life. Total control of death would mean the ability to permanently undo death's effects once a person is physically dead. Medical science can in fact restart a human heart, for example, if it stops beating and bring 'life' back to a person who has been technically dead for a short time. What medical science cannot do is unconditionally undo death when a person has been dead for too long a period of time. Terri Schiavo's case highlighted the ambiguity of this situation as she continued to biologically live in a persistent vegetative state. She was physically alive but portions of her brain had ceased to function and had withered away as a result of oxygen loss during her heart attack.

The politics of death, then, play a significant role in challenging, if not outright politically resisting, state power and indeed not the other way around. A living subject's fear of death often drives biopolitical relations with the sovereign. The fear of life, however, does not pose a great threat to those already dead. That is to say, the sovereign cannot bring the subject's long dead body back to life. What this all suggests is that sovereign power ignores death, and here I am thinking again of Foucault, because sovereign authorities *must* ignore death in order to persist in controlling life. Even though advances in biomedical technology take place on a daily basis, the practical opportunities for totally stopping death remain

---

26   See also Troyer, J. 2013. *Technologies of the Human Corpse*. Durham: University of North Carolina Press.

27   Foucault, *supra* n. 3.

impossible. Yet life, as defined by the Personhood groups, must remain unfettered by anything other than a natural death. The Schiavo case highlighted this very point: that any and all things must be done to keep a person alive, even if that process remains technologically *unnatural*. All said and done, the Personhood groups and the laws they are advocating attempt a political control of the person by radically expanding the definition of life to such an extent that a person's nearly dead body is no longer allowed to die. It is a dying body without death, so much so that the *good death* within this logic is not possible: it is a failure.[28]

Coda: The Federal Personhood Amendment

In August 2009, pro-life groups in Colorado began collecting signatures for a new personhood law. This proposed law eschewed discussions of biological conception altogether and instead it stated that 'the term "person" shall apply to every human being from the beginning of the biological development of that human being'.[29] Interestingly, the leaders of the new initiative, Gualberto Garcia Jones and Leslie Hanks, met in Florida in 2005 while protesting outside Terri Schiavo's hospice. In November 2010, a majority of Colorado voters again voted against adopting the new law. It is unclear at this point in time whether or not these legal campaigns will succeed but more states, including California and Missouri, have active Personhood groups.

Personhood campaigners are planning to offer up an even bigger legal challenge.[30] Many of the new state amendments are modelled after the Federal Human Personhood Amendment (sponsored by the American Life League) and the ultimate goal is to alter the United States Constitution.[31] If that should happen, the amended US Constitution would read:

---

28   For an exceptionally good essay on the limits of medical care for individuals who are dying see Marantz Henig, R. 2005. Will we ever arrive at the good death? *New York Times* [Online, 7 August]. Available at: http://www.nytimes.com/2005/08/07/maga zine/07DYINGL.html [accessed 4 September 2012].

29   Norris, W. 2009. *Anti-abortion activists push new, more radical egg-as-person measures* [Online, 7 July]. Available at: http://www.rhrealitycheck.org [accessed 3 August 2011].

30   To give the reader a sense of the scope the new Personhood groups are now embracing, here is a statement from the California group: 'WHO WOULD BE PROTECTED BY THE CALIFORNIA HUMAN RIGHTS AMENDMENT? Everyone! All human beings, from conception to natural death. That means babies in the womb, frozen embryos in laboratories, children, adults, the handicapped, the dying, and those dependent on feeding tubes and other medical support. All are persons, and therefore due equal protection under the law.' See http://www.californiahumanrightsamendment.com/content/ amendment.

31   This is taken from the California Human Personhood Amendment website available at: http://www.californiahumanrightsamendment.com/content/what-personhood-0:

The term "person" applies to all living human organisms from the beginning of their biological development, regardless of the means by which they were procreated, method of reproduction, age, race, sex, gender, physical well-being, function, or condition of physical or mental dependency and/or disability.[32]

Conclusion

It seems clear that these personhood laws and their advocates will not stop any time soon. What remains less clear is this fundamental question: what happens to a dying or dead person, the death of that person, and the concept of a good death, once one of these laws becomes enacted? At that point, the current American definitions of life and death will be at legal odds with dying persons who are being made to live by state authorities. In short, the current fights over an individual's *right-to-die* in America may establish an entirely different relationship with the nation-state. In order to protect life at all stages of development, a good death (as outlined and detailed in this very book) may itself become unconstitutional.

'The Federal Human Personhood Amendment is unlike all other pro-life legislation in that it guarantees the right to life of ALL people from the moment of creation until natural death. It addresses all of the problems stemming from the culture of death by striking at its root instead of merely trying to treat its symptoms.'

32   *Supra* n. 30.

Chapter 5
Suicide Centres: A Reasonable Requirement or a Step Too Far?

Lynn Hagger and Christoph Rehmann-Sutter

Introduction

In a recent article,[1] we explored the need to have a more permissive regime with respect to assisted suicide in England and Wales (hereafter England for expediency).[2] A critique of the current system was offered followed by an examination of whether the Swiss approach to assisted suicide could be adopted here. Part of the discussion included an assessment of whether the English system should be liberalized to the extent of establishing state-sponsored suicide centres[3] that would respond positively to requests for assisted suicide, regardless of the state of the person's health.

This chapter provides a brief overview of that article, develops some of the ethical arguments in support of change, notes alternative positions and highlights later developments that suggest the controversy surrounding assisted suicide is still very much a 'live' issue. It represents an example of transnational bioethics in that it is a morally complex and sensitive issue that emerges when the jurisdiction of England is compared with that of Switzerland. A considerable number of British residents travel to Switzerland where they can legally get assistance for their preferred death from a specialized, right-to-die organization such as Dignitas. While being tolerant in the way it deals with relatives who assist individuals to travel to Switzerland,[4] the law in England excludes all forms of organized assistance to dying within its territory.[5] This results in a form of international division of labour whose moral legitimacy remains to be questioned. We start from the assumption

---

1   Rehmann-Sutter, C. and Hagger, L. 2011. Organized assistance to suicide in England? *Health Care Analysis*. DOI: 10.1007/s10728-011-0191-y [Online First].

2   Scotland addresses issues concerning suicide through its common law and Northern Ireland addresses these matters under s. 13 of the Criminal Justice Act (Northern Ireland) 1966 as amended.

3   Edwards, E. 2010. An argument in support of suicide centres. *Health Care Analysis*, 18, 175–87.

4   *R (Purdy) v Director of Public Prosecutions* [2009] EWCA Civ 92 (Court of Appeal), para. 6.

5   Crown Prosecution Service. 2010. *Policy for Prosecutors in Respect of Cases of Encouraging or Assisting Suicide*, para. 43(16) [Online: Crown Prosecution Service].

that each country could find a sustainable, socially and ethically sensitive and also legally robust solution for people who seek an assisted death. This, we argue, could include the option of specialized organizations to provide assistance. To do otherwise could force individuals to accept a life under circumstances they wish to avoid: they are prevented from having a 'good death'.

Suicide is not a crime but assisting someone to do so can be.[6] Following the House of Lords' decision in the *Purdy* case,[7] the guidance (guidelines) provided by the Director of Public Prosecutions (DPP) in 2010[8] suggests that assisting suicide in England, or elsewhere, will not be prosecuted provided there is virtuous intent and no active encouragement on the public interest ground: the actions of the suspect must be characterized as reluctant or carried out in the face of a determined wish on the part of the victim to commit suicide,[9] thus resembling the Swiss position.[10]

The central issue of this debate is whether competent individuals should be able to determine the manner of their death in recognition of their autonomous interests, even if this includes being helped by others (an individual or a competent organization).[11] This could be seen as placing pressure on terminally ill people and those dependent on long-term care to end their lives; this runs counter to moral obligations to care for each other's well-being, perforates the ethos of medicine and undermines respect for the sanctity of life principle.[12] It could also interfere with the availability of palliative care.

Appropriate palliative care can obviate the wish for assisted suicide. It can provide reassurance to those who wish to die because they do not wish to be a burden. Even if resource issues are addressed and appropriate care is consistently provided, this will not satisfy all patients because some symptoms, such as incontinence, and indignities such as dependency on others, may be less receptive to palliation.[13] It can be the case that, even where patients are in receipt of high-

---

Available at: http://www.cps.gov.uk/publications/prosecution/assisted_suicide_policy.html [accessed 20 September 2011].

6   Ss. 1 and 2(1) Suicide Act 1961 respectively.

7   *R (on the application of Purdy) v DPP* [2009] 3 WLR 403.

8   *Supra* n. 5.

9   *Ibid.* para 45.

10   Article 115 Swiss Penal Law.

11   Campbell, T. 2006. Euthanasia as a human right, in *First Do No Harm*, ed. by S.A.M. McLean. Aldershot: Ashgate, pp. 450–51.

12   As exemplified by Lord Bingham in *R (Pretty) v DPP* [2001] UKHL 61 (House of Lords) at para. 29.

13   McLean, S.A.M. 2007. *Assisted Dying: Reflections on the Need for Law Reform.* Abingdon: Routledge, at p. 46 and Ahmedzai, S. 2012. Should assisted suicide be legalized? The Exchange, Sheffield Students' Union, 27 March. Professor Ahmedzai is Chair and Head of the Academic Unit of Supportive Care at the School of Medicine in the University of Sheffield and a leading specialist in palliative care who took part in the DEMOS Commission on Assisted Dying noted *infra* at n. 22.

quality palliative care, they still wish to end their lives.[14] Some patients want to be entitled to leave life in their homes with their loved ones around them, at a time of their choosing.

Assisted dying in England continues through, inter alia, medically sanctioned withdrawal of artificial nutrition and hydration and/or deep sedation,[15] as well as the use of the 'double effect' doctrine that allows doctors to administer palliative treatment that incidentally hastens death.[16] Some deaths are the result of the unlawful 'mercy killings' by doctors,[17] but current prosecution policy allows these to go minimally or unpunished,[18] as is also the case with those attributable to assistance from loved ones.[19] At the same time, the government[20] and the General Medical Council[21] have emphasized the importance of valid and applicable advance (and current) decisions that refuse life-saving treatment. Where does this leave the individual requiring assistance to die? It would seem that entirely permissive legislation that provides for assisted suicide is unlikely to be enacted in England in the short term. Even with Lord Joffe restricting the Assisted Dying for the Terminally Ill Bill 2005 to physician assisted suicide where a competent adult has an inevitably progressive, untreatable terminal illness that is likely to result in the patient's death within six months, the Bill was defeated in the House of Lords in 2006. The recent DEMOS Commission on Assisted Dying Report[22] also recommended changes to the law, which was represented as inadequate and incoherent. Despite very clear safeguards in the Report, the current government is refusing to act upon any of the recommendations.[23] However, as indicated earlier,

---

14　Campbell, C.S. and Cox, J.C. 2010. Hospice and physician-assisted death: Collaboration, compliance, and complicity. *The Hastings Center Report*, 40(5), 26–35.

15　Seale, C. 2009. Continuous deep sedation in medical practice: A descriptive study. *Journal of Pain and Symptom Management*, 39(1), 44–53.

16　*Airedale NHS Trust v Bland* [1993] AC 789 at 867 per Lord Goff.

17　Up to 900 per year: Seale, C. 2006. National survey of end of life decisions made by UK medical practitioners. *Palliative Medicine*, 20(1), 3–10.

18　*R v Cox* (1992) 12 BMLR 38.

19　Fletcher, H. 2008. Husband is spared jail for suffocating wife who wanted to die. *The Times* [Online: 2 February]. Available at: http://www.timesonline.co.uk/tol/news/uk/crime/article3292051.ece [accessed 20 September 2011].

20　Directgov. 2010. *Your right to refuse future medical treatment* [Online: Directgov]. Available at: http://www.direct.gov.uk/en/Governmentcitizensandrights/Death/Preparation/DG_10029683 [accessed 26 March 2011].

21　General Medical Council. 2010. *End of Life Treatment and Care: Good Practice in Decision-making*. London: General Medical Council.

22　Demos. 2012. *Commission on Assisted Dying Report* [Online: Demos]. Available at: http://www.demos.co.uk/publications/thecommissiononassisteddying [accessed 2 March 2012].

23　Walker, K. 2012. David Cameron faces new pressure to end ban on assisted suicide. *Daily Mail* [Online: 2 January]. Available at: http://www.dailymail.co.uk/news/article-2080927/Cameron-faces-new-pressure-end-ban-assisted-suicide.html [accessed 4 February 2012].

the guidelines give some parameters of acceptable levels of assistance to suicide but some individuals would prefer more than the making of travel arrangements to avoid having to attend clinics such as those of Dignitas abroad. Further, not everyone has someone to do even this and may need to travel sooner than they would wish while their condition still permits because they need medical intervention.

This paper will explain briefly why the English approach to assisted suicide requires liberalization but not to the extent of establishing state-sponsored 'suicide centres'.[24] The compromise approach that advocates the maintenance of the status quo[25] will be rejected in favour of the 'middle way' offered by the Swiss regime albeit with additional safeguards. Many people in England may assume that the approach of right-to-die societies, which have emerged to offer assistance to suicide on an organizational basis, receive wide endorsement in Switzerland. However, there have been demands for regulatory improvements because some of their actual customs have been controversial, including Dignitas's practice of accepting foreign applicants. Nevertheless, a strong majority in the Canton of Zurich voted against any practice restrictions of right-to-die organizations on 15 May 2011.[26] From the English perspective, it is important to understand the concerns that provided the impetus for the Swiss debate. Some English citizens will continue to avail themselves of the services of Dignitas if they cannot find anyone to help here. They need to know what they face in reality and there may be lessons to be learned more generally: what are the justifiable elements of the 'Swiss model' of regulation that we could possibly embrace in England?

In this chapter, the current restrictive approach that is represented by the legal position in England is examined to illustrate the concerns that suggest a more permissive regime is required. A discussion then follows about whether this should extend as far as state-sponsored suicide clinics,[27] or whether a middle way should be settled upon, whereby aspects of the Swiss approach are transposed here. Such a debate remains helpful because it is clear that the matter has not been settled by the publication of the guidelines.[28] The change advocated in this chapter can, as we believe, be justified ethically and operated within a suitably robust regulatory framework that follows the political imperative of accommodating the plurality of societal values.[29]

---

24   *Supra* n. 3.

25   Huxtable, R. 2007. *Euthanasia, Ethics and the Law: from Conflict to Compromise.* Abingdon: Routledge-Cavendish.

26   The results were that 78 per cent voted against a ban of 'suicide tourism', while 84 per cent voted against a general ban of organized assistance to suicide.

27   *Supra* n. 3.

28   See the discussion at n. 41*ff.*

29   Coggon, J. 2010. Assisted dying and the context of debate: 'medical law' versus 'end of life law'. *Medical Law Review*, 18(4), 541–63.

England: The Current Legal Position of Assisted Suicide and the Pressure for Change

On one side of the euthanasia debate is the argument that legally competent individuals should be able to determine the manner of their death in recognition of their autonomous interests. This finds judicial support in such decisions where it has been stated that an adult competent patient is said to have an 'absolute right' to consent to medical treatment, refuse it or to choose one rather than another of treatments being offered for any or no reason.[30] Competent individuals over 18 may also lawfully end their lives.[31] Further, doctors must comply with a valid and applicable advance refusal of treatment.[32] However, competent patients may require assistance to commit suicide and this is where legal difficulties have arisen.

Although the guidelines[33] followed wide consultation[34] on the DPP's interim guidelines,[35] there has been criticism of the consultation: it has been described as secretive and unduly quantitative not least because of the impoverished notion of 'compassion' in the assisted suicide context.[36] The guidelines focus on compassion as an unselfish motive, rather than as a response to the victim's unbearable suffering, and stating that everyone understands its meaning is a less than impressive response.[37] There has been much comment on the guidelines and the *Pretty* and *Purdy* cases that preceded them.[38] A more restrictive approach could have been advocated by insisting on prosecution in all cases of assisted suicide including helping people to travel to Switzerland. The trend after the guidelines is clearly towards a more liberal stance. The act of assisting suicide remains a criminal offence, but the guidelines suggest that this will not be prosecuted provided certain conditions are met.[39] Public interest factors seem to be interpreted liberally by

---

30   *Re T (Adult: refusal of medical treatment)* [1993] Fam 95 (CA) (Lord Donaldson) 102.

31   S. 1 Suicide Act 1961.

32   *Re B (Adult: refusal of medical treatment)* [2002] 2 FCR 1.

33   *Supra* n. 5.

34   Crown Prosecution Service. 2010. *CPS Public Consultation Exercise on the Interim Policy for Prosecutors in respect of Cases of Assisted Suicide Issued by the Director of Public Prosecutions: Summary of Responses* [Online: Crown Prosecution Service]. Available at: http://www.cps.gov.uk/publications/prosecution/assisted_suicide. html [accessed 26 March 2011].

35   Crown Prosecution Service. 2009. *Interim Policy in Respect of Cases of Assisted Suicide* [Online: Crown Prosecution Service]. Available at: http://www.cps.gov.uk/ consultations/as_policy.html [accessed 2 March 2012].

36   Lewis, P. 2011. Informal legal change on assisted suicide. *Legal Studies*, 31(1), 119–34.

37   *Supra* n. 34, para. 2.15.

38   E.g. Mullock, A. 2010. Overlooking the criminally compassionate: What are the implications of prosecutorial policy on encouraging or assisting suicide? *Medical Law Review*, 18(4), 442–70.

39   *Supra* n. 5, para. 45.

offering tolerance in the way it deals with relatives who assist individuals to commit suicide here or in other jurisdictions, provided there are no self-seeking motives,[40] but the strict interpretation of the evidential test in the Code means the DPP could still pursue a prosecution for inconsequential assistance in suicide where the motives are questionable.[41] Notwithstanding the additional clarity provided by the guidelines, key problems remain: some individuals will still have to travel abroad sooner than they would wish to receive the help they need because the guidelines exclude all forms of organized assistance to dying within its territory[42] and there is no possibility for the caring health professional, who may have developed a close relationship with a particular patient, to assist in such cases.[43]

The guidelines are also only relevant for those suffering from a physical condition that can be seen as untenable if autonomy is supported fully: it is for the individual to decide what constitutes suffering for them even if this is mental anguish. The Swiss National Advisory Commission on Biomedical Ethics (SNACBE, established in 2001) has argued that mental disease is an indicator of a need for treatment rather than a ground for assisted suicide if the wish to die is a symptom of the disease. However, where people with mental health problems have a well-considered and stable wish to die in intervals of competence, they should have the possibility to receive assistance.[44] There is insufficient space to consider the position of competent minors but there should also be a debate about the potential legitimacy of allowing them the right to choose death as is allowed in the Netherlands.[45]

The trend after the guidelines is clearly towards a more liberal approach to assisted suicide. To adopt a more restrictive position could be seen as unfair to those who share a permissive moral view and need help to die. Nevertheless, evidential problems with respect to the guidelines seem inevitable and they will continue to be subject to interpretation and challenge. So uncertainty has been reduced

---

40   *Ibid.* See the discussion about the way the DPP dealt with the Daniel James case in the Court of Appeal in *Purdy*: Rehmann-Sutter and Hagger, *supra* n. 1.

41   Mullock, A. 2009. Prosecutors making (bad) law? decision on prosecution: the death by suicide of Daniel James, 9 December 2008. *Medical Law Review*, 17(2), 290–99, at p. 298.

42   *Supra* n. 5, para. 43(16).

43   *Supra* n. 5, para. 43(14).

44   Swiss National Advisory Commission on Biomedical Ethics. 2006. *Opinion 13/2006, Duty-of-care criteria for the management of assisted suicide, 4.3* [Online: Swiss National Advisory Commission on Biomedical Ethics]. Available at: http://www.bag. admin.ch/nek-cne/04236/index.html?lang=en [accessed 26 March 2011]; *cf* Swiss National Advisory Commission on Biomedical Ethics. 2005. *Opinion 9/2005, recommendation 6* [Online: Swiss National Advisory Commission on Biomedical Ethics]. Available at: http://www.bag.admin.ch/nek-cne/04236/index.html?lang=en [accessed 26 March 2011].

45   Available at: http://www.family.org.au/Journals/2004/dutch.htm [accessed 26 March 2011] and Hagger, L. 2009. *The Child as Vulnerable Patient: Protection and Empowerment.* Aldershot: Ashgate, chapter 2.

rather than removed. As far as the public interest factors are concerned, since the publication of the guidelines at least 30 people have been referred to the Crown Prosecution Service suspected of helping someone to commit suicide but none have been prosecuted.[46] Thus, it could be argued that there is greater certainty with respect to the public interest consideration. The Care Not Killing Alliance opposes the policy and believes there is a risk of 'legislation by stealth' undermining the will of Parliament.[47] Those supportive of the current prosecution policy, such as Lord Falconer who chaired the DEMOS Commission on Assisted Dying,[48] welcome the developments as codifying the significant change in approach that had already begun to take place.[49] His hope appears to be that this means a consensus can be developed for further change. Although the campaigning group Dignity in Dying believe the guidelines are an important step developing patient choice, they want legislation with safeguards for mentally competent patients wanting to commit suicide to afford them stronger protection; at the moment investigation can only take place after the death.[50] The DPP's view is that the law has not been weakened nor has the will of Parliament been undermined with a blanket 'no-prosecution' policy: none of the cases considered raised any doubts about the motivation of the person assisting the suicide.[51] He believes the guidelines are working well not least because they are based on broad consultation.[52] Further, he made it clear that there remains a bright line between assisted suicide and mercy killing, where someone requires someone to take the final steps to bring about their death; the latter would always result in a prosecution.[53]

The chief concerns here relate to individuals who may not have anyone willing to assist their suicide, the need to carry out the act prematurely in some cases while patients are still able to travel, the prohibition on assistance from health

---

46   Gibb, F. 2011. Prosecutors clear way for assisted suicides. *The Times*, 5 September, p. 1.

47   Gibb, F. 2011. I haven't banned mercy killing prosecutions, says DPP. *The Times*, 6 September, p. 10.

48   *Supra* n. 22.

49   *Ibid.*

50   *Supra* n. 41.

51   Starmer, K. 2011. So far, we've got it right on assisted suicide – largely thanks to you, the public. *The Times*, 6 September, p. 22.

52   *Ibid.*

53   Tony Nicklinson, a paralysed man who wants a doctor to be able to lawfully end his life to remove his 'indignity' and have a 'common law defence of necessity' against any murder charge, has been granted the right to proceed with his 'right-to-die' case by the High Court. Mr Nicklinson is seeking a court declaration based on his right to respect for private life under Article 8(1) of the European Convention on Human Rights arguing that, in his circumstances, his right to life included the right to end his life in a humane manner of his choosing: BBC News. 2012. 'Locked-in syndrome' man to have right-to-die case heard [Online: 12 March 2012]. Available at: http://www.bbc.co.uk/news/uk-17336774 [accessed 29 March 2012].

professionals and the exclusion of mental suffering as a justifiable factor for receiving assistance. The next section explores the ethical support for a more permissive regime followed by the highlighting of the main arguments against such liberalization.

Ethical Perspectives on Assisted Suicide

In Support of Liberalizing Assisted Suicide

To provide lawful means for people to be assisted in ending their lives would recognize their autonomous interests.[54] Different questions could be asked about the ethical validity of assisting suicide but, given the prevalence of rights discourse,[55] a legitimate course of enquiry lies in asking whether there is a fundamental right to receive assistance in committing suicide. As Hopkins states,[56] a fundamental right is of a higher order than conventional and legal rights and claims that may exist, regardless of any societal constraints. Formulated in this way, such a right would counter the pursuit of community goals and at least avoid the imposition of criminal sanctions against it. His account is based on the idea that rights are 'practically necessary given the fact of our having interests, or even logically necessary concepts given our experiences of purposive action'.[57] The proliferation of rights and their scope can weaken their meaning. However, if autonomy claims are rational and practical (rather than content-free), the appeal to important, worthwhile and reasonable interests is more grounded and can serve to realize the potential goodness of our lives.[58]

Adopting a human rights perspective allows the interests of vulnerable minorities, such as those who legitimately wish to die with assistance, to be protected against those of 'larger aggregates' of persons or more 'powerful minorities'.[59] Drawing on Dworkin's human rights discourse,[60] Campbell[61] argues that there should be legislative change to avoid the subordination of these important interests to public policies that only protect the interests of these other groups. A

---

54   Dworkin, G. 1988. *The Theory and Practice of Autonomy.* Cambridge: Cambridge University Press.

55   E.g. Campbell *supra* n. 11.

56   Hopkins, P.D. 2008. Is enhancement worthy of being a right? *Journal of Evolution and Technology,* 18(1), 1–9.

57   *Ibid.* at p. 2.

58   Dworkin *supra* n. 54 and Coggon, J. 2007. Varied and principled understandings of autonomy in english law: Justifiable inconsistency or blinkered moralism? *Health Care Analysis,* 15(3), 235–55.

59   Campbell *supra* n. 11, at pp. 450–51.

60   Dworkin, R.M. 1978. *Taking Rights Seriously.* London: Duckworths.

61   Campbell, *supra* n. 11, at pp. 450–51.

liberal and pluralistic understanding of the role of the state[62] would favour a legal solution that does not suppress one group in society over another where they hold competing beliefs, provided there are no higher goods to protect. To do otherwise can mean those who wish to end their lives are subjected to 'a devastating, odious form of tyranny'.[63] Respect for human life is not an abstract matter of principle but must include respect for the person in the situation of dying. 'The value of life is self-determined'[64] and competent disabled individuals who are unable to commit suicide without assistance are subject to discrimination[65] on what will be seen as weak grounds. Avoiding anxiety provoked by medically conducted killing and preserving the relationship of trust between doctors and their patients are important concerns, but anxiety also arises if medicine refuses to help somebody in a desperate situation to die and the relationship of trust can be weakened if the doctor is coerced by law to act against the patient's wish. Where doctors do need to be involved, one or two willing doctors from palliative care or anaesthetics could be assigned to help patients to die. This would release all those health professionals who feel uneasy or outright object to any obligation to be involved. It would also lessen the concerns about undermining the relationship of trust between doctors and patients more generally as well as ensuring they developed sufficient expertise to avoid any failure in administering assisted suicide.[66]

It can be argued that the individual's agency is a complex and dynamic process that cannot be reduced to what a patient declares in one moment because this can change quickly.[67] The wish cannot be seen as an abstraction from the intrinsic ambivalence of the terminal situation. A desire also depends on the social and political context, or on the quality of the relationships with others.[68] When a patient says 'I just want to die' this can mean many different things beyond the face value of these words. Patients may perceive themselves to be a burden, they may be afraid to lose control, they may say this to open up a conversation about

---

62   Coggon *supra* n. 29.

63   Dworkin, R.M. 1993. *Life's Dominion: An Argument about Abortion and Euthanasia.* London: HarperCollins, at p. 217; and Singer, P. 1993. *Practical Ethics.* 2nd edn. Cambridge: Cambridge University Press, at pp. 1194–6.

64   Huxtable, *supra* n. 25 and Harris, J. 1997. Euthanasia and the value of life, in *Euthanasia Examined: Ethical, Clinical and Legal Perspectives*, ed. by J. Keown. Cambridge: Cambridge University Press, pp. 6–22.

65   Freeman, M. 2002. Denying death its dominion: Thoughts on the Dianne Pretty case. *Medical Law Review*, 10(3), 245–70.

66   'Suicide research', *The Times*, 28 July 2009.

67   Pabst Battin, M. 2010. The irony of supporting physician-assisted suicide: A personal account. *Medicine, Health Care & Philosophy*, 13, 403–11; Ohnsorge, K., Gudat, H., Widershoven, G. and Rehmann-Sutter, C. 2012. 'Ambivalence' at the end of life: How to understand patients' wishes ethically. *Nursing Ethics* (forthcoming).

68   Downie, R.S., Fyffe, C. and Tannehill, A. 1990. *Health Promotion: Model and Values.* Oxford: Oxford University Press, at pp. 18–19.

how they will die, they may see their life coming to its natural end and so on.[69] In many cases, those wishing to die will have discussed this with those close to them and considered the impact upon them.[70] With reference to the principle of respect for autonomy we can still argue that it is entirely appropriate for the final decision to be one for them alone, bearing all these other aspects in mind, but made in the way that best serves their needs.

This thick account of freedom, we believe, contains the most important ethical argument for legalizing a form of assisted dying. It is the argument from respect: respecting the ultimate judgment of an individual that her or his own life is marked by unbearable suffering expresses a moral recognition of the individual as a sensitive and reflecting person and incorporates an attitude of mercy.[71] In a legal framework that creates special situations, where there are no alternative options of legally ending the life in a dignified way, refusing to accept the wish for assistance in dying is equivalent to saying 'individuals should live through their suffering even if they find it unbearable and long to die'. We doubt that in a liberal secular state there are sufficient convincing reasons to defend this position. It is not coherent with the general recognition of citizens as persons who are capable of taking actions based on their personal values and beliefs.

The argument from respect will, however, not support an unrestricted liberalization of assisted suicide for two reasons: (1) there are conditions under which a person who wishes to die must be protected from those who could exploit this wish that might not be in harmony with the best interests of the individual affected; (2) the expressed (and acutely felt) wish to die by assisted suicide in one given situation does not necessarily represent the best interests of that person in other circumstances.

The first of those reasons leads to the view that assistance to dying should remain a criminal offence if it is done for reasons other than the interests of the individual affected. The vulnerability of the individual who wishes to die also emerges because of the second reason: the expressed and acutely felt wish to die does not always represent the best interests of the person concerned because there might be ways to ease the situation (medically, socially, economically and so on) that the person concerned is not in a position to see. Sometimes, though not always, others can help to change the situation in such a way that the individual regains confidence and hope. This is the second ethical pole to respect for autonomy suggested by the SNACBE:[72] the principle of care or solidarity. A good decision-

---

69   Coyle, N. 2004. Expressed desire for hastened death in seven patients living with advanced cancer. A phenomenological inquiry. *Oncology Nursing Forum*, 31, 699–706; Ohnsorge, K. and Rehmann-Sutter, C. 2010. Menschen, die sterben möchten. Empirische Studien in der Palliativmedizin und ihre ethischen Implikationen, in *Endlichkeit, Medizin und Unsterblichkeit*, ed. by A. Hilt, I. Jordan and A. Frewer. Stuttgart: Steiner, pp. 249–70.

70   McLean, n. 13, at pp. 34–5.

71   Battin, *supra* n. 67, at p. 406.

72   Opinion 9, *supra* n. 44.

making process includes both respect and a serious attempt to open up more options for the person concerned taking time to ensure the individual is expressing settled wishes. In the end, the two poles of autonomy and care may coincide.

In addition to the argument from respect, there are at least two more ethical arguments for a liberalization of assisted suicide that we find key: first, there is an argument from consistency with regard to suicide and to the refusal of treatment.

The act of committing an attempt to commit suicide is legal so why should assistance to do this be unlawful? This is inconsistent and represents unequal treatment of those who are not in a position to commit suicide without help. This is ethically problematic because it constrains personal freedom in an existentially crucial aspect when an individual is already dependent, restricted and burdened with suffering. The same concerns underpinning opposition to assisted suicide logically require us to contest the right of an individual to refuse life-sustaining medical treatment. We have not been convinced that such refusal should be unlawful, so we should not be persuaded that assisted suicide should be classed as such. The difference between refusal of treatment and assisted dying lies in their passive and active nature and this is ethically relevant in some way. However, we cannot see that it carries enough weight to justify a radically different treatment in law.[73] The refusal of treatment can also lead to a certain death, as does assisted suicide. However, this 'natural' death can, under certain circumstances, be more painful, even cruel, and a legal provision that forces a patient to accept it is thus unjustifiable.

There is a second argument that arises from the limitedness of medicine. Medicine can prolong life but is not always capable of securing an acceptable quality of life throughout the progress of a disease.[74] Not everybody can be convinced that continuing life is worthwhile, even with the best palliative care. There are factors of suffering that cannot be alleviated by palliative care such as the continuous loss of function of important body parts (owing to the disease and the very process of dying), the dependency on caregivers and family, the experience of the meaninglessness of suffering, the loss of perceived 'dignity', extreme fatigue, and also the severe pain for certain patients who do not want to be sedated before dying.[75] The argument frequently proposed by opponents

---

73   Dworkin, G. 2008. Should physician-assisted suicide be legalized? in *Giving Death a Helping Hand. Physician-Assisted Suicide and Public Policy. An International Perspective*, ed. by D. Birnbacher and E. Dahl. Berlin: Springer, pp. 3–9; and Dworkin, G. 1998. Public policy and physician-assisted suicide, in *Euthanasia and Physician-Assisted Suicide. For and Against*, ed. by G. Dworkin, R.G. Frey and S. Bok. Cambridge: Cambridge University Press, pp. 64–80.

74   McLean, n. 13, at p. 46.

75   Admiraal, P. 2008. Physician-assisted suicide: A doctor's perspective, in Birnbacher and Dahl, *supra* n. 73, pp. 131–9; and Admiraal, P. 1999. Listening and helping to die: The Dutch way, in *Bioethic: An Anthology*, ed. by H. Kuhse and P. Singer. Oxford: Blackwell, pp. 332–8.

of assisted suicide that adequate palliative medicine will make assisted suicide unnecessary is not true in all cases.[76]

A key question that needs to be discussed ethically is whether assisted suicide should be restricted to individuals who are terminally ill or profoundly physically disabled. It is worth highlighting the prosecution in the Netherlands of a doctor who assisted the suicide of 86-year-old Mr Brongersma who had 'life fatigue' because this has been cited as further evidence of the 'slippery slope' in action.[77] However, an alternative interpretation of the case could be that this was an appropriate intervention because it was the individual who decided what was unbearable for him rather than the doctor.[78] Similar concerns have been raised in England about the assisted suicide of Nan Maitland who was not terminally ill but suffered from arthritis; she wished to die before she deteriorated further.[79] To restrict lawful assistance to suicide to the terminally ill cannot, we believe, be justified for two reasons: (1) the definition of the concept of 'terminal illness' is necessarily vague. Sometimes doctors can foresee that death must be close, but in other cases death cannot be forecasted and the situation of being close to death can only be established after the individual has died;[80] (2) there are situations where death is clearly not imminent but a request for assisted suicide should be respected for good ethical reasons. This can be where there is increasing multi-morbidity, weakness and advanced age. It can also be when an individual has lost any hope for a future improvement: as Edwards puts it 'can't fulfil "a life plan"'.[81] Alternatively, it can be in a situation of a progressive disabling disease where a serious and understandable wish to die can emerge before the disease becomes terminal in the medical sense.

---

76   Campell and Cox, *supra* n. 14.

77   McLean, *supra* n. 13, at p. 169 and discussed further at n. 77*ff.*

78   *Ibid.*

79   BBC News. 2011. *Right-to-die activist Nan Maitland 'died with dignity'* [Online: BBC News]. Available at: http://www.bbc.co.uk/news/uk-12959664 [accessed 4 April, 2011].

80   Personal communication from Dr D. Bryden, Consultant Intensive Care Physician, Sheffield Teaching NHS Foundation Trust and also discussed in Chapter 3 of this book. The position of the Swiss Academy of the Medical Sciences requiring clinical evidence that death can be expected to come within days or a few weeks seems inconsistent with this epistemological difficulty of forecasting the time of death that is experienced by clinicians: 'wenn er aufgrund klinischer Anzeichen zur Überzeugung gekommen ist, dass ein Prozess begonnen hat, der erfahrungsgemäss innerhalb von Tagen oder einigen Wochen zum Tod führt'; Schweizerische Akademie der Medizinischen Wissenschaften: Probleme bei der Durchführung von ärztlicher Suizidhilfe. Stellungnahme der Zentralen Ethikkommission (ZEK) der SAMW, adopted on 20 January 2012; available at: www.samw.ch.

81   Edwards, *supra* n. 3, at p. 179.

Against Liberalizing Assisted Suicide

To bolster claims about the sanctity of life, evidence is often presented that legislation introducing assisted death would inevitably lead to a 'slippery slope'[82] whereby the chance of morally unjustified acts in the taking of life will increase. This logical form of the slippery slope argument, whereby it is proposed that the legalization of assisted suicide (which may seem justifiable) leads to encouraging death for morally unacceptable reasons,[83] can be dismissed. Coercive or paternalistic suggestions to die are not an inevitable consequence of legalized assisted suicide, if legislation includes provisions to exclude them.[84] The concern, however, that vulnerable members of society may suffer further disadvantage if assisted suicide is legalized does have to be taken seriously.[85] The anticipated expectation, even pressure, subtle or otherwise, on the elderly and disabled to seek assistance to die to avoid being a burden to others as exemplified by Lord Bingham in *Pretty*[86] may be less easy to address. Strict safeguards that protect the interests of those vulnerable to committing suicide, in conjunction with increased valuing of the disabled in society, could ameliorate these fears.[87] Equally, it may be argued that there can be pressures to carry on living because of the legal and practical difficulties in ending one's life as well as the emotional impact on loved ones.[88] Proponents for the facilitation of end of life choices merely see disability as a legitimate factor to be taken into account: it is a matter for the disabled individual and does not entail a devaluing of their lives per se. The disabled person has as much right to have their autonomy respected as anyone else and to assume they are more likely to be coerced does them no service. The experience in Oregon, where assisted suicide is permitted,[89] is that otherwise disadvantaged individuals are no more likely to be targeted for legalized assisted dying than anyone else: it is the

---

82   See Smith, S. 2005. Evidence for the practical slippery slope in the debate on physician-assisted suicide and euthanasia. *Medical Law Review*, 13(1), 17–44; and Smith, S. 2005. Fallacies of the logical slippery slope in the debate on physician-assisted suicide and euthanasia. *Medical Law Review*, 13(2), 224–43.

83   *Ibid.*

84   *Ibid. Cf* Levy, N. 2008. Slippery slope and physician-assisted suicide, in Birnbacher and Dahl, *supra* n. 73, at pp. 11–21.

85   McLean, *supra* n. 13, at pp. 61–70; Golden, M. and Zoanni, T. 2010. Killing us softly: The dangers of legalizing assisted suicide. *Disability and Health Journal*, 3(1), 16–30; Coleman, D. 2010. Assisted suicide laws create discriminatory double standard for who gets suicide prevention and who gets suicide assistance: Not Dead Yet responds to Autonomy, Inc. *Disability and Health Journal*, 3(1), 39–50.

86   *Supra* n. 12, para. 29.

87   McLean, *supra* n. 13, at p. 183 and World Health Organization/The World Bank. 2011. *World Report on Disability.* Geneva: WHO.

88   McLean, *ibid.* at p. 43.

89   Death with Dignity Act 1994. *Cf* Ganzini, L. and Dahl, E. Physician-assisted suicide in Oregon, in Birnbacher and Dahl, *supra* n. 73, at pp. 67–75.

better educated and financially secure who constitute the majority of those seeking physician assisted suicide.[90]

For some, the empirical version of the slippery slope argument also does not withstand scrutiny.[91] McLean believes that closer examination of the evidence suggests that the additional transparency gained by explicit recognition of euthanasia in a regulatory framework is far better than the unregulated practice of assisted death under the guise of the doctrine of 'double effect' or futility practised in England. For example, in the Netherlands, where the legalization of assisted dying is provided by the Termination of Life on Request and Assisted Suicide (Review Procedures) Act 2002, she considers that there is no evidence that increasing numbers of people are being helped to die as a result of their legalized euthanasia policy nor is there a greater tolerance for killing leading to more illicit deaths. However, this is difficult to assert because there was already a wide and morally accepted practice of euthanasia before the legalization:[92] the process in the Netherlands was complex and it is almost impossible to compare numbers before and after the legislation was enacted. In any event, our proposal is restricted to assisted suicide and there is no risk of being killed without explicit request, because then it would not qualify as a suicide.

The idea that legalized physician assisted suicide may undermine the relationship of trust between patients and doctors if the latter take a main role in assisting death has to be considered in the light that (1) the latter already do so albeit obscurely and (2) the relation of trust may even require the doctor to accept a role in assisted dying. A relationship of trust is based on the patient's belief that the doctor will never act against her or his interests and not on the promise that the doctor would never adopt a role in assisting death. If the patient wishes nothing more than to die, to act in the patient's interest means to accept such a role (such as writing a prescription for a lethal drug, organizing the transfer to a suitable location and so on) and not to reject it for the sake of certain professional codices. With regard to (1) we would agree that trust is more likely to be optimized where practices are transparent, appropriately regulated and where the patient is seen as exercising informed and free choices.[93]

The preceding discussion suggests that criticisms of regulation in some other jurisdictions may, in part, be more imagined than real. Concerns that safeguards will fail to be effective do not justify not attempting to put some in place. A more permissive approach to assisted suicide should be taken in England. Options should be explored with patients and appropriate support offered, but if they remain committed to ending their lives and need help to do so, this should be provided. To prohibit health professionals caring for the patient and on right-to-die

---

90   Dahl, E. and Levy, N. 2006. The case for physician-assisted suicide: How can it possibly be proven? *Journal of Medical Ethics*, 32(6), 335–8, 335.

91   McLean, *supra* n. 13, at pp. 170–73 and 183.

92   Admiraal, *supra* n. 75.

93   McLean, *supra* n. 13, at pp. 55–61.

organizations from assisting suicide is unreasonable: patients should not be forced to end their lives prematurely in unfamiliar territory.

Before we consider proposals for publicly supported and accessible suicide centres[94] that would represent the most permissive regime for assisted suicide, it is worth considering whether we should merely maintain the current approach.

The 'No Change' Option

Huxtable suggests that leaving the law largely unchanged eliminates what he calls the 'suicide trap' in English law because it makes it predictable under what conditions those helping a person travel to Switzerland to die do not face a risk of prosecution at home.[95] He notes how epidemiological and demographical changes mean that people will increasingly face difficult end of life decisions in the face of long, terminal illnesses and that continued conflict does not serve them well.[96] Building on earlier calls for defending the middle ground, he believes that conceiving, if not achieving, compromise is a real possibility and one for which we should strive.[97] Huxtable rejects any ideas that 'fresh theorizing' can present satisfactory solutions alone or that achieving consensus on those matters where agreement can be achieved is sufficient, or indeed possible:[98] a consensus position would not necessarily have moral justification and conflict is unlikely to be completely eradicated although it could be minimized.[99] For him, the conceptual framework presented by moral pluralists offers a way through the current quagmire of controversies. It provides an opportunity to acknowledge the nuances of moral dilemmas encountered in practice given the plurality of values that are in a state of constant tension.[100] Compromise differs from consensus because it entails frank concessions on both sides of a debate. Rather than seeing compromise as surrendering integrity, 'we should acknowledge moral conflict as part of living a truly integrated or "whole" life'.[101]

Compromise could be achieved procedurally through bodies reflecting diverse moral views.[102] In the case of assisted suicide under existing law, these could decide

---

94 Edwards, *supra* n. 3.

95 Huxtable, *supra* n. 25.

96 *Ibid.*

97 Huxtable, R. 2009. The suicide tourist trap: compromise across boundaries. *Bioethical Inquiry*, 6, 327–36.

98 *Ibid.* at pp. 145–50.

99 Through e.g. the use of ethics committees.

100 Huxtable, *supra* n. 25, at pp. 151–8.

101 *Ibid.* p 154.

102 Huxtable notes, in particular, the success of the Warnock Committee in addressing the fraught issue of the moral status of the embryo as it contemplated potential laws regulating assisted reproduction (*Committee of Inquiry into Human Fertilisation and Embryology*, DHSS, 1984). The Committee held that those advocating total protection for the embryo, as opposed by those favouring none, were both valid positions. However, they

whether prosecution in the particular case is in the public interest, for example. Governance frameworks should be established to ensure committees operate within more precise criteria against which they are evaluated.[103] Involvement of patients and, in appropriate circumstances, those close to them should be required.[104] Gillon advocates that there should be a voluntary commitment to these ideals unless an audit reveals unsatisfactory outcomes.[105] Should this transpire, then mandatory, universal and centrally-regulated ethical governance should be considered.

More importantly, Huxtable maintains that it is possible to describe the substance of a compromise policy without sacrificing integrity.[106] This may be achieved by recognizing the merits of competing claims but attempting to accommodate and locate a legitimate position between them. Conflicting values can act as checks and balances to avoid any perspective being taken too far. This would also acknowledge the ambivalences that all sides of the debate experience no matter what the apparent strength of their position seems to imply. The inevitable moral discomfort provides a crucial 'moral pause' and will entail victories and defeats on all sides. Compromise provides a legitimate excuse or 'refined moral judgment' in relation to decisions that may not be to the particular taste. This conveys a degree of responsibility but also compassion for all involved. On this basis, Huxtable believes that the current legal approach can be justified provided the relevant end of life practices are conducted with strong procedural safeguards, including clear guidelines.

Adopting a compromise position to suicide specifically,[107] Huxtable develops his ideas on the use of internal practices and rules, and explores what might constitute a legitimate position on the part of the state in the international context. A blanket prohibition on travel to a jurisdiction that permits assisted suicide would unduly affect those requiring such assistance. A universally accepted ethical approach is extremely unlikely to be achieved. Thus, Huxtable concludes that England's de facto permission in allowing travel for these purposes reflects an acceptable compromise between individual freedom and those who would find it hard to countenance the domestic decriminalization of suicide. This position is ethically defensible and justifies any apparent inconsistencies in the law.

Huxtable's claims have a specious appeal but are not ones we are persuaded to support. He is not offering a real compromise because he does not balance

---

adopted a pragmatic position by offering partial protection in that research on embryos was only permissible up till the 14th day of development (*ibid.* pp. 151–8).

103   Larcher,V., Slowther, A.-M. and Watson, A.R. 2010. Core competencies for clinical ethics committees. *Clinical Medicine*, 10, 30–33.

104   The fact that patients may raise issues directly with the Clinical Ethics Forum at Sheffield Children's NHS Foundation Trust is widely advertised, for example.

105   Gillon, R. 2010. What attributes should clinical ethics committees have? *BMJ* 340.

106   Huxtable, *supra* n. 25, at pp. 158–71.

107   *Supra* n. 97.

views within English society but merely evades the issue by allowing travel to Switzerland. Further, we take the view that to maintain the status quo renders the law incoherent and lacking in conceptual rigour. For our part, the law steps in too soon in this model. The practical effect of this is that patients, their loved ones and the health professionals involved are unable to predict with any certainty whether anticipated actions will be compliant with the law. Those who assist in death with good intent should be able to do so without fear of criminal sanction. This would avoid the anxiety experienced by those who assist in suicide while they wait to see whether prosecuting authorities consider that the relevant criteria of any guidelines have been met.

As an indirect approach, Huxtable tries 'to guarantee that the permissive policies in the place of departure reasonably conform to their justifying principles'.[108] However, it has the disadvantage of 'off-shoring' the unpalatable issue of assisted suicide itself, that is, the main practice (the provision of the means for killing, not just travelling assistance) to another jurisdiction, which, for whatever reason, happens to be more permissive and takes over the burden of helping these people die. From the perspective of the receiving country, this approach, if officially endorsed by England, looks like a very 'cheap' solution. Switzerland is too small to provide this kind of service to the whole world. Beyond the problem of justifying off-shoring as a proper solution, developments during 2011 makes this option even more challenging as will become apparent when the Swiss approach to assisted suicide is explored. The country of origin needs to be confident that its citizens seeking suicide will receive appropriate protections. This now cannot be guaranteed because, as is explained in detail below, there is actually, and also in the foreseeable future, no regulatory framework in place in Switzerland that would be defensible in England, even under the premises of a much more liberal basic approach.

To recap here, and putting aside the practical difficulties of determining the imminence of death and level of suffering,[109] we should support the individual's right to decide when and how they want to die to the extent that it is feasible. Only they can determine when life is no longer worth living assuming they are making their choice freely and on an informed basis. Appropriate regulation requiring checks and verification will ensure that the determined few who are likely to ask for such assistance will receive the help they deserve. Safeguards should include sufficient time to ensure that the decision is well pondered and, ultima ratio, that any depression, so often a feature of an incurable condition,[110] is not clouding a person's judgment to the point that their capacity might be in doubt but reflects a permanent lack of hope.

---

108 *Ibid.* p. 335.
109 Watson, M. 2008. The last 48 hours. *Innovait*, 1(4), 267.
110 Finlay, I. 2009. Assisted suicide is fine in a perfect world. We don't live (or die) in one. *The Times*, 1 April.

The discussion now turns to proposals for publicly supported and accessible suicide centres that, as we have said, would represent the most permissive regime for assisted suicide. This is because they would respond positively to requests for assisted suicide regardless of the state of the person's health. The following section explores this option to see if such a proposition is one that should be considered in England.

Suicide Centres: An Obligation or a Step Too Far?

Edwards has proposed the establishment of a network of suicide centres in the UK to assist suicide in cases where a competent person has a definite, sustained intention to end their life, regardless of their state of health.[111] The need is established by a relatively high number of deaths by suicide in the UK (5,554 in 2006), which is exemplified in the media by the case of Daniel James where the Swiss organization Dignitas was involved. However, as Edwards argues, 'the attention given to such cases can lead to a neglect of the problem of how to respond to the vast majority of suicides, in which there is no obvious accompanying health problem'.[112] Professional suicide centres would be places in which people with suicidal thoughts could explore these[113] and then, perhaps, also get the means to commit a safe and painless suicide, without distressing or harming others. The problem with this assessment is that Edwards ignores the fact that the number of suicide attempts is much higher than the number of suicides executed. An organized offer of assistance to end one's life efficiently, safely and without pain therefore could not only affect those who would kill themselves by other means, but also those who only attempt to kill themselves and would otherwise survive. An ethical argument should reflect the needs of both categories of people in suicidal states. To suggest that every person who attempts to commit suicide would be better off if they could successfully die is implausible because of ample evidence of people who, after a failed suicide bid, regain a positive attitude to life.[114] The range of functions of these suicide centres could be broadened to include a form of counselling and help that is primarily directed to find other improvements in the situation so that the wish to die becomes less acute or disappears. If we follow this pathway, there could still

---

111   *Supra* n. 3.

112   *Ibid.* at p. 176.

113   *Ibid.* at p. 177.

114   Hell, D. 2006. Ergebnisse der Suizidforschung, in *Beihilfe zum Suzid in der Schweiz. Beiträge aus Ethik, Recht und Medizin*, ed. by C. Rehmann-Sutter, A. Bondolfi, J. Fischer and M. Leuthold. Bern: Lang, pp. 85–91; and Ernst, K. and Ernst, C. 1995. *Praktische Klinikpsychiatrie*. 3rd edn. Stuttgart: Kohlhammer.

be reasons in support of organizations like the Swiss EXIT or Dignitas, whose practice includes help to alleviate the problems that cause the person's suicidal thoughts and, in consequence, to make the suicide unnecessary.

Edwards' argument from respect for autonomy prima facie counts against the prohibition of suicide centres, because they would give the opportunity to everybody to decide about ending their lives. However, is this really an argument for suicide centres? These are not the only way of providing assistance to dying.

Edwards also uses the 'principle of mercy' invoked by Pabst Battin,[115] the '[…] compassion for the relief of pain and suffering', to support the establishment of suicide centres.[116] However, this principle does not imply that it would be an act of mercy to help everybody who wishes to die. In many cases there will be other options to relieve suffering.

The subjective character of suffering is the focus of Edwards' third consideration. There *are* conditions in which a person can find life in that condition 'worse than death', and the determination of whether or not one's life is 'worth living' is a question of the values of that person themselves.[117] Edwards' argument supports the idea that the perspective of the person concerned should be paramount. However, this does not provide this person with a right to be assisted in a suicide or a right of access to suicide centres.[118]

Edwards also presents the idea of a 'life plan': '[t]he suggestion is that we each of us have a conception of the kind of life we would like to lead'.[119] If this is virtually unattainable they may prefer death. However, this only provides a reason to respect the person's values. Also, life plans are not fixed concepts to be realized or not. They can change and adapt to new situations. If the person feels that others care about them and will do everything to provide them with a new perspective, a new life plan may emerge. It would be a naturalistic fallacy to say that, because of the observable fact that a person in a certain situation prefers death (values death higher than a continuation of an undesired life), it is justified to help her to end this life by providing organized suicide assistance. This view is simplistic. It is conceded that there are *some* circumstances in which a revision of the life plan is impossible, such as where the situation cannot be alleviated in other ways, and a safe and painless death therefore becomes the most desirable way out of an unbearable situation.

Edwards' arguments also do not differentiate between assistance by relatives, other individuals, physicians, or organizations. A key argument in support of the

---

115   Battin, *supra* n. 67.

116   *Ibid.* at p. 403.

117   *Ibid.*

118   Rehmann-Sutter, C. 2007. Was bedeutet das, Recht auf den eigenen Tod? *Schweizerische Ärztezeitung*, 88, 1109–12.

119   Edwards, *supra* n. 3, at p. 179.

organizations is that '[…] although there is reason to suppose that death of a loved one causes anguish to family and friends, there is reason to suppose that death in a suicide centre is a cause for less anguish than death by other means available would be'.[120]

This proposal is partially flawed because it assumes that there are only two alternatives: death in a suicide centre or death by other means. As the experience in Switzerland clearly demonstrates, organizations can also provide assistance at home, where the individual can die in the presence of loved ones. The most compelling part of his argument is that an experienced and well-run organization can create circumstances in which the person can experience a good death, one that they have chosen. This would be considerably less stressful for relatives (and emotionally uninvolved others) than a suicide using other means available. The argument in this chapter supports organizations who adopt a more nuanced approach to assisting suicide as outlined here, but not necessarily centres whose main *raison d'être* is to assist the suicides of legally competent individuals whatever their condition and within the confines of its building.

Edwards supports his perspective with reference to the data from the Netherlands, Oregon and Switzerland identifying that the fact that people know there is an option they can take if they become extremely desperate can make a crucial difference. This is because '[i]f they know there is an escape available, should things become unbearable for them, this fact alone can serve to deter them from actually ending their life' whilst they feel capable of withstanding their situation.[121] An organization may be best prepared to provide such an assurance. A significant proportion of those who successfully go through the evaluation procedure at EXIT and get the recipe for sodium pentobarbital actually never use it. EXIT gets 1,500 requests for assisted deaths per year. In 2010, 421 cases were closely examined (files opened), while only 257 suicides were actually performed.[122] Dignitas reports that about 70 per cent of those with a 'provisional green light' never came back again, with only 13 per cent actually making an appointment to die.[123] In Oregon, in 2010, 96 prescriptions for lethal medications were written under the provisions of the Death with Dignity Act, but only 59 died from ingesting the medications.[124]

---

120   *Ibid.* at p. 181.

121   Dieterle, J.M. 2007. Physician assisted suicide: A new look at the arguments. *Bioethics*, 21(3), 127–39; and Steinbock, B. 2005. The case for physician assisted suicide: Not (yet) proven. *Journal of Medical Ethics*, 31, 235–41.

122   EXIT, 2011. *So viele Beitritte wie noch nie. Medienmitteilung 05. 04. 2011* [Online: EXIT]. Available at: http://www.exit.ch/wDeutsch/ [accessed 12 August 2011].

123   Dignitas. 2011. *So funktioniert Dignitas- auf welcher philosophischen Grundlage beruht die Tätigkeit dieser Organization?* [Online: Dignitas]. Available at: http://www. dignitas.ch/ [accessed 12 August 2011].

124   State of Oregon Public Health Division. 2010. *Oregon Death with Dignity Act, Annual Report 2010* [Online: State of Oregon Public Health Division] [accessed 3 February 2011].

On a pragmatic level, it would be politically difficult to justify *state*-sponsored suicide centres when these would be in direct competition for limited resources with other health services that are perceived as life affirming. This is particularly the case at a time of unprecedented challenge for the NHS, when it is undergoing a massive restructuring exercise within severe financial constraints.[125] Legal challenges to any lack of provision would seem to be futile. Domestic courts are only likely to interfere with rationing decisions where decision-making procedures are found wanting.[126] Arguments using the Human Rights Act 1998 seem doomed to failure also given the European Court of Human Rights' jurisprudence, which clearly shows a reluctance to impose disproportionate burdens on public bodies.[127] This must be all the more so in the case of requests for services to end life.[128] More importantly, the preceding discussion highlights how a well-run right-to-die organization may offer the possibility of a more flexible approach to ensure an individual has a good death than a suicide centre, not least because services could be offered in people's homes where appropriate. Should this type of provision receive Parliamentary approval it would be imperative that safety and quality of care standards are appropriately addressed whether it was offered in the public or private domain. With this in mind, the Swiss approach to assisted suicide is examined in order to ascertain whether it is one that could be adopted in England.

Switzerland: The Current Legal Position and the Pressure for Change

Switzerland has been held up as the best example of supporting individuals in exercising their autonomy.[129] A person commits an offence if, for selfish reasons, he or she incites or assists another to commit suicide under Article 115 of the Swiss Penal Code.[130] This motivational element must be proven by the state as with all elements in any criminal statute.[131] Since the 1980s, right-to-die societies have emerged who offer organized assistance to suicide. These organizations are relatively anonymous, semi-professionalized structures that are able to provide

---

125   Department of Health. 2011. *GP pathfinder consortia by Strategic Health Authority region* [Online: Department of Health]. Available at: http://www.dh.gov.uk/en/Aboutus/Features/DH_122384 [accessed 14 March 2011].

126   *Servier Laboratories Limited v National Institute for Health and Clinical Excellence & An.* [2010] EWCA Civ 346.

127   *Osman v UK* [1999] 1 FLR 193.

128   See the European Court of Human Rights' antipathy to Dianne Pretty's claim: *Pretty v UK* (2002) 35 EHRR 1, 39.

129   McLean, *supra* n. 13, at p. 189.

130   Guillod, O. and Schmidt, A. 2005. Assisted suicide under Swiss law. *European Journal of Health Law*, 12(1), 25–38.

131   Ziegler, S.J. 2009. Collaborated death: An exploration of the Swiss model of assisted suicide for its potential to enhance oversight and demedicalize the dying process. *Journal of Law, Medicine & Ethics*, 37(2), 318–30, at p. 323.

the means to die efficiently and without pain. Two of them (Dignitas and Ex-International) accept applications from other countries.[132] The organization must establish that the person who seeks assistance is capable of understanding the meaning and the implications of committing suicide otherwise the assistance would not fall under Article 115 but would qualify as homicide. However, the last five years have witnessed a debate about whether a statute on assisted suicide is necessary to put the activities of right-to-die societies under state supervision and should include requirements for minimal standards to be met with respect to each request for assisted suicide.

The SNACBE[133] has become one of the leading players in the public sphere after it published an extensive report on assisted suicide in 2005 and a more detailed proposal for regulation in 2006.[134] Although the Commission has proposed an amendment to the law, it has defended the retention of the liberal position in principle to one that does not restrict assisted suicide to physicians, allows right-to-die organizations to play a significant role in facilitating assisted death (but under state supervision), and does not propose to limit assisted suicide to those who are terminally ill or dying. The law should establish the criteria to be used in the evaluation of every request by the right-to-die organizations and in the provision of the suicidal act rather than routinized processes. These should include robust, individual assessment over a period of time, where alternative ways of helping the person should be explored.[135] This would still allow the assistance in suicide of people travelling from other countries to Switzerland, but it would not be done too quickly (for instance during just an overnight stay in Zurich or Bern) and with an evaluation that is based merely on correspondence.[136]

After the publication of the 2005 Report, the Ministry of Law under Federal Councillor Christoph Blocher refused to take action because, it was argued, legal oversight would in effect provide right-to-die organizations with state legitimization.[137] The activity of these organizations has been the object of heated debates in the national media, after controversial cases have become public: for example, EXIT has helped people with mental illness to die; Dignitas, lacking another location, has attended the death of a person from Germany in a car on a parking lot outside the city; and Dignitas has used helium and a plastic bag (over the head) as a suicidal technique to avoid the use of sodium pentobarbital, a

---

132   Baezner-Sailer, E.M. 2008. Physician-assisted suicide in Switzerland: A personal report, in Birnbacher and Dahl, *supra* n. 73, at pp. 141–8.

133   Chaired by one of the authors (CRS) between 2001 and 2009.

134   Opinions 9/2005 and 13/2006 *supra* n. 44; *cf* C. Rehmann-Sutter et al., *supra* n. 114.

135   Opinion 13/2006, *supra* n. 44, at 4.1, 4.4, 4.7.

136   Opinion 9/2005, *supra* n. 44, at 4.10.

137   Blocher, C. 2007. Klare Schranken für die Sterbehilfe. *Neue Zürcher Zeitung*, 26/27, 17: 'Es wäre ausserordentlich gefährlich, wenn der Staat durch ein Aufsichtsgesetz gleichsam nach aussen diese Organizationen und deren Tätigkeit legitimieren oder ihnen gar ein Gütesiegel verleihen würde.'

barbiturate that provides a safe, quick and painless death, but can only be bought in a pharmacy on prescription by a physician. After 2009, the Ministry of Law (now under Federal Councillor Evelyne Widmer-Schlumpf) has been evaluating the results of a public consultation on several options for stricter regulation of such organizations. One suggestion was for a more restrictive version of Article 115 that binds the activity of assisted suicide organizations to a list of criteria, one of which was the closeness of death. Another proposal suggested the organizations should be completely prohibited.[138] The SNACBE has criticized both approaches as being too restrictive.[139] Meanwhile, on 10 July 2009, the Public Prosecutor of the Canton of Zurich published a bilateral regulatory document that contained a list of duty of care criteria and is co-signed by EXIT but not by Dignitas. This was supposed to represent a model for a comprehensive national regulation.[140] However, in June 2010, the Swiss Federal Court declared this document to be invalid.[141] Soon after the referendum in the Canton of Zurich noted above, the Swiss Federal Council finally decided to abstain from any amendments to the law on 29 June 2011.[142]

Against the view endorsed by the Swiss Ministry of Law, we argue that regulating assisted suicide organizations would not give them undue legal legitimacy because Article 115 has been in force since 1942 (in particular its meagre provision concerning inducement and assistance to suicide) and in fact legalizes the practice of such organizations already.[143] Nevertheless, it is valid to state that some of the practices of Dignitas (publicly visible and frequent suicide assistance in residential neighbourhoods, lack of financial transparency and so on), as well as EXIT providing assistance for patients with mental conditions under very narrow conditions, are subject to public concern in Switzerland and abroad.

In the light of the picture in Switzerland, it is not clear whether there is an established 'Swiss model' for dealing with organized suicide assistance. The situation there will probably not change in the near future. This became clear after the decision of the Swiss Federal Council (that is, the executive government), which was explained in public by the new Minister of Law Simonetta Sommaruga

---

138   Eidgenössisches Justiz- und Polizeidepartement EJPD. 2009. Änderung des Strafgesetzbuches und des Militärstrafgesetzes betreffend die organisierte Suizidhilfe [Online: Eidgenössisches Justiz- und Polizeidepartement EJPD]. Available at: http://www. ejpd.admin.ch/ejpd/en/home/themen.html [accessed 27 March 2011 under 'Euthanasia'].

139   Vernehmlassungsantwort der NEK-CNE zu den bundesrätlichen Vorschlägen für eine Änderung von Art. 115 StGB/Art. 119 MStG. 2010. Available at: http://www.nek-cne. ch [accessed 27 March 2011].

140   'Vereinbarung über die organisierte Suizidhilfe' zwischen der Oberstaatsan-waltschaft des Kantons Zürich und *EXIT* Deutsche Schweiz vom 7. 2009. Available at: http://www.staatsanwaltschaften.zh.ch [accessed 27 March 2011].

141   C_438/2009; 16 June 2010.

142   SDA. 2011. Bundesrat will Sterbehilfe doch nicht regeln. *Neue Zürcher Zeitung*, 30 June.

143   Baezner-Sailer, a former president of *EXIT*, points out that its activities are based on this existing law, *supra* n. 132, at p. 132.

on 29 June 2011, to abstain from any explicit regulation of organized assistance to suicide. There were political reasons for this.[144] One of these reasons was that explicit legislation would make the country more attractive for suicide tourists. Switzerland obviously prefers to retain a degree of ambiguity in order to avoid being overwhelmed by numbers of such individuals.

It is likely that (1) assisted suicide will remain legal albeit within constraints; (2) right-to-die societies will continue to play a significant role because they are so well established and they continue to have relatively broad support in society; (3) assisted suicide will not be restricted to physicians, but physicians will have their role in providing the prescriptions for the lethal drug; (4) active euthanasia (voluntary and euthanasia without explicit request) will continue to be a criminal offence without exceptions. As it stands, governance of assisted suicide is to a large extent in the hands of the private organizations that provide the service without adequate oversight. Aside from the questionable practice of 'off-shoring' assisted suicide alluded to earlier, the English government cannot rely on the Swiss legal system to provide adequate protection for its citizens seeking help to die in its jurisdiction, at least not on such a level that would be seen as defensible in the UK.

For the sake of discussion, we can treat the following as the 'Swiss model' de lege ferenda: a complete ban on active euthanasia, but individual and team-assisted suicide within an explicit legal framework that clarifies what standards of care need to be enacted in each individual case should be legal as advocated by the SNACBE. Is this a model that could be transposed to England?

In an important paper of 2009 that contains the results of an extensive comparative and also case-oriented empirical research, Ziegler[145] analyzed the Swiss model with regard to its potential application elsewhere. Although he recognizes that it is not perfect and will probably develop, he sees three key advantages when compared to Oregon and the Netherlands: (1) the Swiss model improves oversight – all cases of assisted death are investigated by the police, and the right-to-die organizations, who manage most of the cases of assisted suicide, are required to document the steps in assisted death, assess decisional capacity, and report the death to the police immediately; (2) the Swiss model reduces physician involvement and increases patient assessment – instead of physician assisted suicide being a doctor-centred approach, the Swiss model is more of a team-assisted approach where one of the five private associations plays a more central role than the physician, and the physician merely needs to write the prescription, which removes the psychological or moral tension for the physician who identifies with a Hippocratic medical ethos; and (3) the Swiss model de-medicalizes death – assisted suicide in Switzerland most frequently takes place at home and in

---

144   http://www.ejpd.admin.ch/content/ejpd/de/home/dokumentation/red/2011/2011-06-29.html.

145   *Supra* n. 131.

the community, which is the preferred location for the majority of the dying, and reverses the trend that more and more people die in medicalized settings.[146]

This chapter contends that the Swiss approach to assisted suicide offers a model that should be considered seriously if respecting autonomy is an important factor as the rhetoric of relevant English cases seems to imply.[147] It is accessible to a wider range of individuals than other regimes allow in that they do not have to justify why they are seeking assistance to die. The main constraint is that the person assisting is not self-serving, such as satisfying their own material, financial or emotional needs.[148] Further, the accusation that end of life decisions have become over-medicalized is avoided because decisions are not left in the hands of doctors. As in other jurisdictions,[149] the permissive Swiss legislation has not led to large numbers of its, or others', citizens being assisted to die, nor has it unduly interfered with the operation of its society.[150] The Swiss system has not been flawless but, despite this, there remains broad public acceptance.[151] Provided domestic concerns are addressed, England could adopt a similar regime with regulation that is transparent and effective so that individuals are not forced to seek assisted suicide in a foreign jurisdiction because they cannot obtain the help they need here. It would also mean that the intervention could be undertaken at an appropriate time. Now, patients with a degenerative condition who cannot find anyone willing to assist them in their suicide will have to travel at a time before their disease progresses to a point when this is no longer an option.

With the appropriate precautions, this chapter argues that an adapted form of the Swiss model should be incorporated into English legislation and consist of four key elements: (1) assistance to suicide becomes legal within explicit

---

146   Münk, H.J. 2009. Suizidbeihilfe in der Schweiz. *Zeitschrift für Medizinische Ethik*, 55, 371; Bosshard, G., Ulrich, E. and Bär, W. 2003. 748 cases of suicide assisted by a Swiss 'right-to-die' organization. *Swiss Medical Weekly*, 133, 310–17; Hurst, S.A. and Mauron, A. 2003. Assisted suicide and euthanasia in Switzerland: allowing a role for non-physicians. *British Medical Journal*, 326, 271–3; Ziegler, S.J. and Bosshard, G. 2007. Role of non-governmental organizations in physician assisted suicide. *British Medical Journal*, 334, 295–8; Fischer, S., Huber, C.A., Mahrer Imhof, R., Furter, M., Ziegler, S.J. and Bosshard, G. 2008. Suicide assisted by two Swiss right-to-die organizations. *Journal of Medical Ethics*, 34(11), 810–14; and Rehmann-Sutter, C. 2006. Zum gegenwärtigen Diskussionsstand um die Beihilfe zum Suizid in der Schweiz. *Zeitschrift für Evangelische Ethik*, 50, 49–53.

147   See e.g. *Re T, supra* n. 30.

148   Swiss Federal Ministry of Justice cited in the Report of the House of Lords Select Committee on the Assisted Suicide for the Terminally Ill Bill, 69, para. 195.

149   E.g. *supra* n. 89*ff.*

150   McLean, *supra* n. 13, at p. 201.

151   Schwarzenegger, C., Patrik Manzoni, P., Studer, D. and Leanza, C. 2010. *Was die Schweizer Bevölkerung von Sterbehilfe und Suizidbeihilfe halt Jusletter* [Online: 13 September]. Available at: http://www.rwi.uzh.ch/lehreforschung/alphabetisch/ schwarzenegger/publikationen/Schwarzenegger_et_al_2010.pdf [accessed 20 September 2011].

constraints that exclude self-seeking motives by assistants such as where the latter stand to gain financially, emotionally or have ideological reasons; (2) private assisted dying organizations can play a role if placed under state supervision in the decision-making processes; (3) assistance to suicide is not restricted to physicians, but they will still have a role in providing prescriptions for lethal drugs; (4) active euthanasia (both voluntary and non-voluntary) without explicit request remains a criminal offence. There should be appropriate education as well as more consistent delivery of high-quality palliative care. This would provide reassurance that all possible physical and emotional support is being offered to patients wishing to end their lives and that robust procedures will ensure the individual is expressing a settled wish. Legislation need not suggest an expression of indifference and abandonment of troubled individuals to an unhappy fate. Rather it reflects clear support for patient autonomy and recognizes that some people prefer a good death at their own hand even with the best palliative care.

Conclusion

The position with respect to assisted suicide in England has gained some additional clarity from the guidelines about whether assisting a loved one's suicide will be prosecuted but remains far too restrictive. If individuals cannot find anyone to assist their suicide, they may have to travel to another jurisdiction prematurely while their condition still allows because of the prohibition of right-to-die organizations and on health professionals directly involved in the care of those wishing to die. We have asserted that legalized physician assisted suicide need not undermine the relationship of trust between patients and doctors if the latter take a main role in assisting death. The relationship of trust may even require the doctor to accept a role in assisted dying in their patient's best interests. Although this chapter supports the liberalization of assisted suicide in England, it finds the proposal for state-sponsored suicide centres wanting, unless they could provide the flexibility of organizations that may be able to offer more appropriate intervention in the person's home. The state is also unlikely to fund such centres at a time of unprecedented financial and organizational challenge for the NHS. Any legal challenge to an adverse resource allocation decision is likely to be unsuccessful.[152]

Assisted suicide can be a dignified way of ending a life. It keeps individuals in control and should not be restricted to those who are terminally ill or profoundly physically disabled. Such respect for autonomy underpins the Swiss model making it ethically defensible and acceptable to broad swathes of Swiss society. This chapter has contended that ethical and legal arguments against legalized assisted suicide do not pass muster unless there is the possibility of exploitation. It is the role of the law to avoid such a possibility by having appropriate safeguards in place including ensuring all other options have been explored to make life more palatable

---

152   *Supra* n. 126.

for the individual, and/or that they are expressing settled wishes. Although robust regulation has yet to be realized fully in Switzerland, the long experience there and in other jurisdictions shows that lawful assisted suicide involving right-to-die organizations can be kept within narrow constraints and does not weaken the taboo on killing. There will be a need to explore the concerns raised in Switzerland not least because of the undermining of local oversight mechanisms after scandals such as that involving Dr Shipman who managed to murder many of his patients.[153] The fact that there are hundreds of Britons on the waiting list for one of the Swiss suicide clinics illustrates the pressing need for reform.[154]

---

153   The Shipman Inquiry Fifth Report. 2004. *Safeguarding Patients: Lessons from the Past: Proposals for the Future.* Cm 6394.

154   Campbell, D. 2009. 800 Britons on waiting list for Swiss suicide clinic. *The Observer* [Online: 31 May]. Available at: http://www.guardian.co.uk/society/2009/may/31/assisted-suicide-reform-uk-switzerland [accessed 20 September 2011].

Chapter 6

Health Economics:
Decisions and Choices at the End of Life

Vincent Kirkbride

Introduction

This chapter will review the recent history of resource allocation within the NHS particularly in the context of how resources are used at the end of life. Although there has been a national body that assesses the clinical and cost effectiveness of new treatments for more than a decade, there are major changes planned by the current government. The ethical arguments for and against resource allocation will be examined as well as a brief background to health economic methodology. The legal and public challenges to the NHS rationing body will also be reviewed together with new approaches and potential solutions, especially for patients with cancer. Although cancer remains an important cause of death, this chapter will also explore whether it has been given undue attention to the detriment of patients who are suffering with other conditions at the end of their lives.

None of us can live forever. However, many of us are now living for longer. We spend a relatively large proportion of the health care budget on patients who are dying. In the United States as much as 12 per cent of the health budget is spent on care at the end of life and in Canada 21 per cent of health care costs is spent on patients in their last six months of life.[1] The 2008 National Audit Office report into end of life care estimated that the cost of providing care to cancer patients in the 12 months prior to their death was £1.8 billion, although only a small fraction of this funded specialist palliative care.[2] For most healthy people there is an expectation that anything that makes us significantly unwell should be treated. There is another group of patients who have reached the 'end of their innings' with a reduced life expectancy and, even though death may be very close, issues remain on how much life-prolonging treatment should be provided. Most people who die are over 75 and the majority of deaths occur in a hospital after a chronic illness. As is argued in Chapter 5 of this book, a 'good death' is one that allows the individual

---

1 Fassbender, K., Fainsinger, R., Carson, M. and Finegan, B. 2009. Cost trajectories at the end of life: the Canadian experience. *Journal of Pain and Symptom Management*, 38, 75–80.

2 NAO. 2008. *End of Life Care* [Online: National Audit Office]. Available at: http://www.nao.org.uk/publications/0708/end_of_life_care.aspx [accessed 4 August 2011].

to choose the manner of their passing. Some will tolerate nature taking its course provided that they feel sufficiently comfortable so that they enjoy a quality of life acceptable to them. Others may insist on life-sustaining treatments even until the very end. Many of these life-sustaining therapies and technologies are new and very expensive. Who should decide which of these treatments should be available or rationed? Should there be an inviolable right to treatments that prolong life irrespective of cost?

One of the reasons that there is such a debate on how much money should be available to provide for a good death as opposed to postponing a premature death is that the costs to the health service are huge. Advances in laboratory and clinical sciences have given rise to a greater expectation that cancer, a major cause of death, is curable. However, it is precisely because of this success that the problem is likely to get worse rather than better. In a recent study from the National Cancer Institute in the US, it is predicted that the enhanced survival rate of many cancers will escalate the cost of care there by \$173 billion in 2020, which is a 39 per cent increase from 2010.[3] However, for any individual with cancer in a health care system that is free at the point of entry, such statistics do little to refute the assumption that the money to pay for treatments somehow will be available.

More recently there has been an extended focus on how resources should be spent. Ethical and economic issues have become more contentious for treatments at the end of life.[4] The magnitude of health care spending at the end of life is striking but this could reflect the clinical challenges in postponing and predicting death[5] as well as political weakness in rationing resources at the end of life. New therapies have revolutionized the care for patients with joint disease, asthma, multiple sclerosis and even conditions such as erectile dysfunction. Who can say no to these treatments? The National Institute for Health and Clinical Excellence (NICE) was established to help decide which of these therapies represent a good investment of the health care budget. For cancer patients in particular, the pain and agony of being denied drugs that are not deemed to be effective is clear to see in the many stories that reach the newspapers. However, it is not just cancer drugs that hit the headlines and NICE has been challenged in the courts for not approving drugs for patients with Alzheimer's disease despite the amount of money available to fund interventions being limited. Good quality palliative care is sometimes not seen as an alternative for those at the end of their lives. The pain and suffering of

---

3   Mariotto, A.B., Yabroff, K.R., Shao, Y., Feuer, E.J. and Brown, M.L. 2011. Projections of the cost of cancer care in the United States: 2010–2020. *Journal of the National Cancer Institute*, 103(2), 1–12.

4   Berry, S.R., Bell, C.M., Ubel, P.A., Evans, W.K., Nadler, E., Strevel, E.L. and Neumann, P.J. 2010. Continental divide? The attitudes of US and Canadian oncologists on the costs, cost-effectiveness, and health policies associated with new cancer drugs. *Journal of Clinical Oncology*, 28(27), 4149–53.

5   Sima, C.S., Panageas, K.S. and Schrag, D. 2010. Cancer screening among patients with advanced cancer. *The Journal of the American Medical Association*, 304(14), 1584–91.

patients who feel obliged to try less effective treatments that prove to be ultimately futile are rarely given the same press coverage. This chapter will examine whether NICE and some of the recent initiatives including the Cancer Drug Fund (CDF) adequately address the question as to whether health care resources are spent wisely or are squandered on patients in an attempt to ensure that they have a good death. It will also explore the economic approach to rationing such treatments and whether any of the proposed changes will improve the experiences of patients with a limited life expectancy, thus ensuring they have a good death.

NICE and the Postcode Lottery

Currently within the NHS there are over 100 Primary Care Trusts (PCTs) who are responsible for budget allocation within certain geographical areas. However, in the White Paper Liberating the NHS,[6] published in July 2010, the new coalition government published its plans for a major overhaul of how health care is delivered. The major impact of these changes will see the abolition of these PCTs and funding passed to general practitioners (GPs) who will reform commissioning groups and perhaps establish up to 50 'super PCTs' or GP consortia in due course. There has already been reorganization of some PCTs in anticipation of these changes but, at the time of writing, the full impact and potential revision to the White Paper are not yet clear. Prior to 1999 each of the PCTs was responsible for deciding which new and existing treatments should be funded within each region. When one PCT gave approval to a drug while another refused, the concept of the 'postcode lottery' arose whereby some people could be denied access to certain drugs just because of where they lived. In 1999, the Secretary of State for Health announced a new organization to overcome this problem and NICE was established. There are new proposals to change (and limit) the impact of NICE as the government plans to get more value for the money it spends on drugs, though the process is not yet clear. The impact that NICE has on cancer drugs has substantially changed as the government has singled out a special fund for these, administered on a regional basis. Although there is substantial scepticism and resistance to these organizational changes, there are already claims that there is a return to postcode prescribing.[7]

Over the last decade the NHS budget has increased substantially. At the same time therapeutic advances and expectations for better health have also increased. Despite new initiatives such as allowing 'top-up payments' for cancer patients,

6   DoH. 2010. *Equity and Excellence: Liberating the NHS* [Online: Department of Health]. Available at: http://www.dh.gov.uk/en/Publicationsandstatistics/Publications/PublicationsPolicyAndGuidance/DH_117353 [accessed 4 August 2011].

7   Graham, J., Guglani, S., Elyan, S., Falk, S., Braybrooke, J. and Roques, T. 2010. Drug rationing in the new NHS. Return of the postcode lottery. *British Medical Journal*, 341, c7389.

choices need to be made as to whether new treatments can be afforded by the NHS. Within the area of health economics one of the key tools used in resource allocation is the Cost Effectiveness Analysis (CEA) explored below. The CEA is at the forefront of the main activities at NICE and is used to debate and inform whether new technologies represent good value for money for the NHS. One of the main issues is that any new CEA represents an opportunity cost for the NHS. As the NHS budget does not increase automatically with every new invention, if a new treatment is to be applied then it means something else must give.

As well as overcoming the postcode lottery, NICE was principally established to promote clinical excellence, clinical effectiveness and the cost-effective use of resources.[8] It has other roles, both in education and assessing quality measures, but it is the work of the Technology Appraisals Committee that is the most contentious and that generates the most publicity. Shortly after the 2010 coalition government was formed, the new Secretary of State for Health announced a special top-up fund (the CDF) to allow patients access to drugs that had a negative appraisal from NICE. The political interference is obvious. Within the original plans for NHS reforms NICE was to lose its ability to refuse new drugs or treatments and its reports would become advisory rather than mandatory. However, the Board of NICE have been in consultation with the Department of Health (DoH): after the NHS Future Forum 'listening exercise' there has been an apparent change of heart and NICE will retain the original role in rationing drugs.[9] The government's response to the listening exercise states that it will uphold all patient rights in the new NHS Constitution, including the right to drugs and treatments recommended by NICE, which will be retained after the introduction of value-based pricing in 2014.[10] There is no clear sign of how the DoH will evaluate, approve or price drugs under this new scheme from January 2014. However, in some form or other there will be a need to use appropriate health economic tools and it is important to have an understanding of the major methodology used to compare cost effectiveness.

Cost Effectiveness Analysis

A CEA looks at both the clinical effectiveness and the economic benefit that one treatment may have over another. If one drug to treat pneumonia needed intravenous administration (and therefore hospital admission) versus a more expensive oral preparation that could be administered in the community, the drug with the most clinical effectiveness and economic benefit would be preferred. NICE adopted a specific variant of a CEA often referred to as a cost utility analysis because it uses

---

8   http://www.nice.org.uk/aboutnice/ [accessed 4 August 2011].

9   Torjesen, I. 2011. NICE will retain drug approval role in government U turn. *British Medical Journal* [Online], 342, d3862. Available at: http://www.bmj.com/content/342/bmj. d3862.full.pdf [accessed 15 August 2011].

10   *Ibid.*

Quality Adjusted Life Years (QALYs) as a comprehensive and universal measure of health outcome.

The QALY combines length of life and health-related quality of life into a single measure. A score of 0 is given for death and 1 for perfect health. NICE compares interventions by calculating the Incremental Cost Effectiveness Ratio (ICER). The ICER is the ratio of the difference in the mean costs of an intervention compared to the next best alternative (which could be no action or treatment) to the differences in mean health outcomes. If a new cancer treatment extended life expectancy by five years with a change in QALY score per year from 0.6 to 0.7 at a cost of £50,000 compared to best supportive care there would be an incremental gain in life years (and life quality) of 5 X 0.7, which would equate to an ICER of just under £14,285 (£50,000/3.5). If the treatment extended life by only two years with a reduced QALY score per year of only 0.5 (owing to, for instance, significant side effects) then the ICER would be £50,000.[11] ICERs are expressed as cost (in £) per QALY gained. In general, when the ICER is £20,000 or less the intervention is considered to be within threshold (and cost effective), and when it is £30,000 or more it is beyond threshold (and ineffective).

Although the economic assessment of new drugs and technologies can be very complex the ICER can be regarded as a bottom line figure as to whether a treatment represents good value for money. The absolute threshold can be set at a certain level allowing judgments to be made about the relative affordability and value of a treatment. However, there are arguments over whether any monetary value should be placed on life (even if it is a key objective of the government to secure treatments with as much value for money as possible). This is discussed further below.

Arguments For and Against the QALY

Harris[12] is one of the strongest critics of the QALY and its economic approach. Harris argues that what matters is not how many life years are saved but how many lives are saved.[13] The terminology of the phrase QALY is very important. The implication is that it is added value – life years – that is important. Harris argues that it is the people that matter and not the mathematical sum of their life years. He also argues that, whilst there clearly is a need to make sure resources are used efficiently, it is the widespread misuse of the QALY itself that is so morally challenging. Harris suggests that life saving dominates over life enhancing in all circumstances, irrespective of QALY benefits. Most people would argue that life saving has priority over life enhancement, although there are some conditions

---

11   This is a simplification of the methodology. There is a variety of techniques and models that factor in other variables including age, other treatment costs and the impact of multiple treatments.

12   Harris, J. 1987. QALYfying the value of life. *Journal of Medical Ethics*, 13, 117–23.

13   *Ibid.*

(such as disseminated malignancy) where to prolong life would be to prolong suffering. Harris states: '[o]ur own continued existence as individuals is the sine qua non of almost everything. So long as we want to go on living, practically everything we value or want depends upon our continued existence'.[14]

When the QALY is used to compare two rival treatments for the same patient then it clearly has a role. However, an argument is that when it is used to consider treating one group of patients over another in terms of priority, it is wrong. In fact, Harris and others[15] argue that the QALY does not value life or lives at all. Harris argues that, as an alternative, apportioning treatment either on a first come, first served basis, or on the toss of a coin, is more reasonable than by economic allocation.[16]

Exponents of the QALY state that QALY maximization is the most efficient way of resource utilization for society.[17] Although it is no longer common practice, there used to be an upper age limit barring elderly patients from intensive care on the grounds that they already had reduced life expectancy compared to younger patients. Unless every new treatment comes with a bigger budget, for a new treatment to be introduced something else must be removed from the overall budget. This is an opportunity cost. For example, a leading group of cancer experts have claimed that we spend more on drugs to treat constipation than we do to treat cancer.[18] Although patients with both conditions deserve to be treated, arguably we cannot make a valid claim to lost opportunity unless we know the comparative value of both treatments. To brandish one as not cost effective without knowing whether all of the other (potentially useless) treatments are cost effective seems unjust.

Harris argues that it is unfair to value the life of an older person as of less value than that of a younger person, as in fact both are equally precious. In particular he argues that age is a completely arbitrary criterion: if there was a fire in a hospital would we really evacuate all the 20-year-olds before the 30-year-olds?[19] Rawlins and Dillon[20] defend the age impact of the QALY on the grounds that, where there is no difference in QALY score, the incremental (ICER) ratio will be the same for an

---

14   *Ibid.* at p. 120.

15   Quigley, M.A. 2007. NICE fallacy. *Journal of Medical Ethics*, 33, 465–6.

16   Smith, R. 2008. Nice decisions on drugs are flawed and tossing a coin is fairer says academic. *The Telegraph* [Online, 23 October]. Available at: http://www.telegraph. co.uk/health/3248107/Nice-decisions-on-drugs-are-flawed-and-tossing-a-coin-is-fairer-says-academic.html [accessed 4 August 2011].

17   Culyer, A. 2001. Economics and ethics in health care. *Journal of Medical Ethics*, 27, 217–22.

18   Waxman, J. 2008. We need cancer drugs. NICE must go. *The Times* [Online, 8 August]. Available at: http://www.timesonline.co.uk/tol/comment/columnists/guest_contrib utors/article4481345.ece [accessed 4 August 2011].

19   Harris, J. 1985. *The Value of Life*. London: Routledge Kegan & Paul, at p. 89.

20   Rawlins, M. and Dillon, A. 2005. NICE discrimination. *Journal of Medical Ethics*, 31, 683–4.

80-year-old as it is for an 8-year-old. However, in many conditions there is an age difference and, although NICE does not value life differentially across the ages, the QALY is different for certain age-related conditions. For example, the ICER for osteoporosis drugs improves with age because complications are reduced and benefits are greater in the older population.[21] Also, in terms of evaluating a new treatment such as a new delivery device for insulin, the effectiveness is judged against the whole population group, be they 8 or 80.

There is also the concept of reverse age discrimination. Consider two patients with a life expectancy of three months with a similar quality of life. An 80-year-old patient has already experienced 80 years of life whereas an 8-year-old has had much less. If the QALY score was the same then some even argue that the QALY is not ageist enough. This is one of the arguments behind the fair innings alternative approach in which all individuals yet to receive a fair innings gain absolute priority over those who have received a fair innings. In a review produced for the House of Commons, Edlin et al.[22] concluded that, by using the QALY as the basis for CEA, the impact of age is subject to constraints. In general, there is limited impact to select patients on the basis of certain characteristics and limited potential for age discrimination. However, older people will largely produce fewer QALYS than younger people. There are several ways to reduce the potential for age-based rationing including a modification as to the way in which the QALY is calculated,[23] but at the moment the focus seems to be on modifying the application of the QALY rather than the formula in general. This may change in the future, especially within the implementation of the CDF.

It is precisely because the QALY involves a financial assessment that it stands out in relation to other issues within health care ethics. Beauchamp and Childress recognize that, although we often do place a monetary value on all sorts of benefit (friendship, recreation and so on), we do not have a moral obligation to do the same with respect to human life.[24] There are no equivalent stringent tests of how well national resources are spent in other areas such as education or social welfare. It is clear that the government disagrees with the thresholds for end of life treatments, which is why it has produced its CDF, thus interfering with the work of NICE. In its commitment to liberating the NHS, the government wants to achieve better value. One way or another it will still need to define upper and lower limits for this value and economic analysis will still need to inform decision-makers involved in this process.

---

21   *Ibid.*

22   Edlin, R., Round, J., McCabe, C., Sculpher, M., Claxton, K. and Cookson, R. 2008. *Cost-effectiveness Analysis and Ageism: A Review of the Theoretical Literature.* Leeds: Leeds Institute of Health Sciences.

23   Kharroubi, S. and McCabe, C. 2008. Modelling HUI2 health state preference data using a non-parametric Bayesian method. *Medical Decision Making*, 28, 875–87.

24   Beauchamp, T. and Childress, J. 2001. *Principles of Biomedical Ethics.* 5th edn. Oxford: Oxford University Press, at p. 208.

Even Harris recognizes that there are some circumstances when it would be appropriate to use the QALY such as when choosing between two treatments for the same patient,[25] but he makes the distinction that what matters is to value individuals and not to value the QALY. However, just because an individual may have an equal claim to a health resource it does not follow that a health resource will be equally effective. For example, if there were two patients both with identical clinical need of a heart transplant, then clinical evidence shows that it is the one who has the closest tissue match who is most likely to benefit. If there was no prioritization or resource scarcity then this would not be an issue but unfortunately this is rarely the case. One way of attempting to resolve such dilemmas would be to adopt Rawls' approach using a 'veil of ignorance'.[26] This is a kind of thought experiment to justify political principles.[27] He argued that society should be organized so that each individual has access to the most extensive scheme of liberties that allows the same liberties to be available to all. Under such a veil, some or many aspects of one's identity are hidden, and all people are then asked to choose how to decide when unable to perceive their own personal benefit. Would a patient insist on obtaining a treatment with a high probability of its being ineffective if he was the wrong tissue type? A group of patients in need of a transplant (who themselves did not know whether they had any benefits) could then argue rationally which treatment thresholds could be used (behind such a veil). So for the heart transplant, would it not be a waste of resources to flip a coin or allocate the donor heart to the first patient who could get to the hospital if that person got much less utility out of the treatment? Mckie et al. argue that when patient characteristics are different, resources would be squandered if allocated on the basis of health utility.[28] Singer et al.[29] disagree with Harris's claim that all lives have equal value. If one of two patients needing a transplant also has a degenerating neurological condition then, whilst that person's life clearly has value, if the goal (of welfare maximization) is to achieve the most good with the resources that are available, the decision to prefer one patient over another is perhaps unfortunate but not unfair.

A GP does not (yet) get his waiting room full of patients to tot up their own respective QALY scores for the morning. Similarly, when deciding on a particular treatment course a doctor and patient give no consideration to any other opportunity costs. The first come, first served or lottery proposal suggested as an alternative can be applied to a new commissioning solution, but in reality such a solution would be difficult to apply. To propose that allocation be on a

---

25   Harris, *supra* n. 12.

26   Rawls, J. 1971. *A Theory of Justice.* Oxford: Oxford University Press, at p. 136.

27   *Ibid.*

28   Mckie, J., Kuhse, H., Richardson, J. and Singer, P. 1996. Double jeopardy, the equal value of lives and the veil of ignorance: A rejoinder to Harris. *Journal of Medical Ethics*, 22, 204–8.

29   Singer, P., McKie, J., Kuhse, H. and Richardson, J. 1995. Double jeopardy and the use of QALYs in health care allocation. *Journal of Medical Ethics*, 21, 144–50.

first come, first served basis would sound egalitarian but there is a risk of some patient groups such as the more mobile, with access to media and technology, and with better communication skills, being more likely to get treatment over the disadvantaged such as the housebound, those with disabilities and those for whom English is not the first language. Also, the idea that a lottery is a fairer approach is open to question. Whilst appearing to be more objective it fails to account for the gravity of a condition. Would one really choose an operation for in-growing toenails over coronary heart surgery on the basis of the toss of a coin? The idea of tossing a coin to decide which patient receives a donor kidney may seem reasonable when a group of patients are identical, but it would surely be a waste of resources to give it to the one the least immunologically matched when the chances of rejection are very high? If such resources were seen to be squandered then it would also have a negative impact on the donor pool, further restricting opportunities for resource allocation in the first place. If there was a health lottery, then how would the rules stand?

Whilst health economists and health ethicists argue, the person on the street still wants to know whether he can access this drug. In the state of Oregon in the US there was a debate and vote on which health treatments should be given priority, which has now evolved into a complicated system that rations treatments within the publicly funded health programme. Although that system has been seen as a model for other health economies, it is not without criticism;[30] but at least most people are aware of what is or what is not allowed. When a new system is established, it is the responsibility of the government to explain its rationale for whatever rationing system it proposes. Should NICE be reconsidered as the best way of deciding upon these issues or is there something better? In harsh economic times would it be foolish to suggest decommissioning the major health rationing body?

The End of NICE?

There is a wide spectrum of opinion about NICE ranging from high regard to utter contempt.[31] Over the last decade there has been extensive criticism of the work of NICE from both the medical profession and the press. NICE is frequently in the headlines. The Chief Executive, Sir Andrew Dillon, has been called 'Dr Death' (even though he is not a doctor). In a review of the 200 most recent press articles, Hawkes comments that all but a few have been highly critical, some 'stretching the boundaries of reasonable comment to breaking point'.[32]

---

30   Alakeson, V. 2008. Why Oregon went wrong. *British Medical Journal*, 337, a2044.

31   Hawkes, N. 2008. Why is the press so nasty to NICE? *British Medical Journal*, 337, aa1906.

32   *Ibid.*

Although the Appraisal Committee is made up of at least 20 members from a variety of clinical backgrounds and experts attend the meetings (after nomination by specialist bodies such as the Royal Colleges), there is a perception that NICE's committees as a whole are run by economists and that there is very little clinical input. In an open letter to the *Sunday Times*, a leading body of cancer experts vented their frustration: '[o]nce again NICE has shown how poorly it assesses new cancer treatments. Its economic formulae are simply not suitable for addressing cost effectiveness in this area of medicine. It is essential that NICE gets its sums right.'[33] This letter was initiated because NICE rejected certain drugs, such as Sutent to treat renal cancer, on the ground that the therapy was outside the ICER threshold. This appraisal was first initiated in 2007 and the second committee meeting was in September 2008. The interim recommendation was that it was not cost effective and that it should not be provided by the NHS. This caused an outcry and there were many articles where affected people felt they were being condemned to die and NICE was pilloried once again. However, new evidence was submitted by the manufacturer and another appraisal meeting was arranged by which time the new end of life guidance would also need to be taken into account. Even though the ICER was in the region of £50,000, by adopting the new end of life guidance Sutent became the first drug to be approved under the new rules in March 2009. For patients with this cancer this is certainly a victory but it comes at a price that increases the end of life costs for the NHS.

There have been many Parliamentary questions tabled over the availability of (mainly) cancer drugs and there has been a House of Commons Select Committee Report on the work of NICE.[34] The Committee focused on NICE because of the changing environment within which the Institute now operates: the rising cost of new drugs and the increased attention it is getting from both the media and the general public in particular. The Committee also wanted to find out what is behind the forceful criticisms frequently levelled at NICE. However, after detailed review, one committee reported that '[m]inisters must support NICE, not seek to undermine it. NICE must not be left to fight a lone battle to support cost and clinical effectiveness within the NHS'.[35]

The Report criticized the time involved in producing an appraisal and also said that it should have available the same information that the pharmaceutical companies are obliged to supply to the licensing authorities. In response, NICE has established an additional Technology Appraisal Committee and in an attempt

---

33   Sikora, K. et al. 2008. Cancer drugs due a review. *The Sunday Times* [Online, 24 August]. Available at: http://www.timesonline.co.uk/tol/comment/letters/article4597132. ece?token=null&offset=0&page=1 [accessed 4 August 2011].

34   HoCHC. 2008. *First Report of Session 2007–8* [Online: House of Commons Health Committee]. Available at: http://www.publications.parliament.uk/pa/cm200708/ cmselect/cmhealth/27/2702.htm [accessed 4 August 2011].

35   *Ibid.* at p. 3.

to improve accountability these meetings are now open to the public and press.[36] NICE looks set to survive, at least in the short to medium term, so the following section explores its approach to the end of life, given that this has a major impact on whether someone experiences a good death.

NICE and New Rules at the End of Life

NICE updated its methods guidance in June 2008,[37] after heavy press criticism continued and it experienced its first judicial ruling against it (discussed below). NICE announced a consultation into end of life medicines in November 2008.[38] The majority of respondents supported the proposal that rejecting proven life-extending treatments on the ground of cost effectiveness was not acceptable. After extensive analysis of the comments, NICE issued new guidance to be used for all ongoing appraisals from 5 January 2009.[39] Thus, public and political pressure forced NICE to adopt new rules and an alternative economic model for patients at the end of life.

The information given to appraisal committees is that the ICER threshold of £30,000 can be breached for treatments that may show some survival benefit over current NHS practice. NICE puts the economic evaluation of a technology at the forefront and has attempted to address key ethical issues by publishing the Social Value Judgments (SVJ) document[40] and by establishing the Citizens' Council, which reported into the use of the QALY. The Council was established in 2002 and consists of 30 lay members who advise NICE on its work as well as producing independent reports.[41] The SVJ document was first published in 2005 and was recently updated in 2008. It recognizes scientific value judgments that interpret evidence from a scientific viewpoint, but is also concerned with other opinions that NICE should adopt within its processes. The second edition of the

---

36   For a description of the Technology Appraisal Committee's role see: http://www.nice.org.uk/aboutnice/howwework/devnicetech/technologyappraisalcommittee/technology_appraisal_committee.jsp [accessed 4 August 2011].

37   http://www.nice.org.uk/media/B52/A7/TAMethodsGuideUpdatedJune2008.pdf [accessed 4 August 2011].

38   Dillon, A. 2008. NICE announces measures on end of life medicines [Online, 6 November]. Available at: http://www.nice.org.uk/newsevents/pressreleases/press_releases.jsp?domedia=1&mid=6C45B250-19B9-E0B5-D4953DA77D9D8314 [accessed 4 August 2011].

39   http://www.nice.org.uk/media/88A/F2/SupplementaryAdviceTACEoL.pdf [accessed 4 August 2011].

40   NICE. 2008. *Social Value Judgments*. 2nd edn [Online: National Institute of Health and Clinical Excellence]. Available at: http://www.nice.org.uk/media/C18/30/SVJ2PUBLICATION2008.pdf [accessed 4 August 2011].

41   http://www.nice.org.uk/aboutnice/howwework/citizenscouncil/citizens_council.jsp [accessed 4 August 2011].

SVJ document was produced following broad public consultation and reports from the Citizens' Council. The bioethical contribution came from a round-table discussion that 'explored the principles in relation to contemporary bioethics and philosophy'.[42] The response to the public consultation and the contribution from its Citizens' Council thus paved the way for the new approach at the end of life. The criteria adopted into the new ICER threshold include that patients must have a life expectancy of less than 24 months, that there should be evidence that the treatment should give an additional three months of life expectancy, and that the treatment is licensed for small patient populations.

Thus it seems that, although NICE has not abandoned the QALY, it has put in a new methodology to allow flexibility in some cases. The consultation into end of life medicines recognized the importance of life to those with terminal illnesses. However, NICE was very specific with its recommendations and stated that treatments that extended life would be considered whereas treatments that improved quality but did not extend life would not. By allowing the ICER threshold to be broken, NICE has further exposed itself to criticism by putting quantitative limits on when it can be broken. The new threshold can only be applied when a patient has less than 24 months to live. Is there really a difference between 24 and 30 months for a patient with a terminal condition? Would it be morally acceptable for a patient with cancer to have to wait for a further few months before he hit this new 'deadline' and be allowed the new treatment? Also, the new directive stipulates that the treatment must extend life by at least three months. Why is three months such a special number? If that is the time that most people would 'need' to get their affairs in order, then should this not be established by research before putting the methodology in place?

Despite these changes, it is clear that the government does not see them as sufficient. As it stated in the CDF consultation report:

> [t]he drugs NICE rejects generally combine high cost with a limited average
> extension of life and/or improved quality of life. These benefits can of course
> be of great importance to individual patients and their families, and it may be
> that current arrangements do not adequately reflect the value society places on
> ensuring that patients in such circumstances have access to drugs that can help
> them.[43]

The importance of the role of the CDF in the resource allocation debate and its implications for patients having a good death merits further examination.

---

42   NICE *supra* n. 40, at p. 6.

43   The consultation on the cancer drug fund ended on 19 January 2011: DoH. 2011. *The Cancer Drugs Fund: A Consultation* [Online: Department of Health]. Available at: http://www.dh.gov.uk/prod_consum_dh/groups/dh_digitalassets/@dh/@en/documents/digitalasset/dh_120931.pdf [accessed 4 August 2011].

The Cancer Drugs Fund

In 2010 NICE examined the cost effectiveness of Sorafenib (Nexavar) versus best supportive care in the treatment of liver cancer. This drug improved median survival by 2.8 months but as the ICER was £52,000 it was not considered to be an effective use of NHS resources, much against the wishes of patient groups and clinical experts. This also reflected a revision to the ICER following a 25 per cent reduction in drug costs offered by the manufacturer as part of a patient access scheme. Despite end of life rules, this particular cancer treatment was still rejected by NICE and once again there was public outcry.

The Secretary of State for Health highlighted the fact that the NHS is ranked tenth for cancer drug spending in Europe.[44] Arguably, one of the blocks to cancer drug funding is the appraisals that are carried out by NICE, which limit the number of new therapies that are approved. As an interim measure the DoH announced a consultation into a permanent CDF that will make funding available for cancer drugs that are otherwise not approved by NICE. The consultation exercise finished at the end of January 2011 and funding of the new scheme has been agreed for three years from April 2011. As well as a review of the role of NICE by 2014, the government is also planning to move to a system of value-based pricing to provide patients with better access to effective and innovative treatments at a price that offers better value to the NHS. There is no longer-term planning for the additional funding of cancer drugs beyond 2014. In the fiscal ice age that is about to hit the NHS, this new spending would equate to 3 per cent of the total £20 billion that is expected to be saved. This sounds like a generous offer from the government, but is it really fair and can we afford it?

By putting the spotlight on cancer the government has failed to notice the deficiencies in funding other treatments: for example, the UK is ranked similarly in its spending on other conditions such as multiple sclerosis, rheumatoid arthritis, osteoporosis and Alzheimer's disease. As three in four of us will die from other conditions then why is cancer so special? Although £200 million seems like a lot of money it is possibly only a quarter of the amount that some cancer specialists would deem to be necessary in order to provide access to all the effective and innovative treatments. One estimate for the ten most 'controversial' cancer drugs is that it would cost £766 million to fund treatment for three months for only 50 per cent of patients for that group of cancers.[45] This includes new drugs recently licensed but not yet appraised by NICE, which are available on a named patient basis, in clinical trials or by payment. In the interim, £50 million was also allocated among

---

44   DoH. 2010. Extent and causes of international variations in drug usage: A report for the Secretary of State for Health by Professor Sir Mike Richards CBE [Online: Department of Health]. Available at: http://www.dh.gov.uk/en/Publicationsandstatistics/Publications/PublicationsPolicyAndGuidance/DH_117962 [accessed 4 August 2011].

45   Sikora, K. and James, NN. 2009. Top up payments in cancer care. *Clinical Oncology*, 21, 1–5.

the ten Strategic Health Authorities (SHAs), who at the time of writing oversee commissioning arrangements to improve access to cancer drugs. Without any clear guidance on the allocation of these amounts each SHA is distributing the funds on a partial first come, first served basis and also according to local need, which could be considered the first step in a return to postcode prescribing. The interim fund was allocated to the ten SHAs on a per capita basis. In South Yorkshire and Humber the allocation was £5.3 million. By the end of March 2011, £1,379,000 had been funded for 54 patients at an average cost of £7,835 per patient.[46] By the end of the financial year there were 181 applications including 33 directly from patients. Approval was given for 178 applications and there were only 2 rejections (although 23 applications were subsequently stopped). It is not yet known whether a patient currently on treatment will be continuously funded, but it is expected that funding will be ring-fenced for at least 12 months for each patient. Out of the 21 drug groups that were approved there were 7 drugs that have not yet even been reviewed by NICE. This supports the notion that the Cancer Drugs Fund has ripped the health economic rule book to pieces and that the government has allowed patients to have any cancer drug they want, whenever they want (in some cases without even the approval of their own cancer specialist). Yet there is still money left in the coffers. Is this bad planning or missed opportunities? When the SHAs cease to exist, the NHS Commissioning Board will be involved in making decisions on how the Cancer Drug Fund is operated and administered. Although it may be a very effective regional distributor of resources it may soon be pilloried by the public and press in the same way encountered by NICE.

Thus, the scene is now set. The government wants things done differently and wants to give more access to cancer patients to new treatments.[47] What about drugs for other conditions? The following section addresses NICE's approach to drugs for Alzheimer's disease (AD). Although the condition is not immediately life-threatening, it does reduce life expectancy and can affect the quality of a person's passing if their dignity becomes compromised through lack of appropriate medication. It was just such an issue that gave rise to the first successful legal challenge to a NICE decision. This legal challenge showed that NICE is not infallible and that the methodology that it uses deserves to be scrutinized, especially for a condition that is likely to affect many towards the end of their life.

---

46 By March 2011 there had been 181 applications. Personal communication from Barnsley PCT Specialist Commissioning Group on 22 June 2011.

47 DoH. 2011. *The Cancer Drugs Fund: Government Response to Consultation* [Online: Department of Health]. Available at: http://www.dh.gov.uk/prod_consum_dh/groups/dh_digitalassets/documents/digitalasset/dh_125721.pdf [accessed 4 August 2011].

Legal Challenges to NICE Drug Appraisals

Although NICE has been carrying out appraisals for over 10 years it is only recently that it has been effectively challenged in court.[48] From March 2000 to November 2010 NICE published 209 appraisals in total, containing 412 individual recommendations. In a small number of appraisals the recommendations were withdrawn. Overall, NICE gave a positive response to 83 per cent; and 24 categories (6 per cent) were recommended only for further research and 46 (11 per cent) were rejected outright. As many as one in three appraisals have been appealed either before or after the final appraisal document was produced. Some appeals were lodged by commissioners who disagreed with a positive outcome but the majority of appeals were by drug companies and pressure groups appealing against negative outcomes. There have been a number of legal challenges, but to date there has only been one appraisal successfully overturned. The appraisal involved the claimant company Eisai, which held the UK marketing authorization for Donezepil (marketed as 'Aricept'). This drug is used for the alleviation of mild-moderate Alzheimer's disease (AD). This drug, together with other similar classes of drug, had been the subject of an earlier appraisal in 2001 and the resulting guidance actually recommended its use for patients with mild to moderate AD. However, when NICE reappraised the evidence it concluded that Aricept should not be available at all to any patients with AD. Not surprisingly, this caused a significant public reaction and there were over 8,000 public responses to the decision and a number of very unsavoury headlines in the British press. As a result of the decision, both Eisai and several other parties (which included the Alzheimer's Society and the Royal College of Psychiatrists) appealed to the Institute's appeal panel on the basis of procedural unfairness, perversity in light of the evidence submitted and acting in excess of powers.

All three grounds of appeal were rejected by the panel and the case finally went to judicial review with a further three grounds.[49] These additional grounds argued that NICE was irrational in not considering carer benefits in its economic model, that the procedural fairness should also allow a full version of the economic model to be available to interested parties and that there was unlawful discrimination in the way that certain patient groups were assessed. In summary, Dobbs J said that all but one of the six grounds of appeal had failed. The court directed that NICE's guidance was in fact discriminatory and that it should amend this to ensure its compliance under the relevant legislation. The focus of the subsequent appeal[50] was that Eisai did not have full access to the economic model that was developed by NICE during the appraisal process. Not having access to the model

---

48   *R (on the application of Eisai Ltd) v National Institute for Health and Clinical Excellence* 98 BMLR 70.

49   *Ibid.*

50   *R (on the application of Eisai Ltd) v National Institute for Health and Clinical Excellence* [2008] EWCA Civ 438.

places consultees at a disadvantage if they wish to challenge its reliability. In the Court of Appeal (CA), Tukey and Jacob LJs agreed and the appeal was allowed. Procedural fairness required release of the fully executable model. NICE appealed to the House of Lords to overturn this judgment. NICE's attempt to appeal further was rejected by the Appeal Committee of the House of Lords on the grounds that it did not raise an arguable point of law and upheld the orders from the CA. Subsequently, the drugs have been the subject of another appraisal. Given further evidence and new economic modelling, the recommendations are now very positive and support the use of such drugs.

Following the first successful appeal against a NICE appraisal there have since been several other judicial reviews and appeals, although none as successful as the Eisai case. Given the recent announcements and new initiatives it is expected that these will all but decline until the new consultations and legislations are in place. The Eisai case has also highlighted the public response to NICE appraisals: the 8,000 Web comments on this appraisal as well as several critical newspaper campaigns showed the extent of public opinion. It is not just spending on drugs to treat cancer that needs to be balanced carefully.

Top-up payments have also been subject to legal challenge. These are not new. Most of us pay additional contributions to optical and dental treatment, for instance. Although there has existed a separate (private) market for health care alongside the NHS, until recently it was difficult and sometimes very expensive to try to obtain care for the same condition in both markets simultaneously. Until 2008, up to 15,000 patients each year were approaching individual PCTs to fund specific drugs not endorsed by the NHS. There have been cases where patients have been charged for NHS care once a PCT has established they were also paying for private care. Some patients contested these charges and counter-challenged the PCTs; a niche market in establishing legal rights to treatments was then developed.[51] After a review by Professor Sir Mike Richards, the National Cancer Director, the government relented and for the first time allowed top-up payments for care (including drugs) to be made both within the NHS and alongside the private health care markets.[52] There are now insurance schemes providing access to new drugs under this scheme.[53] For any patient with unlimited funds or insurance, accessing new treatments has never been easier. However, because of broader media coverage there is also a possibility that some

---

51   *Supra* n. 45: an algorithm is included that outlines specialist law firms in this area.

52   DoH. 2008. *Improving access to medicines for NHS patients: a report for the Secretary of State for Health by Professor Mike Richards* [Online: Department of |Health]. Available at: http://www.dh.gov.uk/en/Publicationsandstatistics/Publications/PublicationsPolicyAndGuidance/DH_089927 [accessed 4 August 2011].

53   For examples of the drugs available on an insurance scheme but not funded in England and Wales see WPA. 2011 [Online: Western Provident Association]. Available at: http://www.wpa.org.uk/general/cancer.html [accessed 4 March 2012].

individuals (or their family) might feel obliged to seek out these treatments, putting further pressure on the NHS.

Although there have been a number of challenges to treatment funding decisions, these have shown how difficult it is to overturn a clinical or operational decision.[54] The legal reasoning in such cases is focused not on the effectiveness of any particular treatment, or on any local health priority setting, but more on the lawfulness of the process in which the decision was determined. However, as the statutory framework by which NHS funding decisions are made is altered, it is possible that additional legal challenges will arise. One-off requests to fund treatments for NHS services outside of normal contracts are called individual funding requests (IFRs). Although the overall numbers are small, each PCT deals with 100 to 200 IFR requests per year. As GPs are now a more significant part of commissioning arrangements, there is the risk of conflict of interest and also a glaring equity issue, as any IFRs for cancer drugs are likely to be funded whereas any other treatment is likely to be subject to even greater scrutiny within the fiscal uncertainty facing the NHS.[55]

One of the less applauded outcomes following unsuccessful appraisals from NICE was the development of Patient Access Schemes (PASs) from pharmaceutical companies. Such schemes either refund the cost of a drug if it is not effective or provide it free or at a reduced cost for the first phase of treatment. This represents a win–win situation: the NHS gets the drugs at a reduced cost and the pharmaceutical companies can continue to provide innovative treatments. However, these schemes have been criticized for their transactional costs and the need to identify treatment failures before reimbursement. By reducing the power of NICE and moving more resources regionally via the CDF it would be unlikely for any drug company to propose a patient access at a lower national price when it can negotiate directly with each regional fund-holder.

As stated earlier, the government is committed to obtaining better value from the drugs it provides. The discussion now turns to how this may be achieved in more detail.

Future Directions for NICE: Getting More Value from Drugs?

It is axiomatic that new goods or services should be obtained at a price that represents good value for money. This is precisely what the government is hoping to achieve by ensuring that the price the NHS pays for a new drug will be based on the value that the drug delivers. Although NICE has won accolades and driven down the

---

54 *R (on the application of Murphy) v Salford Primary Care Trust* [2008] EWHC 1908 (Admin).

55 Russel, J., Greenhalgh, T., Burnett, A. and Montgomery, J. 2011. No decisions about us without us? Individual healthcare rationing in a fiscal ice age. *British Medical Journal*, 342, d3279.

cost of some drugs, it is clear that the current political masters are unhappy with the way it operates. By establishing the CDF, the government has undermined the work of the organization and improved the profits of some of the pharmaceutical companies. Although the UK represents an overall small proportion of worldwide sales, it is thought that the UK drug market price influences up to 25 per cent to 30 per cent of the international market price of a new drug on patent. Negative appraisals from NICE can affect the world market price even in large economies such as China. After the interim measures have passed, the government is hoping to get new drugs and treatments at a price that offers greater value to the NHS. However, there is a major risk that the process would, in effect, drive investment and innovation away from the UK market towards much bigger markets such as Brazil and the US. The total cost for developing a new drug is up to $1 billion, which clearly needs to be recouped by these companies. Being told what price the NHS may pay for these new treatments may infuriate the pharmaceutical industry and shift market focus to other countries. One drug company (Eli Lilly) has already suggested that the scheme could in fact increase bureaucracy and administrative costs and that it could be forced to leave the UK market.[56] The price of open access to such treatments in the US involves a broader inequity and a much larger contribution (from individuals and the state) to health care. This was illustrated by the debate over the US health care reform by the Obama administration.[57]

Notwithstanding ethical and practical concerns, we may also still question the UK's economic approach to resource allocation in the health care setting. Even in the relatively short history of the NHS there have already been many changes. History also has a tendency to repeat itself. The NHS has gone from a policy that prevented postcode prescribing to a position where it is likely to return. The government has stated its commitment to cancer patients boldly by allowing them special access to expensive drug treatments. How long will it be before other groups realize they have not been given the same treatment? Although there are plans to invest more in palliative care, many services are still provided by charities who themselves are under increasing financial pressure. Economic tools can measure the relative merits of drug treatments but the same tools can also measure the benefits of palliative care, both for patients and carers.[58] NICE has produced an economic evaluation of palliative care, but the document has not been

---

56   Prince, R. 2010. NHS reforms could see patients miss out on groundbreaking drugs to cure Alzheimer's, Parkinson's. *The Telegraph* [Online, 2 December]. Available at: http://www.telegraph.co.uk/journalists/rosa-prince/8174456/NHS-reforms-could-see-patients-miss-out-on-groundbreaking-drugs-to-cure-Alzheimers-Parkinsons.html [accessed 4 August 2011].

57   Tanne, J.H. 2010. Protests follow US Congress's passing of health reform bill. *British Medical Journal*, 340, c1771.

58   Vigano, A., Donaldson, N., Higginson, I.J., Bruera, E., Mahmud, S. and Suarez-Almazor, M. 2004. Quality of life and survival prediction in terminal cancer patients. *Cancer*, 101, 1090–98.

modified since 2004.[59] As society becomes more aware of what constitutes a 'good death', the balance of spending sufficient funds to avoid an untimely death versus spending enough funds to achieve a good death becomes even more important.

Conclusion

There are many different models for the provision of health care throughout the world. Although they are funded via a variety of sources there is a consistent concern that there is not enough money to meet the population health demands and, sadly, rationing is ubiquitous. There is a growing elderly population and an increasing number of health technologies to treat conditions that would have been considered untreatable in the past. Prevention may reduce the incidence of some cancers, but better treatments will mean that more patients are surviving with cancer than ever before. Whilst it is acknowledged that there is uncertainty in predicting death there is continued pressure to spend a significant proportion of the health budget in avoiding death.[60] It is clear to see why the government has focused on cancer care as it is a common cause of death. There truly are some 'magic bullet' therapies that have produced very pronounced improvements in both the quality and quantity of life.[61] There are some treatments that may prolong life by only days or weeks with marginal effects on life quality. Although the government is keen to improve survival for common cancers such as lung, breast and bowel, this also needs to be achieved through prevention and earlier detection. At a time when it is more likely that other treatments such as IVF for infertility, joint replacement and other forms of non-essential surgery will become increasingly rationed, is it appropriate to spend more on treatments with borderline improvements in life expectancy and quality?

Perhaps the biggest problem is the politicization of resource allocation pandering more to public opinion than to clinical evidence. A cynic could say that the CDF is a victory for the lobbying power of both drug companies and pressure groups, including cancer charities. It has been noted that some leading cancer specialists have commented that we spend less on cancer drugs than we do on drugs to treat constipation. Against this claim is the evidence that £1.8 billion was spent on cancer patients in the last year of their life. The high usage of expensive medicines does not necessarily equate with better care and outcomes, especially

---

59   NICE. 2004. Improving supportive and palliative care for adults with cancer [Online: National Institute for |Health and Clinical Excellence]. Available at: http:// guidance.nice.org.uk/CSGSP [accessed 4 August 2011].

60   *Supra* n. 5.

61   For example the drug Imatinib in leukaemia appeared on the front cover of *Time* magazine as the first 'magic bullet' drug: Lemonick, M.D., Park, A., Cray, D. and Gorman, C. 2001. New hope for cancer. *Time Magazine* [Online, 28 May]. Available at: http://www. time.com/time/magazine/article/0,9171,999978,00.html [accessed 4 August 2011].

if funds for preventive and palliative care are diverted. By attempting to liberate the NHS the government is clearly at risk of neutering NICE. Cancer is important but three out of every four of us are more likely to die from other conditions. By attempting to address some of the problems of access to certain cancer drugs there is a significant chance that the postcode lottery could return.

On the whole, patients are perhaps more conservative than their doctors. It is possible that those who are dying from chronic conditions such as multiple sclerosis, Parkinson's disease or congestive cardiac failure are even less demanding of life-sustaining treatments compared to cancer sufferers. Patients in the former group might prefer more being spent on a better quality death through enhanced palliative care services. Whilst acknowledging the excellent work done by professional groups, pressure groups and charities, there should be more discussion over this balance between the extreme costs of life-saving treatments against this investment in palliative care.

Never before has it been more important to get the decisions right. The balance should be addressed by the greater voice of all patients facing death and more equitable public consultation. If we do spend a significant amount of an individual's health budget in the last six months of life, is it not too much to ask that this money be spent wisely on a good death?

Chapter 7

The 'Good Death', Palliative Care and End of Life Ethics

Simon Woods

Introduction

This chapter explores the concept of the good death within a philosophical framework based upon axiology. Axiology is the theory of value, and in this context the possible 'good-making' characteristics or parameters of the good death are considered. A number of different thought experiments are used to explore and 'test' some intuitions about the good death, the natural death and the engineering of our dying. Sections of the chapter will seek to clarify the key concepts associated with the values and goals of palliative care, and the extent to which these are seen as part of or distinct from the values and goals of medicine. The chapter will also address the meaning and role of autonomy in defining the parameters of a good death and in particular it will address what currently is open for individuals to decide for themselves and what, by parity of reasoning, ought to be open for them to decide in forming the nature of their own death. The chapter will draw upon historical and contemporary accounts of palliative care and definitions of care pathways for dying and will examine the goals of palliative care alongside the claim that deliberate control over one's own dying is a morally defensible means to a good death.

The idea that there is such a goal as achieving a good death may strike readers as macabre. However, after only a moment's reflection, most people will realize that they have a number of quite particular intuitions about this thought.[1] For many people, the idea of a good death will consist in a *negative* conception and will almost certainly focus upon the dying process rather than death itself. The negative conception is likely to be based upon the avoidance of particular 'bad-making' characteristics such as undignified dying in which pain, fear, anxiety, loss of control and loneliness may feature. Most such fears are fuelled by the uncertainty and mystery of death and dying but also by a lack of familiarity, since death is largely hidden away in the developed world. Aries characterized the history of death in the West as shifting from the assurance and unity of a shared religious faith to uncertainty, individualism and death denial, a view shared by

---

1 For a much wider consideration of these issues see Woods, S. 2007. *Death's Dominion*. Maidenhead: Open University Press/McGraw-Hill.

other commentators.[2] In the past, death by trauma or infection was often swift, but a feature of modern medicine has been to render dying a drawn-out process. Death is now caused by a chronic disease, or combinations of such, and dying will likely take place within a number of institutions, under the supervision of a variety of health professionals but rarely within the home.[3] Thus, for the dying person and their family the dying may be protracted and in situations in which it is difficult to have personal preferences fulfilled.

Contemporary commentators have described a variety of plausible approaches to the good death including the least worst death, or the good enough death, the personally ideal death, and the quality of life until death.[4] However, the overarching message is that it is impossible to give a singularly adequate account of the good death in a world of heterogeneous values.[5]

In contrast, the philosophy of palliative care, from its origins within the modern hospice movement, has drawn upon a consistent and coherent historical tradition. The philosophy of palliative care articulates a set of values within which the idea of a good death can be framed.[6] A key feature of this tradition is the concept that a person has intrinsic moral worth and therefore that the life they have is of value until its end.[7] This is of course a position that requires some teasing out; however, the basic idea that life is an intrinsic good has important implications for ethics at the end of life. There have been several cases in which there has been serious, and public, deliberation about how the end of life ought to be managed. Challenging cases where the individual is unable to speak for him or herself, such as those of Anthony Bland[8] and Terri Schiavo,[9] have required others to determine

---

2   Aries, P. 1976. *Western Attitudes Towards Death: From the Middle Ages to the Present*. London: Marion Boyars; Kubler-Ross, E. 1969. *On Death and Dying*. London: Tavistock; Walter, T. 1991. Modern death: Taboo or not taboo? *Sociology*, 25(2), 293–310; and Bauman, Z. 1997. *Postmodernity and Its Discontents*. Oxford: Polity Press.

3   Walter, T. 2003. Historical and cultural variants on the good death. *British Medical Journal*, 327, 218–20.

4   Pabst Battin, M. 1994. *The Least Worst Death*. New York: Oxford University Press; McNamara, B. 1998. A 'good enough' death? in *Health Matters: A Sociology of Illness, Prevention and Care*, ed. by A. Peterson and C. Waddell. Sydney: Allen and Unwin, pp. 169–84; and Randall, F. and Downie, R.S. 1999. *Palliative Care Ethics: A Companion for All Specialties*. 2nd edn. Oxford: Oxford University Press.

5   Sandman, L. 2005. *A Good Death: On the Value of Death and Dying*. Maidenhead: Open University Press.

6   The philosophy of palliative care is captured in particular within the writings of Cicely Saunders (e.g. *infra* n. 18) but see the discussion in Woods *supra* n. 1 for a fuller discussion of the evolution of these ideas.

7   Saunders, C. 1996. Into the valley of the shadow of death: A personal therapeutic journey. *British Medical Journal*, 313(13), 1599–1601.

8   Singer, P. 1994. *Rethinking Life and Death*. Oxford: Oxford University Press.

9   Gostin, L.O. 2005. Ethics, the constitution and the dying process: The case of Theresa Marie Schiavo. *Journal of the American Medical Association*, 293, 2403–7. See also Troyer, Chapter 4 in this volume.

what is best for those individuals. Such decisions have been made but often in the face of considerable dispute and disagreement. In other cases individuals with life limiting conditions have spoken for themselves about the kind of control they wish to have at the end of their life.[10]

One of the strongest statements of the underpinning values of palliative care was given in the evidence to the House of Lords by the Association of Palliative Medicine (APM).[11] The statement affirmed that life has value and meaning and that '[e]uthanasia poses the risk that an opportunity for growth will be lost and that life will be devalued'.[12] The APM emphasized the importance of respect for patient autonomy but also that '[t]he doctor should show respect for life and acceptance of death by understanding that: treatment should never have the induction of death as its specific aim'.[13]

More recently, the House of Lords Select Committee on the Assisted Dying for the Terminally Ill Bill[14] heard evidence from members and supporters of the palliative care community. In his statement to the Committee, John Finnis emphasized the long-established prohibition against killing the patient:

> That is the Law, it is the long-established common morality, it is the ethic of the health care professions [...] There is a "bright" line, and though like other laws and principles it is not invariably respected it is not the least artificial or brittle; it rests on a rational principle that a person's life is the very reality of the person, and whatever your feelings of compassion you cannot intentionally try precisely to eliminate the person's reality and existence without disrespect to the person and their basic equality of worth with others.[15]

So from the outset it is possible to establish that the ethical stance of palliative care is in line with a traditional morality, one that seeks to accept death without weakening the value of life.[16]

---

10   Boyd, K.M. 2002. Mrs Pretty and Ms B. *Journal of Medical Ethics*, 28, 211–12. See also DEMOS. 2012. *Commission on Assisted Dying Report* [Online: Demos]. Available at: http://www.demos.co.uk/publications/thecommissiononassisteddying [accessed 2 March 2012].

11   House of Lords Select Committee on Medical Ethics. Session 1992–93. HL Paper 91–viii. London: HMSO.

12   *Ibid.* p. 4.

13   *Ibid.* p. 2.

14   House of Lords Select Committee on the Assisted Dying for the Terminally Ill Bill – First Report. Session 2004–05. Available at: http://www.publications.parliament.uk/pa/ld200405/ldselect/ldasdy/86/8602.htm [accessed 29 August 2011].

15   *Ibid.* at 553.

16   See the European Association of Palliative Care's Task Force statement on palliative care and euthanasia, and the range of commentaries published in *Palliative Medicine* 2003, 17.

Palliative Care: History and Values

The traditional morality alluded to above is plausibly strongly influenced by, if not co-terminus with, Christian moral traditions, and there is no doubt that palliative care, the heir to the hospice movement, has been strongly influenced by Christian morality and the Christian tradition of caring for the sick and dying.[17] However, with the establishment of palliative care as a health discipline and as a medical specialty specifically, there has been a shift towards the secular ethics that predominates within medicine.

Homes for the care of the dying were established in the nineteenth century under the auspices of Catholic religious orders in Ireland and France, and Anglicans in England, and in other countries were mostly operated under one Christian denomination or another.[18] The modern hospice movement that began in the 1950s and 1960s was in part a continuation of this tradition and in part an attempt to bring modern methods of medicine and nursing care to bear on the problem of the 'bad death'. There was a growing recognition, certainly in the UK, that the quality of dying was poor.[19] Many nurses shared the perception that mainstream medicine was failing the dying specifically in relief of pain and symptoms, and hospitals were failing to provide basic nursing care and spiritual support.[20] Cicely Saunders, writing as a nurse, produced a series of highly influential articles in the *Nursing Times*, eventually published as a supplement entitled 'Care of the Dying',[21] where she addressed some of the key concerns, including symptom control, the need for psycho-social and spiritual care, and specifically the need to resist any form of euthanasia.[22]

---

17   Saunders, C. 1993. *Oxford Textbook of Palliative Medicine*. Oxford: Oxford University Press.

18   Clark, D. and Seymour, J. 1999. *Reflections on Palliative Care*. Buckingham: Open University Press.

19   Joint National Cancer Survey Committee of the Marie Curie Memorial and The Queen's Institute of District Nursing. 1952. *A Report on a National Survey concerning Patients with Cancer Nursed at Home*. London: Marie Curie Memorial. See also Hughes, G.H.L. 1960. *Peace at the Last: A Survey of Terminal Care in the United Kingdom*. London: The Calouste Gulbenkian Foundation.

20   Woods, S. 2001. The contribution of nursing to the development of palliative care, in *Palliative Care in Europe*, ed. by H.A. ten Have and R. Janssens. Amsterdam: IOS Press, pp. 133–42. The conception of the 'good' death within these early hospices was essentially a *passive* one, allowing nature to take its course in the best possible circumstances.

21   Saunders, C. 1960. Care of the dying. *Nursing Times Supplement*. London: *Nursing Times* reprint.

22   One needs to exercise caution and distinguish Saunders' personal religious conviction, as expressed in her earlier writing, from her later articulations of an underlying philosophy of hospice care with its aim to bring practical and rational solutions to the problems of pain and distress in the dying. David Clark's annotated bibliography of Saunders' writing up to 1967: Clark, D. 1998. An annotated bibliography of the publications of Cicely Saunders – 1: 1958–67. *Palliative Medicine*, 12, 181–93. See also Woods, S.,

In articulating the values of hospice care it became clear that the good death was reliant upon the provision of holistic care, an approach that seeks to meet the whole needs of a person as a physical, psycho-social and spiritual entity, a philosophical commitment that came to be regarded by some as problematic when one turned to consider how such commitments might be delivered as a service.[23]

In addition to the psycho-spiritual needs of the dying, poor pain control was regarded as one of the major obstacles to a good death, and thus the regular administration of oral opiates was one of the practical and active forms of intervention that came to characterize some of the best and innovative forms of terminal care. Whilst the evil of inadequate pain relief was plain for all to see, many practitioners were also worried about the risks of over-treatment: a justified anxiety in circumstances in which the quality of the drugs was not standardized and little was known about the metabolism of the drug within the patient. As a wider range of technology and pharmaceuticals became available then the ethical implications of the use, withholding and withdrawal of such interventions raised questions both about the aims of palliative care and the obligations and duties of health professionals.[24] Questions concerning the nature, appropriateness and proportionality of medical interventions have continued to be a significant feature of the debates about the nature and purpose of palliative care.[25] These debates have to an extent intensified as palliative care has evolved from the hospice, with an almost exclusive focus upon terminal care in the last few weeks of life, to palliative care, with its focus upon the management of progressive chronic disease.

This evolution from hospice to palliative care was a gradual one, and in order to explore any parallel change within the concept of the good death it is necessary to trace the gradual change in emphasis over the same period. Although the change from hospice to palliative care was gradual it is likely that the term 'palliative care' was first used in 1973 to describe a hospital terminal care unit established by Balfour Mount in Montreal.[26] Although located within a hospital, the very institution many blamed for failing dying patients, it was clear that Mount

Webb, P. and Clark, D. 2001. Palliative care in the United Kingdom, in *Palliative Care in Europe, supra* n. 20, 85–98.

23   Randall, F. and Downie, R.S. 2006. *The Philosophy of Palliative Care: Critique and Reconstruction*. Oxford: Oxford University Press.

24   Kelly, G. 1951. The duty to preserve life. *Theological Studies*, 12, 550; and Jonsen, A. 1990. *The New Medicine and the Old Ethics*. Cambridge: Harvard University Press.

25   Major contributors to these debates include: Ashby, M.A. and Stoffell, B. 1991. Therapeutic ratio and defined phases: Proposal of ethical framework for palliative care. *British Medical Journal*, 302, 1322–4; Ahmedzai, S. 1996. Making a success out of life's failure. *Progress in Palliative Care*, 4, 1–3; Randall and Downie 2006, *supra* n. 23; and Ellershaw, J.E. 2002. Clinical pathways for care of the dying: An innovation to disseminate clinical excellence. *Journal of Palliative Medicine*, 5(4), 617–23.

26   Hamilton, J. 1995. Dr. Balfour Mount and the cruel irony of our care for the dying. *Canadian Medical Association Journal*, 153(3), 334–6; and Billings, J.A. 1998. What is palliative care? *Journal of Palliative Medicine* 1(1), 73–81.

intended to apply what he had learned at the pioneering St Christopher's where he had spent some time working with Saunders.[27]

There were a number of reasons for the eventual adoption of the term palliative care over hospice care. One reason was the recognition that 'hospice' does not retain the same connotation across cultures as it has within the Anglo-Christian tradition. Another is the association of hospice care with the passive care of the person close to death whereas palliative care strove to be regarded as an active form of treatment for chronic progressive disease and not exclusively concerned with dying. Saunders was herself persuaded to adopt the new terminology because she saw that the principles of care she had helped to develop within the hospice could be applied wherever the patient was located.

There were other, more ideological influences on this evolution. For example, hospice care was essentially a nursing initiative whereas palliative care came to be led by a medical speciality, palliative medicine. Palliative medicine is both active and evangelical, characterized by a greater willingness to use active and sometimes aggressive forms of treatment. Evangelical, because palliative medicine has application in all areas of chronic disease and has thus turned to face away from the terminal phase and to look upstream towards earlier and earlier points of intervention within chronic illness.[28]

Some commentators have argued that the evolution of palliative care has been under the shadow of medicalization to the detriment of the values and goals that underpinned the hospice movement.[29] Medicine has continued in the task of providing a strong evidence base for palliative care, particularly in the use of opiates for pain relief.[30] There has also been continuity, with the emphasis placed upon the respect owed to the dying person up to the point of death, a strong stance

27   Mount, B. 1997. The Royal Victoria Hospital palliative care service: A Canadian experience, in *Hospice Care on the International Scene*, ed. by C. Saunders and R. Kastenbaum. New York: Springer, pp. 73–85; Clark and Seymour 1999, *supra* n. 18; Clark, D. 1999. An annotated bibliography of the publications of Cicely Saunders – 2: 1968–77. *Palliative Medicine*, 13, 485–501; Clark, D. 2002. *Cicely Saunders: Founder of the Hospice Movement. Selected Letters 1959–1999.* Oxford: Oxford University Press.

28   Clark, D. 2002. Between hope and acceptance: The medicalisation of dying. *British Medical Journal*, 324, 905. See also the World Health Organization's (WHO) definition of palliative care as: 'The active total care of patients whose disease is not responsive to curative treatment' (WHO. 1990. *Cancer Pain Relief and Palliative Care.* Geneva: Technical Report series 804) and ten Have, H.A. and Clark, D. (eds). 2002. *The Ethics of Palliative Care: European Perspectives.* Buckingham: Open University Press.

29   James, N. and Field, D. 1992. The routinization of hospice: Charisma and bureaucratization. *Social Science and Medicine*, 34, 1363; and Biswas, B. 1993. The medicalisation of dying, in *The Future for Palliative Care*, ed. by D. Clark. Buckingham: Open University Press.

30   Twycross, R. and Lack, S. 1993. Oral Morphine in Advanced Cancer. Rev. 2nd edn. Beaconsfield: Beaconsfield Publishers.

against euthanasia and the recognition of the multidisciplinary team approach in which nursing remains a core discipline.[31]

The Evolving Values of Palliative Care

The history of modern palliative care reflects a movement that offered a vision of a better way of dying when dying people had seemingly been abandoned by mainstream medicine. The early Christian notions of offering hospitality to strangers and a stopping place for pilgrims evolved to become a transferrable philosophy of care for people with chronic progressive disease. Palliative care has maintained the belief that it still has a substantive good to offer even in secular and diverse modern cultures.[32] The key ethical values inform the practices of palliative care in terms of what can and cannot be offered towards achieving a good death. The prohibition on the intentional and active ending of life remains a moral cornerstone even where palliative care services operate within jurisdictions that permit assisted suicide and euthanasia.[33] The belief that all human beings matter morally, and are of value until they die, is closely associated with the prohibition on assisted dying, as is the conviction that people have the capacity to benefit from life lived to its natural end. The most powerful interventions within the palliative pharmacopeia, opiates and their analogues, sedatives and psycho-active medications are used in appropriate measure as proportionate means to the permissible end – a letting die.[34] However, the idea that palliative care can offer a better way of living life to its end is becoming increasingly hard to sustain. The particularly Christian spiritual dimension of the early hospices no longer has resonance in a diverse and increasingly secular society. The Christian *ars moriendi*[35] has become diluted into the amorphous and secular notion of attention to 'spiritual' aspects. Similarly, as the goal of the hospice was the good death, the goal of palliative care has drifted towards the less substantial goal of quality of life;

---

31   To an extent the continuity is reflected within the work of Cicely Saunders who became medically qualified and forged a bridge between nursing and medical approaches. She wrote: 'All the work of the professional team – the increasingly skilled symptom control, the supportive nursing, the social and pastoral work, the home care and the mobilization of community resources [–] enable[s] people to live until they die': Saunders, C. 2005. Foreword, in *Oxford Textbook of Palliative Medicine*, 3rd edn, ed. by D. Doyle, G. Hanks, N. Cherny and K. Calman. Oxford: Oxford University Press.

32   National Council for Hospices and Specialist Palliative Care Services, 1995. *Specialist Palliative Care: A Statement of Definitions*. Occasional Paper 8.

33   E.g. assisted suicide is not a crime in Switzerland: see Chapter 5.

34   Included in the WHO definition of palliative care is: 'intends neither to hasten nor postpone death' (WHO. 2002. *Cancer Pain Relief in Palliative Care*. Geneva: Technical Report series).

35   *Ars moriendi* is the Christian 'art of dying' captured in a body of literature, see http://www.deathreference.com/A-Bi/Ars-Moriendi.html.

although, in fairness to those who still cling to the founding values of palliative care, much has been done to incorporate key principles into service standards. In the UK, for example, the National Service Framework, end of life care planning and the Gold Standards Framework for community palliative care have ensured that planning for death, including some choice of place of death, is now a routine aspect of health care.[36] Care pathways, including the Liverpool Care Pathway, have brought terminal care back into mainstream hospitals and reminded health care professionals what seemed to be forgotten 60 years previously, that is, that death is a natural part of life, and that in the final days or hours of life medicine should recognize that it has not failed but has finished its work, a fact that should be marked by the withdrawal of all but that which is necessary to keep the patient comfortable.[37]

The influence that palliative medicine has come to exert over the evolution of palliative care philosophy is very clear. Medicine has always been good at defending its territory and lobbying for its interests. To a large extent palliative care has been thoroughly colonized by medicine and, as with any colonizing strategy, there have been benefits and costs. Benefits include the professional and political recognition of a discipline, and its cause, which has helped to place the concerns of palliative care on the national and international policy-making agenda. The establishment of an evidence base for palliative care interventions has given the discipline greater credibility, and the evolution of specialist palliative care alongside palliative care principles has given the discipline a lead into all areas of health care concerned with the management of chronic progressive disease. However, some critics are concerned that the upstream turn has changed the focus of palliative care away from caring for dying people. Recent criticisms and calls for the revision of palliative care philosophy by Randall and Downie have been met with further concern that the suggested revisions will further narrow the focus of palliative care from the holistic care of patient and family to consensual agreements between doctor and patient, that is, the standard medico-legal model.[38]

Palliative medicine, like medicine in general, has also to face up to the cult of individualism that pervades Western societies. Within such cultures autonomous

---

36   National Health Service Confederation. 2005. *Improving End of Life Care.* London: NHS Confederation Publications. The Gold Standards Framework for Primary Care is a systematic approach to improving the quality and organisation of care for all people nearing the end of life. See http://www.goldstandardsframework.org.uk/GSFInPrimary+Care. Thomas, K. 2003. *Caring for the Dying at Home: Companions on the Journey.* Oxford: Radcliffe Medical Press.

37   Ellershaw, J.E. and Wilkinson, S. 2003. *Care of the Dying: A Pathway to Excellence.* Oxford: Oxford University Press; and Ellershaw, J.E. and Ward, C. 2003. Care of the dying patient: The last hours or days of life. *British Medical Journal*, 326, 30–34.

38   Randall and Downie 2006, *supra* n. 23.

individuals define their own good life and expect to achieve it.[39] Translated into the context of medicine, patient rights become more akin to consumer rights. In the context of palliative care this means a greater pressure to respect the wishes of the patient in determining how their lives might end.[40] Although medicine is resisting, the 'bright line' that John Finnis remarked upon is perhaps less bright than it once was: there is a creeping acceptance of assisted suicide and euthanasia and a growing body of evidence that palliative care and assisted suicide can exist side by side, which suggests that a compromise is possible.[41]

What palliative care is at liberty to offer is a negative conception of the good death, the ideally 'palliatized' death. The ideally palliatized death allows death to happen: it 'intends neither to hasten nor postpone death'.[42] Palliative care on this model is wedded to an ideal of the 'natural death' in which people die of an underlying condition rather than by human intervention. With the belief in the value of natural death there comes a normative requirement to die a natural death and this imposes restrictions on what the individual can request for themselves.[43] For palliative care it is imperative that the distinction between the natural and the engineered death can be cleanly maintained; but this also requires a certain construction of what legitimate medical interventions aim at. This often appears as a distinction between assisting death and letting die that requires a casuistic argument to sustain: perhaps most prominent is the denial that there is any moral parallel between the withdrawal of life sustaining treatment and assisted dying.[44] In the light of such arguments ideally palliatized death therefore becomes itself not a natural, but a socially constructed, form of dying.

---

39   Laurie, G. 2006.The autonomy of others: reflections on the rise and rise of patient choice in contemporary medical law, in *First Do No Harm*, ed. by S.A.M. McLean. Aldershot: Ashgate.

40   Although ironically, despite frequent claims for a majority public support in favour of assisted dying, death remains a taboo with only 34 per cent of the public discussing their end of life preferences: see ComRes Poll conducted on behalf of BBC Panorama programme January 2010. Available at: http://news.bbc.co.uk/1/shared/bsp/hi/pdfs/01_02_10_Poll_results.pdf [accessed 23 August 2011].

41   See Huxtable, R. 2007. *Euthansia, Ethics and the Law*. London: Taylor and Francis, for a fuller discussion of potential compromise in end of life care goals.

42   WHO 2002, *supra* n. 34.

43   Although of course there are also legal constraints on what can be offered in most jurisdictions but palliative care is nevertheless wedded to the conviction of the natural death.

44   Randall, F. 2005. *Letter to House of Lords Select Committee on the Assisted Dying for the Terminally Ill Bill. Vol. II: Evidence*. London: HMSO; and Randall and Downie 2006, *supra* n. 23.

Axiology and the Idea of a Good Death

This section turns now from the very specific history and context of palliative care to a broader and more philosophical account of the good life (good death). Axiology is the study or theory of the good life and as a traditional philosophical discipline it is concerned with formal or theoretical properties rather than empirical ones. The traditional formal approach of axiology has been somewhat overshadowed by contemporary empirical approaches to quality of life. However, with a little digging beneath the surface it is quickly apparent that so-called quality of life tools also presume that certain general principles hold, since most such tools have physical, mental and social domains with the implication that the quality of life is an aggregate of how we feel, think and interact socially.[45]

Axiology does not aspire to describe the perfect life with attention to the painted in detail of a particular form of life. Whilst a life of sunbathing, champagne and caviar may appeal to some, it will certainly not appeal to all and probably any description, no matter how comprehensive, will fail to satisfy every person. Axiology tries to identify the underlining structure of any candidate description of a good life. So the idea of a good life consisting of good things to eat and drink is premised upon the principles that the fulfilment of basic needs, the satisfaction of appetites, and the stimulation of sensual pleasures are some of the, possibly, necessary elements of a good life. Axiology is not concerned with moral goodness, although inevitably there is a sense in which the pursuit of the good life through particular kinds of lifestyle must inevitably be justified in moral terms.

So far the talk has been of the good life, yet the focus of this chapter is the good death. However, it could reasonably be claimed that, if there are plausible foundations to the good life, then these same foundations will apply to the good death. Of course it must be made clear that when referring to the 'good death' what is really being discussed is the quality of dying, since this chapter has nothing to say about the nature of death itself or the possibility of experiences after death.

It would take more than a brief chapter to develop an axiological theory of the good life that was anywhere near adequate to the task, so an appeal to a number of intuitions regarding candidate foundations to, or, alternatively, parameters of, a good life will be made. It has already been noted that conceptions of a good life require the satisfaction of certain basic needs such as food and warmth. So when Fast describes his fictional slave Spartacus's attitude to survival he describes someone seeking to achieve the brute minimum: '[a]nd all around him are the movements and breathing and chewing of other men and children who do exactly as he does, and within him the expert organs of his body help him and expertly extract what they need from the little food and little water. He picks the last grain of food from his bowl, drinks down what is left, and licks the inside of the wood.

---

45   Parfit, D. 1991. *Reasons and Persons*. Repr. Oxford: Clarendon Press; and Bowling, A. 1995. *Measuring Disease: A Review of Disease Specific Quality of Life Measurement Scales*. Buckingham: Open University Press.

He is not conditioned by appetite; food is survival; every small speck and stain of food is survival'.[46] Although Spartacus may have the basic needs satisfied, a good life is not merely about the mere satisfaction of basic needs but is also, for human beings at least, about the meaning and pleasure to be derived from the ways in which those basic needs are satisfied so that they become more than mere satisfaction. So the enjoyment and pleasure of food goes way beyond the mere satisfaction of hunger or nutritional needs. For human beings at least the enjoyment of food extends to a culture of cultivating food, cooking, eating, and sharing a meal. The good life is therefore one in which there is a rich tapestry of goods beyond basic survival.

The idea that an account of the good life consists in cultivating, pursuing and satisfying experiential desires has been long recognized and discussed by philosophers under the guise of hedonism. Hedonism is the philosophical theory that gives priority to how things feel, that is, the quality of experience when judging the goodness of a life. The experiential aspects are usually evaluated in terms of either their positive or negative dimension: positively, through the pursuit of pleasure, broadly construed; and negatively, by the avoidance of pain, discomfort, unhappiness, or however the opposite of pleasure might be construed. The idea of hedonism does fit with some basic intuitions about the good life even if, for many people, the idea that pleasure is the ultimate good seems rather shallow. Dworkin makes use of this way of thinking about the good life.[47] Although he recognizes the importance that a person's 'experiential interests' play in contributing to the goodness of a life, he also argues that the 'felt' qualities of a person's life are secondary to the overarching or abiding interests that give shape and meaning to a life; what he calls a person's 'critical interests'.

In what way are these rather abstract and theoretical ideas relevant to the good death? The claim central to this chapter is that the idea of a good death should be understood in the same way that claims about a good life are made. So, for example, the satisfaction of basic needs and the quality of one's experiences more generally are arguably equally significant in one's dying as in the rest of life, albeit with some account given to changes in need and the intensity of desire and satisfaction.

Other writers have used these ideas to elaborate the goals of palliative care, for example, seeking to achieve a good death through a deliberate use of the principles of negative hedonism, by taking measures to avoid or ameliorate unpleasant experiences such as pain and other symptoms so that death occurs in the 'least unpleasant way'.[48] Although less explicitly described there is also a cautious but very clear agenda within palliative care's holistic approach to actively and

---

46 Fast, H. 1951. *Spartacus*. Armonk, New York: Northcastle Books, at p. 75.

47 Dworkin, R. 1993. *Life's Dominion: An Argument about Abortion, Euthanasia and Individual Freedom*. New York: Alfred A. Knopf.

48 Randall and Downie 1999, *supra* n. 4, at p. 74.

positively enhance the experiences of terminally ill people. This is a point for further discussion later in this chapter.

Parameters of Good and Bad Death

The possible characteristics or parameters of a good death require an exploration of a number of intuitions that might render death 'good' or 'bad'.[49] For example, imagine the sudden death of a seemingly healthy individual, a person who dies with no awareness or anticipation of their death, no pain and no other sensation other than the feeling of falling into a deep sleep. This example of sudden death seems to meet many of the hedonistic concerns one might have about dying since there is no morbid and distressing anticipation of death, no pain or other unpleasant symptoms. Although the thought experiment satisfies a number of potential concerns about dying it nevertheless seems inadequate if one takes into account, to use Dworkin's terminology, both experiential and critical interests.[50] Sudden death may be experientially good but it is such a devastating thwarting of a person's critical interests that this will overshadow any positive evaluation.

Three features of this form of sudden death are striking: one is that in focusing exclusively upon the experiential aspects the death is seen as a negative good, good only in the sense that the person does not suffer; another is that, by making the evaluation from an entirely first person perspective, the impact of the death on others who know and care about the person and are likely to be devastated by the event are not taken into account;[51] and a third is that, although the dead person ceases to have a perspective, it nevertheless makes sense to say that the bluntness of death's interruption of a life in full flow is also a 'bad-making' feature. As a general idea it seems bad when a life ends so abruptly, since part of the intrinsic value of one's life is to have the sense that one is engaged in projects that give shape and meaning to life, fulfilling ambitions, seeing relationships flourish, careers progress, family grow and develop and so on. Of course, whilst it is true that there are no certainties in life, life is lived with a degree of open-endedness. The bluntness of sudden death, with no possibility of adjustment, has a capacity to render a life incoherent.[52]

Unless there are miraculous breakthroughs in science that enable us to postpone death indefinitely, we shall all die, approximately, within our eight decades of lifespan. So whilst we can all expect to die it is not unreasonable to consider the ways in which our dying might be made better. Taking the idea of sudden death, one might consider the ways in which the appealing aspects of sudden death –

---

49   Woods 2007, *supra* n. 1.

50   Dworkin 1993, *supra* n. 47.

51   Since, plausibly, the goodness of my life, and death, is not a solipsistic fact.

52   This is not an argument that sudden death *necessarily* renders life incoherent. For a more complete discussion see Woods 2007, Chapter 2, *supra* n. 1.

lack of awareness, fear and distress – might be made to fit a form of dying in which other important aspects are also realized. Take, for example, a person with a chronic progressive disease who is, as far as it is possible to predict, within months of death. Let us presume that this individual has become reconciled to their death, has taken measures to put their life in order, to take their leave of loved ones and face the inevitability of their end. Now consider the scenario in which this person dies suddenly and peacefully in their sleep, several months before their death was expected. This state of affairs could be seen as better, in several respects, than the first account of sudden death. Knowing that death is imminent, and being reconciled to that fact, diminishes, at least to an extent, the anxiety and existential distress of knowing that one is dying, along with the opportunity such knowledge provides to put one's affairs in order, to initiate goodbyes with friends and family, and to exploit the exercise of one's autonomy to at least recover some control and coherence from the shadow of death. The foreshortening of the dying period might also be seen as a good since from the experiential perspective of the dying person there is less time in which to experience pain and other unpleasant symptoms, and no period of lingering decline with its potential for erosion of dignity. From the perspective of others there is less time in which they must witness the decline and suffering of their loved one.[53]

Axiological Trajectories

The 'thought experiment' about different kinds of death described above has drawn upon a growing empirical literature that has begun to plot so-called 'illness trajectories'. These trajectories are themselves conceptual tools informed by the natural history of common progressive diseases and are an aid to planning future care needs as well as being a means of addressing one of the most common yet most difficult questions to answer: what will happen next?[54] The trajectories are essentially plotted graphs that indicate the rate and magnitude of the decline in

---

53   It is noted that the foreshortened period also means there is less time for enjoying remaining pleasures, and that such a period before death is not necessarily one of pain and erosion of dignity. Nevertheless, the intuition remains plausible and sits with some empirical evidence that people would rather trade off a longer period of poor quality of life for a shorter period of better quality of life. See: Buxton, M. and Ashby, J. 1988. The time trade-off approach to health state evaluation, in *Measuring Health: A Practical Approach*, ed. by G. Teeling Smith. London: John Wiley & Sons, pp. 69–87. See also Swarte, N.B., van der Lee, M.L., van der Bom, J.G., van den Bout, J. and Heintz, A.P.M. 2003. Effects of euthanasia on the bereaved family and friends: a cross-sectional study. *British Medical Journal*, 327, 189–94.

54   Lynn, J. and Adamson, D.M. 2003. *Living Well at the End of Life. Adapting Healthcare to Serious Chronic Illness in Old Age.* Washington: Rand Health; and Murray, S.A., Kendall, M., Boyd, K. and Aziz, S. 2005. Illness trajectories and palliative care. *British Medical Journal*, 330, 1007–11.

quality of life until death for a number of common diseases. In theory there is such a graph for every person's trajectory to death and one could also imagine that by extending the time frame of the graph and the number of parameters plotted one could map the whole of a life.[55]

In the previous discussion about sudden death a number of 'good-making' characteristics or parameters were identified. So between the two forms of sudden death the parameters that seemed to make a difference included the fit or coherence of the death with the rest of the person's life and, related to this, the timing of the death, the quality of the experiences of the dying person, and the experiences of others who cared about the dying person.

Sudden death presents us with an abrupt squaring-off of the predicted trajectory of life and how 'good' or 'bad' this is might plausibly rest upon the kinds of parameter identified. Sudden death in one's prime seems worse than sudden death towards the expected end of life. If one imagines that the trajectory for all lives involves a tapering of the curve towards zero (death) then the quality of life lived in this 'tail' period may have profound implications for the way in which an individual values their life during this time period. If the tail represents a lingering dying then this time may be regarded as bad hence the intuition that the second form of sudden death is better than a longer period of suffering before death.[56] It is by no means a necessary truth but there is a strong intuition that a short period of rapid decline may be preferable to a lingering death.

The examples of sudden death discussed so far might be described as examples of *natural* squaring-off, but of course squaring-off can also be engineered in the form of euthanasia or assisted dying. There is, of course, a massive literature and ongoing debate about the morality of assisted dying; but this chapter is neither an analysis of those debates nor is it an argument for or against euthanasia and assisted dying.[57] It is, however, necessary to touch upon assisted dying since it represents one form of deliberate intervention that aims to control the quality of dying and, at least in some instances, seeks to bring about a good death. In this sense the *raison d'être* of assisted dying can be seen as sharing something in common with the *raison d'être* of palliative care, in that both seek to influence the quality and course of dying towards a good death. Palliative care operates within normative boundaries and one such boundary determines that the kind of death that one has ought to be a 'natural' death, a matter of moral luck rather than human intervention. Although palliative care interventions may nudge the dying process along its least arduous path, the aim is to ameliorate what may be bad in the dying process but not to fundamentally change the nature of the 'natural' death. Of course, whether a death that follows a battery of palliative interventions remains

---

55   There are, of course, severe limitations as to what can be represented by a simple two-dimensional diagram; therefore this a merely heuristic device for the sake of the analysis at this point.

56   Lynn and Adamson 2003, *supra* n. 54.

57   See Chapter 5 in this volume for a rehearsal of some of these issues.

in any sense a natural death is an interesting debate. This hypothetical exploration of axiology and death trajectories may seem far-fetched but such reflections help to throw into relief some of the important intuitions about the nature of a good death. The following and final sections of this chapter will explore other possible means of manipulating and engineering the good death.

Death Analogue

If the pursuit of a good death requires the deliberate control of the bad-making features of a natural death but short of taking life, then an alternative to squaring-off by killing is that of deep and permanent sedation until death. An induced coma of this kind would in effect be a death 'analogue' since the advent of the sedation would end a person's experiences.[58]

If we ask directly what constitutes a good death then there are many influences that tend towards a defence of the norm that a complete and coherent life is a life lived to the point at which the curve touches the baseline. We can make sense of this position in secular terms by invoking the concept of coherence discussed earlier. There is a sense in which living life to its 'natural' end could be seen to render the whole coherent and complete. Let us stay with this intuition for the moment: a good life is a coherent and complete life, a life lived to its natural end. Defending this intuition seems to offer a means of grounding the argument that justifies preserving the moratorium on assisted death. In contrast, if the analysis of the good death gives prominence to its experiential aspects then it could equally be argued that living a life to its 'bitter end' where this includes many 'bad' experiences adds no value to a life and may even positively detract from the quality and coherence of a life. In this case a 'better' death may be achieved by active human intervention.

Some of the ethical debate around deep sedation of the kind described here has focused on the possibility that sedation is not an alternative to euthanasia but rather euthanasia in disguise. It is interesting that the rationale for deep sedation within palliative care is usually couched in cautious and pragmatic terms that seek to distinguish the intentions from the effects. Thus Randall and Downie justify the use of sedation:

---

58   The ethical issues associated with sedation, or more specifically terminal sedation, in palliative care have generated an extensive literature but see Materstvedt, L.J. and Kaasa, S. 2000. Is terminal sedation active euthanasia? *Journal of the Norwegian Medical Association*, 120(15), 1763–8; Broekaert, B. 2000. Palliative sedation defined, or why and when terminal sedation is not euthanasia. Abstract 1st Congress RDPC. *Journal of Pain and Symptom Management*, 20(6), S58; and T. Tännsjö (ed.). 2004. *Terminal Sedation*. Kluwer Academic Press, *passim* for an introduction to the issues.

[If] distress is so severe as to require greater sedation if it is to be relieved, then there is a significant risk that life may be shortened [...] The benefit of alleviating severe distress is considered by patients and carers to outweigh the possible harm by shortening the duration of the terminal illness. Sedation sufficient to alleviate distress is used. Intentional overdoses of either analgesics or sedative medication are not morally justified.[59]

This statement is, however, an unambiguous affirmation of the time trade-off reasoning alluded to earlier, with both the patient's and third parties' interests forming part of the justification for the intervention. So, although deep sedation may shorten life, the intention is to have an effect upon the patient's mental state. The objective of having a direct and more or less controlled influence over the mental states of terminally ill people has been a long-established and routine part of palliative care; but what, if any, is the moral boundary to such a strategy?

The admittedly strong claim that palliative care routinely aims to influence patients' mental states needs some elaboration and defence. The idea that the quality of a person's mental state has relevance to the quality of their death has an ancient history. The Christian tradition of ars moriendi emphasized the importance of being alert and prepared for death. However, alertness, clarity of mind, reconciliation and acceptance are mental qualities commonly described as elements within contemporary accounts of good dying.[60]

In considering what may or may not be justified when using measures that affect mental states, there are normative implications to consider. Normative values are often implicit within other distinctions such as the distinction between positive and negative forms of intervention. Thus a good death can be negatively characterized in terms of the relief, and therefore the absence, of symptoms such as, pain, restlessness, depression and anxiety. Yet there seems to be greater restraint in the endorsement of positive measures towards a good death. Euthanasia may be one extreme example, but others, such as aiming to deliberately enhance the experiences of the dying person in a positive way by

---

59   Randall and Downie 1999, *supra* n. 4, at p. 119. See also their statement: 'Health care practitioners may justifiably hasten death as a foreseen but not intended effect of treatment whose aim is the relief of pain and distress at the end of life [...] In the philosophy of palliative care, as in health care ethics and the law generally, letting die must be permitted. Letting die here means withholding or withdrawing a life-prolonging treatment when its harms and risks exceed its benefits. Health care practitioners who act in this way neither intend nor cause the patient's death' (Randall and Downie 2006, *supra* n. 23, at p. 221).

60   Kubler-Ross 1969, *supra* n. 2; McNamara, B., Waddell, C. and Colvin, M. 1994. The institutionalization of the good death. *Social Science and* Medicine, 39(11), 1501–8; and, for example, Saunders warns of the potential 'stuporose' effects of opiates, sedatives and alcohol in terminal care: Saunders, C. 1969. The moment of truth: Care of the dying person, in *Death and Dying: Current Issues in the Treatment of the Dying Person*, ed. by L. Pearson. Cleveland: The Press of Case Western Reserve University, pp. 49–78.

enhancing or inducing a 'better' mental state, are either morally condemned at worst or at best regarded as unnecessary.

To put this simplistically, if pain is taken as a token bad mental state, then pain has the potential to create a moral claim that positive mental states (pleasure) do not. In health care ethics the duty not to cause harm and to relieve pain are seen as duties related to beneficence and non-maleficence. Yet, arguably, the same emphasis is not given to a duty to give pleasure or to enhance the quality of a person's experiences. In the medical context, enhancement, at least above the norm, is regarded as supererogatory, and in many medical fields the blurring of the boundary between treatment and enhancement is regarded as problematic, if not unethical.[61] There is a long history in Western culture that regards the pursuit of pleasure as morally suspect. With regard to enhancing pleasurable experiences specifically in the medical context, this notion might well be regarded as dubious and incompatible with medical goals. It could even be seen as abusive, blurring the distinction between substance use, such as morphine for pain relief, and abuse, such as heroin use for 'kicks', for example. However, the idea of positively enhancing experiences, whilst seemingly suspect because of an association with frivolous hedonism, might in fact have a role within palliative care: palliative care's commitment is not only to symptom relief but also to the possibility of the personal development of the dying person. Both may be assisted by several strategies, including the use of pharmacy.

One of the major goals of the modern hospice movement was to address the problem of pain often by the administration of morphine and elixirs whose basic ingredients might include morphine, cocaine, alcohol and chloroform. It would be a distortion of the truth to suggest that the primary use of such substances was their notorious side effects, but there is no doubt that such effects were regarded as also potentially beneficial. The use of narcotics might therefore be described in terms of the desired effect, pain relief, which may only be achieved alongside the effects that are not desired yet tolerated, irrespective of whether such effects are pleasant or not.[62] However, if one considers the very wide range of therapies and interventions employed by contemporary palliative care, then many of these can be seen as deliberate attempts to enhance or induce certain mental states.[63]

Many medications used in the treatment of pain, such as opiates and steroids, have effects that alter the conscious state of the person, changing their perception

---

61   Hagger, L. and Hagger-Johnson, G. 2011. 'Super kids': Regulating the use of cognitive and psychological enhancements in children. *Law, Innovation and Technology*, 3(1), 137–66.

62   This parallels the tolerance of death as an undesired (intended) side effect of sedation. This fits with the secondary or 'double effect' justification noted in Chapter 5.

63   Complementary therapies as disparate as massage, aromatherapy, and neuro-linguistic programming are aimed at enhancing, either through a pleasant physical sensation, or through psychological effects, the quality of the experiences as well as the quality of life of the recipient.

of the pain by dulling or 'distancing' it but also by inducing and enhancing other sensations such as mild euphoria or a feeling of well-being. There has even been speculation and some early research about the possible clinical application of lysergic acid diethylamide (LSD) or similar 'psychedelic' drugs in terminal care with a view to enabling the patient to come to a peaceful acceptance of their death.[64] Cicely Saunders was also interested in the possible applications of such experimental drugs as LSD in terminal care with a view to utilizing any means to enable patients to die in 'a spirit of quiet serenity and acceptance'.[65] Deliberately aiming to alter mental states might therefore be judged appropriate where the patient desires this, and where the effect is temporary and does not become a dominant end in itself in the way that a narcotic addiction might. Thus it is possible to envisage a goal of positively enhancing the experiences of the dying person in a way that maintains integrity with the goals and moral boundaries of palliative care.

Good Life, Good Death, Good Endings

This chapter has explored the concept of a good death from a number of perspectives: from that of the changing demographics of death, which reflect the changes in cause, management and even the experience of death, and from an analysis of the underpinning values that have informed the contemporary approach to managing death and dying. It has chronicled the emergence of the modern hospice movement with its clear links to Christian values and has shown how this became the foundation for the secular and scientific approach characteristic of palliative medicine. However, in spite of its secularism and rationalism, contemporary palliative care still clings to the moral boundaries that strive to maintain the divide between the active management of dying and actively bringing about death. The philosophical and other critical analyses of palliative care introduced in this chapter have shown that maintaining such a divide results in a strain upon the coherence and logical consistency of palliative care values as well as creating a tension between traditional values and changing contemporary norms.

To some, the idea of a positive concept of the good death is nonsense and this chapter has outlined some of the debates on this issue.[66] Much, of course, hinges upon what is meant by 'a positive good death'. The growing consensus on the good death seems to be one that has a negative conception: the least worst

---

64   Kurland, A. 1985. LSD in the supportive care of the terminally ill cancer patients. *Journal of Psychoactive Drugs,* 17(4), 279–90.

65   Clark 2002, *supra* n. 28.

66   Hart, B., Sainsbury, P. and Short, S. 1998. Whose dying? A sociological critique of the 'good death'. *Mortality*, 3(1), 65–77; McNamara, B. 1998. A 'good enough' death? in *Health Matters: A Sociology of Illness, Prevention and Care*, ed. by A. Peterson and C. Waddell. Sydney: Allen and Unwin, pp. 169–84; and Clark and Seymour 1999, *supra* n. 18.

death. However, the constraints on how well a positive conception might be realized arise not only from ethical concerns about direct interference through sedation, assisted dying or even deliberate enhancement of mental states but also from a creeping acceptance of the liberal plurality that there is no single good end. However, in exploring the axiological approach, the possibility of a new ars moriendi has been shown to be at least plausible and quite possibly consistent with the goals and ideals of palliative care. This chapter has but merely scratched the surface of a complex problem of moral, legal and social issues of a kind that will not be easily resolved, if indeed they are resolvable. The morally pragmatic way forward is to seek clarity about the desirable goals for end of life choices, to be robust when challenging both new demands and established norms, and to seek the complementary and potentially compatible aspects of the entrenched opposites that inform the contemporary landscape.

Chapter 8
Children, Law and a Good Death*

Lynn Hagger

Introduction

Facing life and death decisions gains particular poignancy where children are concerned. Not being in a position to survive childhood always has an air of untimely tragedy for the children and their families alike. However, making a decision that means that death occurs sooner than if nature was allowed to take its course may mean that, for children, and their families, the death for them is 'good'. Not to avail children of all the benefits modern medicine can bring to extend their lives may seem counter-intuitive, but if interventions are unduly burdensome or against deep and long-held beliefs, this may be a legitimate approach to take. Of course, such decisions are not reached lightly and, in some cases, a consensus about an appropriate course of action cannot be achieved. This is where the law has a clear role. There may be disagreement between parents and/ or health professionals about the decision being made. The law has a responsibility to establish the parameters of appropriate decision-making not least to provide guidance as to how parental responsibility should be exercised and how health professionals should be involved in the process to ensure younger children also experience a good death. Where competent children are concerned, the same interested parties may hold differing views as to how much account should be taken of the former's wishes. Ultimately, the courts will need to be the final arbiter as to what is in a child's best interests, even to the extent that they could decide this is a matter for the child to determine. This chapter will explore how the courts currently resolve areas of contention about end of life matters in the paediatric setting and how judicial deliberations could be improved. This has particular resonance in relation to mature minors where the approach of the courts will be shown to be too cautious. The chapter will also discuss how what happens after a child has died will affect parents' perception as to whether the death was good or otherwise for them. Before these areas are explored, the chapter commences with a discussion of incompetent child patients. There may be disagreements about whether a medical intervention is in the best interests of the child in practice but it

---

* A more detailed version of this chapter may be found in Hagger, L. 2009. *The Child as Vulnerable Patient: Protection and Empowerment.* Aldershot: Ashgate, chapters 2 and 3. See also Chico, V. and Hagger, L. 2011. The Mental Capacity Act 2005 and mature minors: a missed opportunity? *Journal of Social Welfare and Family*, 33(2), 157–68.

will be proposed that the courts adopt a justifiable position albeit one that needs to take greater account of parental wishes in some cases.

Incompetent Children and End of Life Decisions

Where children are deemed to be legally incompetent, those with parental responsibility[1] have the capacity to consent to their medical treatment and this must be exercised in the child's best interests.[2] Not seeking appropriate medical treatment can amount to a criminal offence or lead to care proceedings.[3] Where more than one person has parental responsibility the consent of one will usually be sufficient.[4] Responsible parenting should involve taking the child's views into account. International legal instruments suggest that even very young children should be involved in the decision-making process to an optimal extent.[5] This is supported in domestic law[6] and professional guidelines.[7] All children, whatever their age and circumstances, can provide valuable perceptions that can improve their clinical care.[8] It has been indicated that even young children are more

---

1   S. 3(1) CA.

2   *Gillick v West Norfolk and Wisbech Area Health Authority* [1986] AC 112 at 127. It is arguable that all that a parent is required by the law to do is act in a way that is not against a child's best interests: in *S v S* [1972] AC 24 it was considered that to allow paternity testing against the mother's wishes would not be against the child's interests and was justifiable in the general public interest Following this principle would give parents authority to consent to certain non-therapeutic interventions on their children (Pattinson, S.D. 2006. *Medical Law and Ethics.* London: Sweet and Maxwell, at p. 165).

3   See e.g. s. 1(1) and (2) of the Children and Young Person's Act 1933. From the doctor's perspective, in the case of more routine treatment, consent should be obtained from parents. Where this is not feasible, the defence of necessity would justify an emergency intervention. However, it would be wise to seek consent from parents or court authorization if time permits. If not, they may intervene even where parents object (*Re O* [1993] 2 FLR 149). Anyone caring for a child may do 'what is reasonable in all the circumstances of the case for the purpose of safeguarding or promoting the child's welfare' under section 3(5) Children Act 1989 (CA) and this appears to allow consent to be given for medical treatment (*B v B* [1992] FLR 327). It is unlikely that this provision would extend to major interventions that are not emergencies or where there is parental objection.

4   S. 2(7) CA.

5   See e.g. Articles 12 and 13 of the United Nations Convention on the Rights of the Child 1989.

6   S. 1(3)(a) CA 1989.

7   General Medical Council (GMC). 2007. *0–18 years: Guidance for Doctors.* London: GMC.

8   See e.g. Alderson, P. 1993. *Children's Consent to Surgery.* Buckingham: OUP; Eiser, C. 1985. Changes in understanding of illness as the child grows. *Archives of Disease in Childhood*, 60, 489–92 and Hammond, L. 1993. *Children's Decisions in Health Care and Research.* London: Institute of Education.

competent than is traditionally perceived,[9] particularly where they have experience of a long-term illness.[10] With appropriate techniques, children as young as four can make helpful comments about their experiences of health services[11] and like to be involved in this way.[12] Where they have an opinion, it may not be given in an expected way. They need to be empowered through creative means and allowed originality in their views. However, this represents good practice and the law does not require parents to involve their children in making decisions. It is only when the court becomes involved that the child is given a certain opportunity to have their needs and wishes addressed and the parent's decision may be challenged as being contrary to their child's welfare.

Authorization must be sought from the court for some procedures,[13] where parents refuse to consent to life-saving procedures, and may be advisable wherever there is any uncertainty or disagreement about a particular intervention.[14] The courts will resolve disputes by making an assessment of what is in the welfare of the child taking wide-ranging factors into account that encompass medical, emotional and other welfare factors,[15] including the psychological and social benefits to the child.[16] The court must have regard to the wishes and feelings of the child concerned as far as they can be ascertained according to their age and understanding.[17]

---

9   See e.g. Woodward, A.L., Sommerville, J.A. and Guajardo, J.J. 2001. How infants make sense of intentional action, in *Intentions and Intentionality: Foundations of Social Cognition*, ed. by B. Malle, L. Moses and D. Baldwin. Cambridge MA: MIT Press, at pp. 149–69; Mandeltzoff, A.N. 1999. Origins of mind, cognition and communication. *Journal of Communication Disorders*, 32(4), 251–69.

10   See e.g. Mandler, J.M. 1990. A new perspective on cognitive development in infancy. *American Scientist*, 78, 236; Pinker, S. 2002. *The Blank Slate: The Modern Denial of Human Nature.* London: Penguin Books; and Bluebond-Langner, M. 1978. *The Private Worlds of Dying Children.* Princeton: Princeton University Press, *passim.*

11   Curtis, K., Liabo, K., Roberts, H. and Barker, M. 2004. Consulted but not heard: A qualitative study of young people's views of their local health service. *Health Expectations*, 7(2), 149–56.

12   Elliott, E. and Watson, A. 1997. But the doctors aren't your mum. *Health Matters*, 30, 8–9.

13   Sterilization, change of surname and male circumcision would constitute such procedures; see, for example, *Re C (a child) (immunisation: parental rights)* [2003] 2 FLR 1095, paras. 15–17.

14   From the High Court under its inherent jurisdiction or for a specific issue order under s. 8 CA to determine the appropriate way forward. Judicial sanction is a legal requirement where a child is a ward of court when important steps are being considered: see e.g. *Re J* [1991] Fam 33.

15   *Re A (Male Sterilisation)* [2000] 1 FLR 549 *per* Dame Butler-Sloss P at 555. Although this is a case concerning an adult, the approach towards establishing the best interests of children is similarly broad.

16   *Re Y* [1997] 2 WLR 556 at 562.

17   S. 1(3)(a) CA.

Recently, the courts have been enthusiastic about adopting a balance sheet approach whereby a list is drawn up of benefits and burdens of proposed courses of action and the approach is followed that has the greatest overall benefit.[18] That notwithstanding, relying on an application of the welfare principle can be seen as unpredictable, lacking in substance, susceptible to bias, and can mean that a child's interests are insufficiently acknowledged.[19] As James has pointed out,[20] the courts can be only too ready to 'deny children's ability to behave and decide responsibly and to set aside their wishes and feelings, [and] it also demonstrates the power of the language of welfare and how it can be used to deny children's agency'.[21]

The views of the parents will also be taken into account as part of the assessment of a child's welfare. The nature of judicial reasoning often means that, rather than seeing parents as having a fundamental interest in their children's welfare, their interests are seen as in conflict with those of their child. However, not only do parents possess unique, detailed knowledge of their child, but they also have high levels of empathy, and a stake in the child's well-being.[22] Parents will usually support treatment to keep the child alive on the basis of medical opinion and will generally act in accordance with the best scientific information in the interests of their child's health. Paediatric health professionals often see the family as the 'patient'.[23] The familial and social context has to be acknowledged as playing a role in caring for the child. To do so is the preferred holistic approach. Nowhere is the care offered to families more evident than when a child reaches the end of their life. There are many eloquent testaments about the support families receive. An example of this may be found in chapters 9 and 10 of this book.[24] In Chapter 10, Isabel's mother speaks of the time taken in helping her and her husband to reach decisions about treatments that were

---

18   See e.g. *Wyatt and another v Portsmouth Hospital NHS Trust and another* [2005] EWCA Civ 1181.

19   Reece, R. 1996. The paramountcy principle: Consensus of construct? *Current Legal Problems*, 49, 267, at p. 303.

20   James, A. 2008. Responsibility, children and childhood, in *Responsibility, Law and the Family*, ed. by J. Bridgeman, H. Keating and C. Lind. Aldershot: Ashgate, discussing *Re W (Contact: Joining Child as Party)* [2001] EWCA Civ 1830.

21   *Ibid.* at p. 153.

22   See the discussion with respect to *An NHS Trust v MB* [2006] 2 FCR 319 discussed *infra* n. 146*ff.*

23   Personal communication from a range of health professionals throughout my 25 years of NHS experience.

24   E.g. personal communication from Sabine Vanacker and David Kelly, the parents of Isabel who suffered from Tay-Sachs disease and was treated at Sheffield Children's NHS Foundation Trust. Their experience of support from the hospital was recorded and presented at 'The Value of Life, the Value of Death', ETHOX Annual Conference, Sheffield, 21 May 2008.

right for them. In the sad event that a child dies, the families often continue to receive support through bereavement counselling.[25]

Notwithstanding the common practice of taking time to help families make decisions, parents may still disagree with doctors' views of what is in the child's best interests and either demand treatment against the prevailing clinical opinion or, less commonly, refuse to consent to treatment. Such tensions are particularly vivid where life-sustaining treatment is concerned. If such disagreement cannot be resolved locally, a court will be asked to determine the appropriate way forward.[26]

The courts have taken parental views of the quality of a child's life into account when determining best interests but have not allowed these to be the sole determinants of such issues. The case of *Re T (Wardship: Medical Treatment)*[27] has been seen as an aberrant decision,[28] or, conversely, as more progressive than most:[29] aberrant if viewed as a reversion to the idea of the natural rights of parents; progressive because it took into account the important aspect of the caring relationship.[30] Here, in view of the mother's perception that a liver transplant was not in the child's best interests, contrary to those of the health team involved, the court decided not to overrule her wishes. This was understandable given the level of post-operative care that would be required of her.[31] The sacrifices required would have been very significant because the parents lived abroad.[32] If she was less than fully supportive such care would, undoubtedly, have been compromised. In addition, the mother's view was within the band of acceptable decisions a reasonable person could take, that is, she was making an informed and educated decision.[33] Further, the child had already undergone an unsuccessful operation that had caused pain and distress. Nevertheless, some commentators have regarded this decision as a regressive step because, inter alia, the interests of the child and the mother were not fully articulated.[34] Great care needs to be taken when considering the views of parents.[35] There may be occasions when parents do not

---

25   This may also be true in cases involving the loss of an adult patient, of course.

26   Note that doctors will not be compelled to act against their clinical judgment: *Re C (a minor) (medical treatment)* [1998] 1 FLR 384.

27   [1997] 1 WLR 242.

28   Bainham, A. 1997. Do babies have rights? *Cambridge Law Journal*, 56, 48–50 and Michalowski, S. 1997. Is it in the best interests of a child to have a life-saving transplantation? *Re T (Wardship: Medical Treatment)*. *Child and Family Law Quarterly*, 9, 179–89.

29   Bridgeman, J. 2007. *Parental Responsibility, Young Children and Healthcare Law*. Cambridge: Cambridge University Press, at pp. 137–42.

30   The ethic of care is explored in Hagger, L. 2009. *The Child as Vulnerable Patient: Protection and Empowerment*. Aldershot: Ashgate, chapter 5.

31   *Supra* n. 27 at 251.

32   *Ibid.* at 252.

33   *Ibid.* at 250.

34   See the discussion in Bainham and Michalowski, *supra* n. 28.

35   Bainham, *supra* n. 28.

have a child's interests truly at heart and it cannot be assumed that the interests of parents and children are exactly aligned.[36] However, this mother was not seen as anything less than a loving parent.[37] Recognition of the caring relationships is to be welcomed, although there is a need to be clear about how they should be valued and acknowledged[38] and it should not be forgotten that there is the option of finding a foster carer or adoptive parent if the parent no longer wishes to carry out the parental role.[39]

In some cases parents of extremely ill children have insisted on inappropriate (so-called 'futile') medical treatment for children. No doubt, in such cases, it is extremely difficult for parents to relinquish the child to its fate. There will always be a need to have sensitive discussions with families. Decisions subsequent to *Re T*[40] have adopted an approach that focuses on the child's best interests, rather than appearing to conflate these with those of the parents. The traditional approach adopted a presumption in favour of prolonging life while weighing up the pain and suffering involved in further treatment against the quality of life that would result from it.[41] Treatment would only be withheld or withdrawn if, from the child's perspective, the child's life would be intolerable.[42] More recently, the 'intolerability' point was addressed in the *Wyatt* case, where Hedley J was explicit that this was not an additional test to best interests but part of the process for determining what these might be[43] with the test sometimes providing a 'valuable guide in the search for best interests in this type of case'.[44]

In *R v Portsmouth Hospitals NHS Trust ex parte Glass*,[45] Lord Woolf MR[46] established important principles of law requiring the courts to take into account 'the natural concerns and the responsibilities' of parents.[47] However, the parents' views will be overruled where they are seen to be in conflict with the best interests of the child. In this case, the mother disagreed with the medical team that her severely disabled 12-year-old son David, who had a limited life span, should be given no more than palliative care. Following a respiratory tract infection the doctors prescribed diamorphine to make him comfortable but this has the effect of further depressing lung function. To make matters worse, they placed a 'Do

---

36 Michalowski, *supra* n. 28.

37 *Supra* n. 27 at 246.

38 Fox, M. and McHale, J. 1997. In whose best interests? *Modern Law Review*, 58, 700–709.

39 Bainham, *supra* n. 28.

40 *Re T, supra* n. 27.

41 *Re J (Wardship: Medical Treatment)* [1991] 2 WLR 140 drawing on *Re B (a Minor) (Wardship: Medical Treatment)* [1981] 1 WLR 1421.

42 *Re J, Ibid. at* 147–9 *per* Taylor LJ.

43 *Portsmouth NHS Trust v Wyatt* [2004] EWHC 2247 at para. 24.

44 *Supra* n. 18 at paras 75–76, 87 and 91 *per* Wall LJ.

45 [1999] 2 FLR 905.

46 As he then was.

47 *Supra* n. 45 at 911.

Not Attempt Resuscitation' order on his medical notes without discussing this with his mother. The family forcibly intervened and took him home where he was successfully treated by the family doctor.

Mrs Glass sought a declaration from the court as to the intervention her son could expect on further admittance to the hospital. The Court of Appeal declined to give such an anticipatory authorization because it would unduly restrict the doctors involved. The ideal is for doctors and parents to agree in a climate of consultation and full information but, where this is no longer possible, the court should only be called upon to adjudicate on actual facts as they occur at the time. At that point, the court would determine the best interests of the child.

The *Glass* case was then brought before the European Court of Human Rights,[48] where the Court was particularly critical of the Trust's failure to seek an earlier authorization from the High Court or otherwise defuse the situation.[49] In many ways this case has proved to be a salutary lesson for the health and legal professions alike not least because, as one of the judges noted in the European Court, 'maternal instinct has had more weight than medical opinion':[50] despite the prognosis David had survived for more than six years following these events. Notwithstanding the judges' remarks in this case, the decision does little to improve overall decision-making in these cases of very dependent children. The obligation of doctors to consult with David Glass's family was made clear. However, the concern remains that if the parents do not agree with the doctors and a court order is sought, then undue judicial deference to medical opinion means that the doctors' views will carry much the greater weight in the court room.[51] In particular, there is a worry that the medical perception of quality of life, seen very much from the able-bodied perspective, will rule the day whereas the views of the disabled person themselves should be a major determining factor.[52] Where this is not possible, those caring for them on a day-to-day basis, should they be relatives, carers or health professionals, should make a significant contribution in determining these matters.[53] Of course, doctors understand better than most the most suitable clinical approach to the prevention, cure or relief of disorders. However, it is the patient and/or their carers who understand their temperament, experience of other medical interventions and other important factors.

More recently, *An NHS Trust v MB*[54] provides another unusual example of where the courts have recognized the parents' views as to the quality of their

---

48   *Glass v UK* [2004] 1 FLR 1019.

49   *Ibid.* at para. 79.

50   (2004) 39 EHRR 15, 364 (Separate Opinion of Judge Casadevall).

51   *Re J, supra* n. 41.

52   This was the concern of the Disability Rights Commission expressed in *R (on the application of Burke) v GMC* [2005] QB 424.

53   Asch, A. 1998. Distracted by disability. *Cambridge Quarterly of Healthcare Ethics*, 7, 77–87.

54   *NHS Trust v MB* [2006] 2 FCR 319.

child's life, notwithstanding the profound disability of spinal muscular atrophy. At the time of referral to the court, MB was artificially ventilated, had very limited movement but was said to be cognitively aware by the parents. The extent of this was uncertain, as was the amount of pain the child experienced,[55] which made decision-making very challenging. The mother's view was that it was not in the child's interests to have ventilation removed and her opinion was supported by the court. This was despite the fact that there were opposing opinions from no fewer than 14 consultants. This would accord with Jonas's[56] view that where levels of pain or the extent of an infant's higher-order interests such as autonomy cannot be established, parental views about treatment should prevail notwithstanding any resource implications. Parents have strong claims in decisions for infants because they usually have their best interests at heart. These decisions also have a profound and enduring impact on them so their views should be taken seriously: '[t]hey rejoice when their child flourishes and grieve when her welfare deteriorates'.[57] Where a parent disagrees, more weight should be given to the opinions of the primary care giver.

The Religious and/or Cultural Dimension

Religious and/or cultural views about specific interventions are often at the heart of disputes between doctors and parents about a child's best interests.[58] In *Re C (a minor) (medical treatment)*,[59] Orthodox Jewish parents argued that their 16-month-old daughter, who suffered from muscular atrophy, should continue to be ventilated. This was contrary to medical opinion, which considered such intervention to be futile because ventilation would only prolong the child's life by a few days. The parents' faith dictated that all efforts should be made to preserve life, but the court preferred the doctors' views. The courts have generally demonstrated an unwillingness to order doctors to carry out medical intervention that parents seek but that the doctors believe to be medically inappropriate.[60] Where parental views include adherence to religious and/or sub-cultural views, it may be easier to be dismissive of these as being less than rational in the light of clinical judgment.

Further examples of the religious context arise in relation to Jehovah's Witness families. Currently, the courts usually support the doctor's view as to what is in the child's best interests although the parents' genuinely held beliefs that they *are*

---

55   Jonas, M. 2007. The baby MB case: Medical decision-making in the context of uncertain infant suffering. *Journal of Medical Ethics*, 33, 541–4.

56   *Ibid.*

57   *Ibid.* at p. 546.

58   See Macaskill, M. 2008. Parents of ill vegan girl may face police. *The Sunday Times* [Online, 8 June]. Available at: http://www.timesonline.co.uk/tol/news/uk/scotland/article4087734.ece [accessed 9 August 2011] for an interesting example of parental beliefs in a particular diet proving to be severely detrimental to their daughter's health.

59   *Supra* n. 26.

60   *Supra* n. 26.

acting in the child's best interests are acknowledged.[61] This means that there have been a number of cases where doctors have been authorized to give children a blood transfusion, despite the religious objections of their Jehovah's Witness parents and, sometimes, the child.[62] The approach of the courts could be challenged under the HRA, focusing on the rights under Articles 8(1) and the right to freedom of thought, conscience and religion under Article 9(1), neither of which are absolute rights.[63] Given the courts' commitment to the sanctity of life and best interest considerations with respect to children, the ability to derogate under Article 8(2) or 9(2)[64] would be relied upon to protect the child. The courts will not allow parents to make martyrs of their children in the name of religion[65] and they have had little appetite to permit mature minors to refuse life-saving treatment.[66] So any attempt to use these Articles to further a child's right to manifest their religion would seem doomed to failure notwithstanding Johnson J's obiter remarks in *Re P*,[67] where he suggested that there might be cases where *older* children would be permitted to refuse to receive blood products.

There are examples of good practice where NHS Trusts engage in constructive dialogue with the Jehovah's Witness community through their hospital liaison committees, which have resulted in useful guidance for health professionals dealing with children from these families.[68] This guidance contains consent forms for parents to sign whereby parents are relieved of their agonizing decision-making. There is an acknowledgement that they would never agree to the use of certain blood products but equally recognize that the medical team may decide it is in the child's best interests to do so. This proves acceptable to the Jehovah's Witness community who then do not ostracize a family whose child does receive blood products. The reaction of the religious community has been a key influence on parents in this situation.

Apart from the decisions in *Re T*[69] (which, arguably, turned on its own particular facts and was subject to widespread criticism),[70] and *An NHS Trust v. MB*,[71] the

---

61   See the discussion in Bridgeman, *supra* n. 29 at pp. 143–9.

62   See e.g. *Re R (A Minor) (Blood Transfusion)* [1993] 2 FLR 757, *Re S (a minor) (medical treatment)* [1993] 1 FLR 376 and *Re O (a minor) (medical treatment)*, *supra* n. 97.

63   See *R (Williamson) v Secretary of State for Education and Employment and Others* [2005] 2 FLR 374 where it was held that religious beliefs did not justify allowing corporal punishment.

64   Which, inter alia, provide for the protection of the rights and freedoms of others.

65   *Re E (A minor) (Wardship: medical treatment)* [1993] 1 FLR 386.

66   *Ibid.*

67   *Bro Morgannwg NHS Trust v 'P' and others* [2003] EWHC 2327 (Fam) (*Re P*).

68   Personal communication from J. Reid, Director of Clinical Operations, Sheffield Children's NHS Foundation Trust.

69   *Supra* n. 27.

70   See e.g. *supra* n. 28.

71   *Supra* n. 54.

courts generally support medical opinion[72] and thus far the HRA has failed to challenge this approach to any significant degree.[73] However, the HRA does provide a much stronger means whereby families may challenge any perceived lack of involvement in the health care decision-making process under Article 8(1).[74] This means that more account should be taken of the parental perspective both in practice and in future judicial decision-making.

An important aspect of the responsibilities of parents is to ensure their children achieve competent adulthood. The natural tendency of parents is to try to maintain a strong influence on the behaviour of their children not least to protect them from harm. The desire to safeguard children does not diminish as they approach adulthood. However, parents do not fulfil their duties if they do not gradually relinquish their proxy decision-making role so that their maturing offspring are given opportunities to make their own decisions, practising their skills on the road to reaching 'a capacity where they are able to take full responsibility as free, rational agents for their own system of ends'.[75] This can mean that they decide to refuse life-saving treatment where this is against their devout beliefs and/or is unduly burdensome. The following section explores the extent to which the law acknowledges mature minors' autonomy in the end of life context.

Competent Children and End of Life Decisions

While children's decision-making should not be unfettered, it is important that their right to autonomy receives appropriate recognition. When competent, children have the right to more than mere consultation about their views. Strong statements of this legal principle are essential in the light of increasing recognition of children's rights[76] and persuasive empirical evidence that children are more capable of making decisions than is generally thought to be the case.[77] The ability of a child to make very significant decisions such as refusing life-saving interventions will be explored in relation to this point. Unfortunately, practice remains inconsistent and incoherent with conservative assessments of children's ability to be involved in

---

72   See *NHS Trust v (1) A (A Child) (Represented by an Officer of CAFCASS as Child's Guardian) (2) Mrs. A (3) Mr A* [2007] EWHC 1696 (Fam) for an example where the court agreed with the medical team that the 50 per cent prospect of a full, normal life with painful treatment for a 7-month-old child against certain death before 18 months without treatment outweighed all other considerations notwithstanding the parents' faith that God would cure the child and their concern about further suffering.

73   See the discussion in Hagger, *supra* n. 30, Chapter 2.

74   See e.g. *Glass, supra* n. 45.

75   See Freeman, M. 1983. *The Rights and Wrongs of Children.* London: Pinter, at p. 57.

76   Discussed *infra* n. 93*ff.*

77   *Supra* n. 8*ff.*

decisions about their medical treatment remaining the norm.[78] Of course, problems only arise when there is disagreement about the course of action to be adopted. There is anecdotal and other evidence that where parents and health professionals agree with a child who does not wish to receive even life-saving treatment, the child's decision is allowed to stand.[79] It is only when there is no such concurrence that the courts will have to decide whose opinion should prevail.

This section will provide an overview of a realistic version of autonomy that can recognize the position of children before addressing whether they have a right to have this respected. It will then explore the current legal status of mature minors' decision-making to establish whether the law requires further attention.

The Nature of Autonomy

Rights are important because they enable claims by persons to be treated as dignified subjects of respect on the ground of desert rather than relying on the whim of others to act benevolently.[80] Autonomy has become the predominant concept in the biomedical context[81] even though its ascendancy over other ethical principles may be challenged.[82] There is no universally accepted definition of autonomy and it has been argued that its equivocal nature allows judges to achieve outcomes that reflect their values: where they empathize with a patient the latter's interests are more likely to receive support.[83]

Dworkin's account of autonomy requires the promotion and improvement of reflective and critical faculties, but no particular substantive content.[84] He notes

---

78　Alderson, P. and Montgomery, J. 1996. *Health Care Choices: Making Decisions with Children.* London: Institute for Public Policy Research, discovered this to be the case based on a 1993 research project generally and more recent evidence suggests this is still so: BMA. 2007. *Consent, rights and choices in health care for children and young people* [Online: British Medical Association]. Available from: http://www.bma.org.uk/ethics/ consent_and_capacity/Consentchildren.jsp [accessed 9 August 2011]. This seems to be the case even in specialist children's settings: see Healthcare Commission. 2007. *State of Healthcare,* London: Healthcare Commission, at p. 71; and personal communication from Dr J. Wales, Consultant Paediatrician, Sheffield Children's NHS Foundation Trust.

79　See Hagger *supra* n. 30, Chapter 2 for evidence of this.

80　Feinberg, J. 1966. Duties, rights and claims. *American Philosophical Quarterly,* 3(2), 1 at p. 8.

81　See, for example, Laurie, G.T. 2004. *Genetic Privacy: A Challenge to Medico-legal Norm.* Cambridge: Cambridge University Press, at p. 194; and Beauchamp, T.L. and Childress, C.F. 2001. *Principles of Biomedical Ethics.* 5th edn. Oxford: Oxford University Press, at p. 177.

82　Laurie, *ibid.* and Foster, C 2009. *Choosing Life Choosing Death: The Tyranny of Autonomy in Medical Ethics and Law.* Oxford: Hart Publishing.

83　Coggon, J. 2007. Varied and principled understandings of autonomy in English law: justifiable inconsistency or blinkered moralism? *Health Care Analysis,* 15(3), 235–55.

84　Dworkin, G. 1988. *The Theory and Practice of Autonomy.* Cambridge: Cambridge University Press, at pp. 30–32.

how all moral theories have some idea of treating others as equal in certain ways to oneself, that actions require moral justification and that what we do must reflect the preferences of those who are affected by what we do. In addition, these theories accept that some element of choice exists so that, for example, each person is seen as the best judge of their own interests. He believes that inherent in these common assumptions is a shared conception that a person consists of their life-plans and that by pursuing autonomy the person gives meaning to their life. This will not be the same for everyone so autonomy cannot have substantive content. In their ability to define themselves, all deserve moral respect although this may be subject to a limit.[85] His version of autonomy takes account of the person as situated in a social and relational context[86] that enables self-determination.[87] Perhaps the single most important extrinsic factor for autonomy is relational, in that the extent to which one can expect one's own autonomy to be respected is relative to the right and freedom of others to act autonomously. This implies that an individual's autonomy is enhanced by and dependent on others in that they may provide essential information or may manipulate the environment to that person's advantage or otherwise. This aspect of Dworkin's approach to autonomy has particular resonance in the health care setting. Thus, there is harmony with theories that hold that autonomy does have a substantive content and requires that individual choices accord with certain values. This principled autonomy[88] with its notions of constraint, obligations and responsibility[89] is perhaps best exemplified by Kant: autonomy is achieved when a level of rationality is reached by the individual so that they unreservedly impose rational laws upon themselves because they are applicable for all rational beings.[90]

The English courts claim that autonomous medical decisions do not need rationality to be deserving of respect[91] but, in reality, it can be argued that the

---

85   *Ibid.* at p. 31.

86   See e.g. Mulhall, S. and Swift, A. 1997. *Liberals and Communitarians.* 2nd edn. Oxford: Blackwell.

87   Kymlicka, W. 2002. *Contemporary Political Philosophy.* Oxford: Oxford University Press citing Taylor, C. 1991. Shared and divergent values, in *Options for a New Canada*, ed. by R. Watts and D. Brown. Toronto: University of Toronto Press, at p. 216.

88   O'Neill, O. 2002. *Autonomy and Trust in Bioethics.* Cambridge: Cambridge University Press.

89   Veitch, K. 2007. *The Jurisdiction of Medical Law.* Aldershot: Ashgate, at p. 100.

90   Ansell-Pearson, K. 1991. Nietzsche on autonomy and morality: the challenge to political theory. *Political Studies*, 39, 270–86, at p. 273.

91   Lord Donaldson said '[t]his right of choice is not limited to decisions which others might regard as sensible. It exists notwithstanding that the reasons for making the choice are rational, irrational, unknown or even non-existent' in *Re T (Adult: refusal of medical treatment)* [1993] Fam 95, at 102. Relying on traditional conservative and objective reasoning, the courts appear to adopt this content-neutral conception of autonomy, which may seem appropriate given prevalent patients' rights discourse: Veitch, K. 2007. *The Jurisdiction of Medical Law.* Aldershot: Ashgate, at p. 100.

courts do require that some patients demonstrate the rationality of their decisions to have their autonomy recognized: patients must be 'responsible'.[92] Thus, the courts may enquire into the rationality of decisions to reject treatment, even where the patient is demonstrably competent as in *Re B*: Ms B had to show that her decision to refuse treatment was instrumentally rational in that it represented her genuine desires. However, she did not have to prove substantive rationality in the sense that the decision had to accord with objective values: her refusal was respected even though it was at odds with the beliefs of her carers.

It can be argued that the courts do require minors' decisions to be substantively rational to deserve respect. Mature minors are at particular risk of having their autonomy interfered with when their decision appears irrational on the basis that it is contrary to medical advice. Before the law as it pertains to the medical decision-making of children is examined, the basis of children's claims to autonomy will be explored.

Do Children Have a Right to Autonomy?

International instruments such as the United Nations Convention on the Rights of the Child (UNCRC) recognize the importance of protecting children's autonomy by promoting their rights.[93] Children need to be provided with opportunities to develop into autonomous adults but this does not necessarily entail that children have a right to autonomy and the UNCRC rights may be seen as merely claims to further children's needs[94] and rights to participate. However, the wide acceptance of the UNCRC suggests that states accept the idea that children possess rights that should be acknowledged and the language of rights is a useful rhetorical device to ensure that these claims are conceded and satisfied.[95]

---

92   *Ibid.*

93   For example, Articles 12, 13 and 14 of the United Nations Convention on the Rights of the Child.

94   Feinberg, J. 1966. Duties, rights and claims. *American Philosophical Quarterly*, 3(2), 1 at p. 8.

95   Feinberg, J. 1980. *Rights, Justice and the Bounds of Liberty.* Princeton: Princeton University Press, at p. 153. However, it should be noted that, although the UNCRC underpins the UK's legal framework, some of its key Articles, especially those concerning children's participation in decision-making, are not fully reflected in law, policy and practice: James, A. and James, A.L. 2004. *Constructing Childhood: Theory, Policy and Social Practice.* Basingstoke: Palgrave Macmillan; and Hargreaves, D.S. and Viner, R.M. 2011. Children's and young people's experience of the National Health Service in England: A review of national surveys 2001–2011. ADC Online First: 10.1136/archdischild-2011-300603. The UK Children's Commissioner has also expressed disappointment at the continuing lack of progress made on children's rights in the UK: UK Children's Commissioner. 2008. *Report to the UN Committee on the Rights of the Child* [Online: UK Children's Commissioner]. Available at: http://www.niccy.org/uploaded_docs/UNCRC_REPORT_FINAL.pdf [accessed 21 September 2011]. The Scottish government *has* published a consultation on the Rights

Identifying and balancing children's rights where these are disputed is challenging but an interest theory of rights can accommodate the idea that children have rights notwithstanding their lack of adult capacities. MacCormick holds that a person may be seen as having rights where their interests are protected by '[legal or moral] normative constraints on the acts or activities of other people with respect to the object of one's interest' and enforcement can be seen as a separate issue that does not preclude the establishment of rights.[96] O'Neill prefers the concept of 'obligations' owed to children by others,[97] which can embrace the relationship between children and their parents. However, children's and parents' interests are not necessarily the same and mechanisms are needed to ensure that children's views receive an adequate hearing. MacCormick's proposition that a moral right is 'a good of such importance that it would be wrong to deny it to or withhold it from any member of C [a given class]'[98] is persuasive because it supports notions of children's rights. Nonetheless, translating interests into moral rights that could then become legal rights has also been problematic. Eekelaar has suggested that society should behave towards children as if they have rights that would then define the rights children should have.[99] Their right to choose is promoted in his theory of 'dynamic self-determinism', which should 'bring a child to the threshold of adulthood with the maximum opportunities to form and pursue life-goals which reflect as closely as possible an autonomous choice'.[100]

In practice, the balance to be struck between the child's need for protection vis-à-vis the importance of promoting their capacity for self-determination will always be a consideration. Requiring instrumental rationality so that decisions are backed by reasons rather than the decision itself being deemed objectively rational may be reasonable. Requiring the decision to be substantively rational in the case of children where they have met tests for legal competence is repressive and contrary to the approach taken with most adults.

The Legal Position: Autonomy and Children

In English law the clear commitment to patient autonomy has been less evident with respect to mature minors. Competent 16 and 17-year-olds can consent to treatment under section 8(1) of the Family Law Reform Act 1969. The capacity of anyone over 16 is now determined under the Mental Capacity Act 2005 (MCA).[101]

---

of Children and Young People with a view to providing greater clarity about compliance with the UNCRC in legislation.

96   MacCormick, N. 1982. *Legal Right and Social Democracy: Essays in Legal and Political Theory.* Oxford: Clarendon Press, at p. 154.

97   O'Neill, *supra* n. 88 at pp. 38–9.

98   MacCormick, *supra* n. 96 at p. 160.

99   Eekelaar, J. 1991 *Regulating Divorce.* Oxford: Clarendon Press, at p. 103.

100   Eekelaar, J. 1982. The emergence of children's rights. *Oxford Journal of Legal Studies*, 6, 161 at pp. 170–71.

101   S. 2(5).

Arguably, the relationship between the two statutes is unsettled on the point of refusing interventions as is noted below. There is a rebuttable presumption of capacity under the MCA,[102] which is determined with respect to the decision to be made[103] so that a more serious and/or complex decision will require a higher level of competence.[104] There is also a requirement to take all practicable steps to help the individual make that decision,[105] which may be significant.[106] Under section 3(1), the patient must be able to understand the information relevant to the decision, to retain that information, to use or weigh that information as part of the process of making the decision and to communicate their decision by some means. Only being able to retain the information for a short time or expressing ambivalence about the decision being made will not necessarily mean the patient is incompetent[107] but they will need to understand the implications of deciding one way or another or not at all.[108] Additionally, a person is not to be assumed to lack capacity merely because of their age or appearance[109] or because others believe they have made an unwise decision.[110] For individuals aged 16 and 17 years, the MCA does make some key distinctions. They cannot make advance directives to refuse treatment,[111] nor can they appoint a Lasting Power of Attorney to manage their affairs in the event they become incompetent.[112]

With respect to the under 16s, *Gillick v West Norfolk and Wisbech Area Health Authority*[113] was hailed as an important case in the development of respect for children's autonomy[114] because the case more broadly established the right of children under 16 to consent to medical interventions provided they have 'sufficient understanding and intelligence to enable him or her to understand fully what is proposed'.[115] However, subsequent cases established that competent minors of *all* ages have no corollary right to refuse life-saving treatment.[116] With respect to those

---

102   S. 1(2).

103   Ss. 1(3), 1(4) and 3(1) in particular.

104   As in *Re T supra* n. 91, per Lord Donaldson at 102.

105   S. 1(3).

106   There are onerous requirements contained in Part 2, Chapter 3 of the Code of Practice in some detail as to what might be expected including appropriate settings and the use of aids.

107   S. 3(3).

108   S. 3(4).

109   S. 2(3).

110   S. 1(4).

111   Ss. 24–26.

112   Ss. 9–13.

113   *Supra* n. 2.

114   See e.g. Bridge, C. 1999. Religious beliefs and teenage refusal of medical treatment. *Modern Law Review*, 62(4), 585–94 at p. 585.

115   *Gillick, supra* n. 2, per Lord Scarman at 189.

116   *Re R (A Minor) (Wardship: Consent to Medical Treatment)* [1991] 4 All ER 177 and *Re W (A minor) (Medical treatment)* [1993] Fam 64.

over 16, the empowering MCA provides an opportunity to challenge the status quo.[117] In the meantime, the consent of those with parental responsibility and the consent of the courts will protect the doctor if the child refuses treatment.[118]

The approach of the courts to the mature minor's refusal of treatment is in direct contrast to the attitude adopted towards adults where the latter's decisions are apparently to be respected no matter how irrational they appear to others unless it concerns an issue of competence.[119] This is particularly contentious in the case of mature, intelligent minors with no mental disorder who are perceived to be making unwise decisions by refusing medically appropriate treatment on the basis of long-held, deep religious beliefs. In such cases, the courts have sought to find reasons to deem the minor incompetent rather than honestly acknowledging that, although the minor is capable of achieving capacity, the decision will be overridden if it is seemingly imprudent.

In *Re E*,[120] a 15-year-old Jehovah's Witness suffering from leukaemia refused a blood transfusion necessary to save his life. Ward J acknowledged his 'intelligence', his 'calm discussion of the implications' of his decision and, crucially, his 'awareness that he may die as a result' of the refusal but considered him to be unable to understand the implications of refusing a blood transfusion thus lacking competence.[121] It was presumed that E lacked understanding of the pain and breathlessness that would ensue but neither the doctors caring for E, nor the courts had explained this to him thus preventing the opportunity for 'full understanding' as required by *Gillick. Re L*[122] concerned a refusal of life-saving blood transfusion by a 14-year-old Jehovah's Witness girl, whom the court felt had serious commitment and maturity.[123] L had an advance directive, drafted only two months earlier, refusing blood. Sir Stephen Brown decided that she was not '*Gillick* competent' because she too had not been given all the information about the death that she would suffer if she continued to refuse blood transfusions, preventing an understanding of the relevant risks and benefits.[124] In both cases, the provision of full, accurate and accessible information could have addressed some of the concerns.

In *Re M*,[125] a 15-year-old girl's refusal of a heart transplant was overridden without expressly commenting on her capacity status. Nevertheless, it seems Johnson J did consider her to satisfy the *Gillick* criteria because he thought that she

---

117   See Hagger, *supra* n. 30, Chapter 2 on this point.

118   Parental consent will not be sufficient in cases of non-therapeutic sterilizations, abortion, or donation of non-regenerative tissue in which cases court authorization must be sought.

119   See e.g. *Re T, supra*, n. 91.

120   *Supra* n. 65.

121   *Ibid.* at 391.

122   *Re L (Medical treatment: Gillick competency)* [1998] 2 FLR 810.

123   *Ibid.* at p. 811.

124   *Ibid.* at p. 813.

125   *Re M (a child) (refusal of medical treatment)* [1999] 2 FLR 1097.

could potentially have given a valid consent.[126] Nevertheless, the court overruled her wishes. M's statement that she would 'rather die than have the transplant'[127] indicates her clear grasp of the fact that she would die without treatment. She demonstrated her ability to absorb and retain the information, to believe it and to weigh that information balancing risks and needs.[128] M was ambivalent[129] but this can be seen as only being relevant if it genuinely strikes at the root of the mental capacity of the patient.[130] Respect for autonomy requires clear, consistent and principled decision-making and should not be usurped on the basis of subjective judgments of the patient's possible future feelings. For all those who might subsequently express gratitude that their decision was ignored, there may be many others who feel angry and violated. For the young man in *Re E*,[131] he refused blood transfusions on attaining the age of 18 and died believing he had committed an 'ungodly' act,[132] the very antipathy of a good death.

The decisions concerning children's refusal of treatment accord little weight to the child's autonomy. As Devereux et al. say this shows '[…] the catch 22 by which patients whose competence is in doubt will be found rational if they accept the doctor's proposal but incompetent if they reject professional advice'.[133] In considering Lord Donaldson's approach to refusals of treatment by mature minors in the post-*Gillick* rulings, Kennedy has said:

> His failure to accept that the power to refuse is no more than the obverse of the power to consent and that they are simply twin aspects of the single right to self-determination borders on the perverse.[134]

This view is presented more forcefully by Harris: '[…] the idea that a child (or anyone) might competently consent to a treatment but not be competent to refuse it is a palpable nonsense'.[135]

Of course, notwithstanding the support for children's involvement in decision-making preferred here, there will always be those who adopt a more protectionist stance. Some commentators believe that encouraging children to make mature

126   *Ibid.*

127   *Ibid.* at 1100.

128   *Ibid.*

129   *Ibid.*

130   *Re B (Adult: refusal of medical treatment)* [2002] 2 FCR 1 per Dame Butler-Sloss, at para. 35.

131   *Supra* n. 65.

132   Pattinson, *supra* n. 2, at p. 162.

133   Devereaux, J.A., Jones, D.P.H. and Dickenson, D.L. 1993. Can children withhold consent to treatment? *British Medical Journal*, 306, 1459–61.

134   Kennedy, I. 1992. Consent to treatment: The capable person, in *Doctors, Patients and the Law*, ed. by C. Dyer. Oxford: Blackwell, pp. 44–71 at pp. 60–61.

135   Harris, J. 2003. Consent and end of life decisions. *Journal of Medical Ethics*, 29, 10 at p. 12.

decisions unnecessarily redraws the boundary between childhood and adulthood and that the focus should be on the child in the present.[136] There are also many advocates of intervening in the lives of children for the sake of their future autonomy, their 'right to an open future' where a child's decision or behaviour is such that this is threatened.[137] However, this proposal is problematic from the perspective of those who seek to empower children through children's rights theories. It distinguishes children and adults but there is no fixed correlation between age and capacity for autonomy.

Using only age[138] and traditional measures of general intelligence are weak assessments of a child's capacity to understand and meaningfully engage with medical information.[139] Cognitive maturity is often related to age but this provides only a very general indicator because children develop at different rates across a range of situations.[140] Research[141] highlights how young children's cognition appears to be 'hardwired' enabling them to process and interpret the demands of their world when very young. Notwithstanding the emphasis the judiciary places on understanding the implications of a decision, using age to determine capacity continues, even in institutions that purport to focus on the individual child's rights.[142] This fails to acknowledge the importance of contextual factors in cognitive development including any particular perspective a child may have gained, perhaps from the experience of having a chronic illness or disability.[143] The latter are more indicative in assessing competency than age.[144] Psychologists who adopt contemporary, mainstream thinking in this area prefer to assess profiles of children's cognitive competencies in both broad and specific abilities.[145] Adopting children's perspectives about their treatment will lead to more appropriate health care as perceived by *them*.[146]

---

136   Campbell, T. 1992. The rights of the minor, in *Children, Rights and the Law*, ed. by P. Alston, S. Parker and J. Seymour. Oxford: Clarendon Press.

137   Feinberg, J. 1992. *Freedom and Fulfilment: Philosophical Essays*. Princeton: Princeton University Press at pp. 76–98 and Maclean, A. 2008. Keyholders and flak jackets: the method in the madness of mixed metaphors. *Clinical Ethics*, 3, 121.

138   As suggested by s. 1(3)(a) CA.

139   Alderson and Montgomery, *supra* n. 78.

140   Flavell, J.H. 1971. Stage-related properties of cognitive development. *Cognitive Psychology*, 2(4), 421–53.

141   See e.g. Mandler and Pinker, *supra* n. 10.

142   *Supra* n. 3.

143   Fielding, D. and Duff, A. 1999. Compliance with treatment protocol: Interventions for children with chronic illness. *Archives of Disease in Childhood*, 80, 196–200; and Alderson, P. and Montgomery, J. 1996. What about me? *Health Service Journal*, 22–4.

144   Hammond, *supra* n. 8.

145   Deary, I.J. 2000. *Looking Down on Human Intelligence: From Psychophysics to the Brain*. Oxford: Oxford University Press, *passim*.

146   National Children's Bureau. 2005. *Children and Young People's Views on Health and Health Services: A Review of the Evidence*. London: National Children's Bureau.

Aside from the overly cautious assessments of children's capacity, making a child wait to have their autonomy respected assumes the decision is one that can be delayed. It also supposes that overriding current autonomy can be justified by stating that a refusal in the future can be permitted if a relevant situation arises. This takes no account of the grounds for the refusal and how a patient may feel violated. In addition, the mature minor will not necessarily become more competent. The *Gillick* competent minor must 'understand fully' the implications of what is proposed, which is at least equivalent to that of an adult, if not more.[147] For those over 16, they have to satisfy the adult test of capacity under the MCA. *Practice* may differ. There is anecdotal and other evidence that where parents and health professionals agree with a child who does not wish to receive even life-saving treatment, the child's decision is allowed to stand,[148] but practice is inconsistent.[149] As Wicks has proposed, to treat young people under 18 as incompetent *in law* simply because they refuse treatment is unacceptable because

> [...] it involves an assumption in favour of treatment; it destroys any possibility
> of a competent minor making an autonomous choice (the power to say yes is
> not a power to choose) and it prioritises the legal protection of the medical
> profession over the rights of the vulnerable patient.[150]

By limiting a mature minor's right to a right to consent, the courts only respect their decisions when they are substantively rational as perceived by others. However, in *Re W*, Lord Donaldson said: 'I personally consider that religious or other beliefs which bar any medical treatment or treatment of particular kinds are irrational, but that does not make minors who hold those beliefs any the less "*Gillick* competent"'.[151] If we adopt the position that children's rights are important, we should allow those children who are capable of demonstrating instrumental rationality (by, for example, providing deep reasons for their decisions), to make their own decision whether they want to forgo their future autonomy in favour of their present autonomy. For some, this choice will involve choosing not to live with a particular condition.[152]

The Human Rights Act 1998 (HRA) has begun to emphasize the importance of children's autonomy. By largely incorporating the provisions of the European Convention on Human Rights (ECHR), the HRA provides an opportunity to challenge traditional notions of children's ability to make decisions. Articles 3 and 8 have particular relevance for respecting children's autonomy. Currently, a failure

---

147   Pattinson, *supra* n. 2, at p. 175.
148   Hagger, *supra* n. 30.
149   *Supra* n. 78.
150   Wicks, E. 2007. *Human Rights and Healthcare.* Oxford: Hart Publishing, at p. 114.
151   *Supra* n. 116, at 88.
152   See e.g. *Re B*, *supra* n. 130, at para. 94.

to assess competence accurately is unlikely to constitute a breach of the right not to be subject to inhuman and degrading treatment under Article 3 of the ECHR. However, if this is followed by very significant medical intervention, then it could be regarded as a form of harm. Generally, therapeutically *necessary* treatment without consent would not constitute inhuman and degrading treatment[153] unless there is undue compulsion.[154] The focus here is on Article 8(1), which requires respect for private and family life. This would be at the centre of any claim now made by the mature minor who believes their autonomy has received insufficient recognition: there may have been a failure to consult them on their views or they may wish to argue that their refusal of treatment should not be overridden by the court and/or their parents. The broad reading given to Article 8(1) includes 'attacks on his physical or mental integrity or his moral or intellectual freedom'.[155] In the context of children this is relevant because the imposition of treatment can undermine their right to make such a decision.

The judiciary is now suggesting a stance towards the mature minor's autonomy that is more aligned to the liberal interpretation of *Gillick*. In *R (Axon) v Secretary of State for Health (Family Planning Association intervening)*,[156] *Gillick* was revisited in the light of Mrs Axon's right to family life under Article 8(1) of the HRA[157] in that she wished to be informed if either of her daughters, then aged 12 and 15, sought an abortion. Citing Articles 16(1) and 12(1) of the UNCRC and the judgment of Thorpe LJ in *Mabon v Mabon*,[158] Silber J indicated that the international instruments illustrate '[…] that the right of young people to make decisions about their own lives by themselves at the expense of the views of their parents has now become an increasingly important and accepted feature of family life'.[159] With respect to Mrs Axon's argument based on Article 8(1) in particular, Silber J concluded that:

---

153   *Herczegfalvy v Austria* (1992) 15 EHRR 437.

154   Case law under the Mental Health Act 1983 illustrates how the HRA adds a further protection to existing barriers to compulsory treatment in cases where patients resist it. See, for example, *R (on the application of PS) v G (RMO) and W (SOAD)* [2003] EWHC 2335 (Fam) regarding unnecessary compulsory treatment and *Keenan v UK* (2001) EHRR 38 with respect to unreasonable physical force.

155   Velu, J. 1973. The European Convention on Human Rights and Right to Respect for Private Life, the Home and Communications, in *Privacy and Human Rights*, ed. by A.H. Robertson. Manchester: Manchester University Press, at p. 92.

156   *R (Axon) v Secretary of State for Health (Family Planning Association intervening)* [2006] EWHC 37 (Admin).

157   In relation to Guidance for Doctors and other Health Professionals on the Provision of Advice and Treatment to Young People under 16 on Contraception, Sexual and Reproductive Heath (29 July 2004), Gateway Reference No 3382. Relevant parts of the Guidance are set out at [2006] EWHC 37 (Admin), at paras. 22–4.

158   *Mabon v Mabon et al.* [2005] 3 WLR 460.

159   *Axon, supra* n. 156, at para. 80.

[…] any right to family life on the part of a parent dwindles as their child gets older and is able to understand the consequence of different choices and then to make decisions relating to them […]. [The child's] autonomy must undermine any Article 8 rights of a parent to family life.[160]

More recently, in *Re P*,[161] Johnson J was prepared to acknowledge that there *might* be cases where older children would be permitted to refuse to receive blood products. Further cases decided less unequivocally would encourage a further shift in attitudes because cases such as *Mabon*,[162] which purportedly protects child autonomy, also has a strong focus on child welfare. Indeed, in that case, Thorpe LJ says:

> In testing the sufficiency of a child's understanding I would not say that welfare has no place. If direct participation would pose an obvious risk of harm to the child arising out of the nature of the continuing proceedings and, if the child is incapable of comprehending that risk, then the judge is entitled to find that sufficient understanding has not been demonstrated.[163]

In addition, Silber J's judgment in *Axon* suggests that the guidelines for assessing competence[164] require a very high level of understanding of the decision to be made.

Respect for children's autonomy and their decision-making powers has particular force in the case of the experienced child patient who is suffering from a chronic condition where the treatment may offer a limited prospect of success and/or the treatment itself is very distressing.[165] To do so will empower the child to influence their own (good) death within the legal restraints that apply to any person.

---

160 *Ibid.* at paras. 129–30.
161 *Supra* n. 67.
162 *Mabon, supra* n. 158, at para. 29.
163 *Ibid.*
164 Laid down in *Gillick, supra* n. 2.
165 Rosenbaum, P. 2008. Children's quality of life: Separating the person from the disorder. *Archives of Disease in Childhood*, 93(2), 100–101. See also Morrow, A.M., Quine, S., Loughlin, E.V.O. and Craig, J.C. 2008. Different priorities: A comparison of parents' and health professionals' perceptions of quality of life in quadriplegic cerebral palsy. *Archives of Disease in Childhood*, 93, 119–25, which highlights how parents and health professionals need to communicate well to ensure the latter have a better understanding of a child's emotional and social well-being; and Wolff, A., Brown, J. and Whitehouse, W.P. 2011. Personal resuscitation plans and end of life planning with disability and life-limiting/ life-threatening conditions. *Archives of Disease in Childhood*, 96, 42–48 for an example of where this is done well and includes the child. Involvement of children in personal health care decision-making remains patchy: see e.g. Kilkelly, U. and Donnelly, M. 2011. Participation in healthcare: The views and experiences of children and young people. *The International Journal of Children's Rights*, 19(1) 107–25.

Children suffering from cancer who come out of remission know only too well how unpleasant further treatment will be and it is not always possible to ameliorate their symptoms. Do we really want these children to be prevented from having the dignified and peaceful passing they may desire until they reach the age of 18? An empowering position may be less palatable in some cases. Where there is clear evidence that the young person lacks capacity as a result of mental illness, this should be acknowledged and appropriate use of mental health legislation instigated to ensure they are provided with the safeguards this brings. Some jurisdictions do allow mature minors to refuse treatment within prescribed parameters. For example, in the Netherlands, children between 12 and 16 must normally have their parents' consent before they may request euthanasia. However, in 'exceptional' cases such as those involving serious and incurable disease or intolerable and unrelenting suffering, a doctor may agree to such a child's request even without parental request. Requests by children aged 16 and 17 do not require parental consent although parents should be involved in decision-making.[166] It is worth noting that the Age of Legal Capacity (Scotland) Act 1991 could be interpreted to admit the possibility of competent children refusing even life-saving treatment.[167] Forcible treatment, which may involve restraint or even detention, needs strong justification. The reality for practitioners is that, without the cooperation of the mature minor, many procedures will be impossible to administer without force.

The proposal here is that the use of a human rights framework can recognize children's right to autonomy within their social context: such an approach can establish the parameters of autonomy to the extent that this is possible. This does not need to undermine their relationships with others or deny any need for protection. Respecting children's self-determination does not mean we are expressing indifference rather than concern or that we are abandoning them to an unhappy fate. It is according them the same rights enjoyed by competent adults where there is evidence they are similarly capable. This evidence may be derived from a process that assists their decision-making to the extent offered by the MCA's Code of Practice to the over 16s, which includes formal, expert assessment. Even where there is a very strong commitment to optimize the autonomy of adolescents, it will be hard to resist the idea that '[... w]here a choice has irreversible consequences the temptation to take some account of defects in

---

166 http://www.family.org.au/Journals/2004/dutch.htm. The US state of Virginia has now passed a law (VA Code No 63.2-100 (2007)) allowing parents of a child at least 14 years old with a life-threatening condition to refuse medically recommended treatment where the parents and child made the decision jointly, the child is sufficiently mature to have an informed opinion on the treatment, other treatments have been considered and they believe in good faith that their choice is in the child's best interests: Mercurio, M.R. 2007. An adolescent's refusal of treatment: implications of the Abraham Cheerix case. *Pediatrics*, 120(6), 1357–8.

167 Discussed in Hagger, *supra* n. 30.

stability is nigh on irresistible'.[168] The HRA can balance competing claims when a potential interference with a child's rights is under consideration.[169] This can be done on a non-confrontational basis and will ensure all relevant interests are adequately addressed. Once all pertinent issues have been explored, there must be a commitment to allowing competent minors with devout beliefs, and/or where a treatment is unduly burdensome, to make the ultimate decision even if this means their death will inevitably follow. Such an approach optimizes their chance of having a good death.

A rights-based approach where the focus is on the individual child, at least initially, can help to redress the balance so that more attention is paid to children generally[170] and their need to be involved in decision-making is emphasized. The plea for specific legislation, with a code of practice, dealing with all aspects of children's health care decision-making should be supported. Any departure from the code of practice should require justification through formal procedures.[171] The MCA could have made improved decision-making with children under 16 along these lines if they had been included within its remit.[172] In the absence of empowering measures, it is even more important that the courts adopt a robust approach to the need to hear young children's views. The use of rights language is having a positive influence on the way in which public bodies deal with more vulnerable members of society[173] and judicial pronouncements that acknowledge younger children's rights to be heard would help further to foster a culture in which this becomes commonplace.

Noting Dworkin's account of autonomy that places the individual in a social and relational context,[174] it would be remiss in a chapter such as this to neglect the sense of parental responsibility that remains with parents following a child's death and how what happens after a child has died will affect their perception as to whether the death was good or otherwise. If evidence is needed, one only has

---

168   Brazier, M. and Bridge, C. 1996. Coercion or caring: Analysing adolescent autonomy. *Legal Studies*, 16, 84 at p. 93.

169   As is the case when considering autonomy interests under Article 8(1) vis-à-vis those contained in Article 8(2): see, for example, the discussion in *Axon, supra* n. 156.

170   James, A. and James, A.L. 2004. *Constructing Childhood: Theory, Policy and Social Practice*. Basingstoke: Palgrave Macmillan. See also *UK's Children Commissioners' Report to the UN Committee on the Rights of the Child*, 2008, on the continuing disappointing level of progress made on children's issues.

171   Alderson and Montgomery, *supra* n. 78.

172   See also guidance to this effect in DoH consent forms and accompanying documentation: www.doh.gov.uk/publications, December 2001.

173   British Institute for Human Rights. 2007. *The Human Rights Act: Changing Lives*. London: British Institute for Human Rights: this report shows how the language and ideas of the HRA are being used to change the approach taken in dealing with more vulnerable members of society, for example.

174   N. 84*ff.*

to consider the scandals revealed by the Bristol and Alder Hey inquiries[175] and the consequences for affected families.

Parental Responsibility Following a Child's Death

The Inquiry set up to investigate the paediatric cardiac service at Bristol Royal Infirmary[176] revealed that organ and tissue retention post-mortem was common practice across the UK. It was used (or often not) for a wide range of (sometimes valuable) purposes including audit, medical education and research. It became apparent that the largest collection of hearts was at the Royal Liverpool Children's Hospital and this led to the Alder Hey Report,[177] which underlined the fact that the practice was pervasive and long-standing.[178] Removal of children's organs and tissues was often done without the consent, or even knowledge, of parents and thought to be acceptable practice at the time. This is perhaps unsurprising given that the law concerning the removal of body parts was complex and unclear. Relying on the provisions of the Human Tissue Act 1961,[179] hospitals assumed they could remove organs and tissue for research and education purposes if no family member objected. There was an assumption that whether a relative was 'complete' or not would not be of concern to families, that discussing removal of the material would add to their distress and that progressing science should be an overarching objective. However, the subsequent reaction of families after the revelations is an indication that the removal was ethically unsound.

Where removal was discussed with families, they often did not understand to what they were consenting or that they could object. When the extent of the retention was revealed there was a public outcry. It was not that parents did not recognize the need for such material but that their consent was not obtained for its use.[180] It was thought this indicated a lack of respect for them and their deceased relative. There was resentment about the lack of control over the disposal of their

---

175   *The Report of the Public Inquiry into Children's Heart Surgery at the Bristol Royal Infirmary 1984–95: Learning from Bristol* (Cmnd 5207 (1) 2001 and *The Royal Liverpool Children's Inquiry Report*, HC 12-11, 2001 (the 'Alder Hey Report').

176   *Ibid.*

177   *Ibid.*

178   *Cf.* McLean, S.A.M. (Chairperson). 2001. *Independent Review Group on Retention of Organs at Post-mortem* Report. Scottish Executive: Edinburgh discussed *infra* n. 178*ff.*

179   Especially s. 1(2) provides that the hospital may authorize removal and retention of body parts if after '[…] such reasonable enquiry as may be practicable, there is no reason to believe: (a) that the deceased had expressed an objection to his body being so used after his death […] or (b) that the surviving spouse or any surviving relative objects to his body being so dealt with'.

180   Brazier, M. 2003. *Medicine, Patients and the Law.* 3rd edn. London: Penguin Books, at p. 470; and personal communications from affected families and teams of NHS

remains. This sometimes had a religious basis. It is imperative for the Jewish and Muslim faith, for example, to bury the body intact. Even where this was not an issue, the feeling for many families was that they could not lay their loved one to rest if they were incomplete. In some paediatric cases, the body may well have been a 'shell' given the amount of organs and tissues removed. Above all, the reaction of families clearly indicates the close connection they continue to feel with the deceased. This is particularly the case where a child has been lost. Parents continue to feel responsible. They feel that an appropriate burial is the last thing they can do for their child. Many felt this was denied to them as a result of this practice. The removal of body parts interfered with families' image of their loved one who was still a person to them, not merely a useful object.[181]

The Human Tissue Act 2004 has now been enacted in an attempt to deal with the shortcomings of its predecessor. In particular, the position of parents' rights with respect to the use of their child's remains has been strengthened. Section 2 provides that where a child is competent they can make an advance decision concerning their consent to the removal and use of their human material. Such a decision must be respected. If the child was incompetent, the person with parental responsibility can consent for the child, apart from the use of the body for anatomical examination: this requires consent from the child. Where the child has died leaving no one with parental responsibility, someone in a 'qualifying relationship' can consent to the removal, storage and use of the material.[182]

It should be noted that the Scottish Report on Retained Organs at Post-mortem[183] recommended that the term 'authorization' should be used in this context[184] rather than consent. This proposal is persuasive because intrinsic to the notion of consent given by proxies is that this is done on the basis of acting in the particular child's best interests. This cannot be relevant to a post-mortem examination. The Report took the view that the use of the word 'authorization' rather than 'consent' strengthens the role of parents in decision-making about the way in which their children should be dealt with and clarifies the scope of the (legally valid) decision-making powers that they have in respect of such children in these circumstances.[185] Further, a valid consent is generally expected to follow the provision of information. Authorization is not constrained by this requirement and this meets the concerns of those parents who do not wish to receive information

---

staff, who were involved in supporting them through the scandal at Sheffield Children's NHS Foundation Trust.

181 BMA. 2004. *Medical Ethics Today*. London: BMA, at p. 417.
182 S. 2(7). The hierarchy of qualifying relationships is set out at s. 27(4).
183 *Supra* n. 178.
184 *Ibid.* paras. 6, 28, 47 and 59–72 for example.
185 *Ibid.* at Section 1, para. 17.

about post-mortem examination and/or the subsequent removal and retention of organs or tissue, but who do not object to this.[186]

It was noted earlier how paediatric health professionals support the whole family at the end of a child's life.[187] When the child dies, the families often continue to receive support through bereavement counseling,[188] and health professionals sometimes accompany parents when they visit their child in the mortuary because they want to help the relatives. They also wish to spend time with the child with whom they have often formed a relationship. The new legislative provisions mean that a similar level of care must be taken when examination of the child's human material can offer some benefit. When this is properly explained to families, they are usually only too willing to assist. This underlying wish to help is confirmed by the statements made by affected parents during the Bristol Inquiry.[189] Their complaints centred on the lack of respect shown to them and their relative. They thought their loved one was treated with contempt: as a mere convenience.

As Mrs Susan Francombe, mother of Rebecca, said:

> I know I felt if another baby could be helped by the retention and, if that was the reason, then we would have said yes; but the fact that they were kept without our knowledge [...] came as a very, very big shock.[190]

Conclusion

To have a 'good death' can be proposed as an entitlement of all human beings.[191] To ensure children experience the 'good death' domestic law should more closely reflect the international trajectory of respect for children's autonomy and the

---

186   *Ibid.* Notwithstanding these arguments, this is not a view shared by their counterparts in England and Northern Ireland for example (see Brazier, M. 2002. Retained organs: ethics and humanity. *Legal Studies*, 22(4), 550–69, at p. 556), does not represent English law and is '[...] of academic rather than practical significance': Mason, J.K. and Laurie, G.T. 2006. *Law and Medical Ethics.* 7th edn. Oxford: Oxford University Press, at p. 494. The latter view is supported in Department of Health. 2002. *Human Bodies, Human Choices.* London: Department of Health, at p. 52. However, if language is seen as an important instrument of social change as suggested *supra* at n. 95 and in Hagger, *supra* n. 30, Chapter 2, the use of the term authorization has relevance with respect to parental decision-making more generally. This is beyond the focus here and does not, in any case, detract from the more general observations about children and consent that are made throughout this book.

187   N. 23*ff.*

188   This may also be true in cases involving the loss of an adult patient, of course.

189   *Supra* n. 175.

190   *Ibid.* at para 27.

191   Seale C. and van der Geest S. 2004. Good and bad death: Introduction. *Social Science and Medicine*, 58(5), 883–5.

empirical evidence of their decision-making abilities. Respect for the autonomy of the child, and the decision-making powers that would flow from it, would empower the child to influence the nature of their own dying. Where statute and/or guidance is lacking, the judiciary should be robust in their response in relevant cases. Where a child has satisfied rigorous tests of legal competence using sophisticated tools of assessment, they should be allowed to refuse even life-saving treatment. Where such competence cannot be demonstrated, the child should nevertheless participate in decision-making as much as possible in a context that recognizes the unique perspective of their parents and the latter's sense of responsibility. Account must also be taken of the continuing sense of duty felt by parents in the event that their child suffers an untimely end.

Chapter 9

Practical Realities of Decision-making Relating to End of Life Care

Jeff Perring

Introduction: Theory versus Practice

Ethical considerations around the care of children with severe disability or progressive illness are an everyday reality within health services, particularly in areas such as paediatric intensive care (PIC), neurology and oncology. These ethical considerations often concern the realities of withholding or withdrawing life-supporting treatment. Problematic decisions relating to end of life care are not new. In *R v Arthur*[1] the doctor, Leonard Arthur, faced with a newborn infant with Down's syndrome who had been rejected by his mother, prescribed care based upon analgesia and 'nursing care only', which would lead to the child's inevitable death. This withholding of life-supporting treatment led to a charge of attempted murder from which he was acquitted. Although the case of Leonard Arthur is extreme, and maybe more so now because the boundaries of acceptability have moved, withholding or withdrawing life-supporting treatment will inevitably be close to the boundaries of moral and legal acceptability. Such decisions require exploration: who is involved in the decision-making process; on what basis are the decisions made; can parents insist on demanding treatment; and what should be the response of the medical teams who may consider the provision of that treatment to be unduly burdensome and prevent the child from having a 'good death'? This chapter focuses on decision-making relating to end of life care within PIC, some of the consequences of these decisions and how disagreements between parents who want their child to receive ongoing medical interventions and medical teams who believe this would fulfil no purpose should be resolved. Two case studies explore decision-making processes and the ethical dilemmas these raise. Although these case studies are fictional, they have been developed from a number of real cases to demonstrate the types of decision regularly made in the care of children with severe disability and progressive illness. Both case studies relate to children in a paediatric intensive care unit (PICU) where a high proportion of these decisions are made.[2]

---

1   *R v Arthur* (1981) 12 BMLR 1.

2   In one study from Great Ormond Street Hospital the proportion of hospital deaths occurring on the PICU increased from 80 per cent to 91 per cent between 1997 and 2004.

Case Study 1: Child H

H was four years old when she presented for the third time to the PICU with a chest infection. She had been born prematurely at 25 weeks' gestation. Her first few months of life were difficult: for many weeks she needed support with her breathing and she had a number of serious infections. For a while H's parents were not sure if she would survive to go home with them. However, she pulled through and was discharged home albeit with a number of longer-term problems. H still required oxygen to help her breathing and a feeding tube because she was unable to take a bottle. Her hearing and eyesight were also thought to be impaired.

H only remained at home for a week before she presented at 4 a.m. to the local Emergency Department with apnoeas, brief periods when she stopped breathing. These were subsequently found to be due to a viral infection. She required invasive ventilation for five days and continued to require oxygen upon her discharge home. H had a further admission to PICU six months later with another chest infection and on this occasion took over a fortnight to wean from the ventilator. At one point the consultant intensivist asked her parents if they thought it was appropriate to continue with treatment. Her parents were adamant that they wanted intensive care to continue.

H remained relatively well over the next few years although she did require a number of admissions to hospital with further chest infections. During this time her level of disability became clearer. She continued to be dependent upon her parents for everything but had started to develop a personality of her own. She was blind and required hearing aids to provide her with some limited hearing. She had also had an operation to have a permanent feeding tube inserted through the wall of her stomach as she continued to be unable to feed herself.

This admission to PICU was different. It was clear that H was very poorly: she not only required ventilation to support her breathing as she had previously but had also become shocked and required aggressive treatment to support her heart and circulation. She was developing renal failure and it was likely that she would require support for her kidneys.

As part of his conversation with H's parents, the intensivist discussed the appropriateness both of continuing with the level of care that she was receiving and of the escalation of treatment that would be required if she needed support for her kidneys. Her parents made clear their wish that everything possible should be done for H and the intensivist agreed. H continued with the drugs to support her heart and later that day was started on renal replacement therapy.

H slowly improved over the following fortnight and reached the point where she no longer required support for her breathing. In view of her illness, it was not clear to the team caring for her that she would cope without this support. These concerns were expressed to H's parents and following discussion it was agreed

Ramnarayan, P., Craig, F., Petros, A. and Pierce, C. 2007. Characteristics of deaths occurring in hospitalised children: changing trends. *Medical Ethics*, 33, 255–60.

that she would be put back on to the ventilator should she be unable to cope on this first occasion. H was taken off the ventilator but struggled to cope after a few hours and was therefore put back on. Further discussions were held with H's parents before a second attempt was made. Her parents made clear their wishes that they wanted H to go home with them and that every effort should be made to make this possible. This was agreed and a further attempt to remove respiratory support was made. This was successful and H was subsequently discharged first to the ward and then home.

H's parents made the decision with their own doctor that they did not want her to go through another period of intensive care especially having gone though such a difficult time with her last admission. She lived another six months before she had a further infection, which was treated supportively with symptomatic treatment. She was admitted to her local hospice where she died shortly thereafter.

Case Study 2: Child M

M was a normal two-year-old child when she was involved in an accident that caused her cervical spine injury. She stopped breathing immediately. No one knew how long it was before she was resuscitated, first by a passer-by and then by paramedics.

On arrival in the Emergency Department her breathing continued to require support but her heart was working well. She was sedated and taken to the PICU for further care. Over the next 24 hours the extent of M's injuries became clear. She had a C1-C2 spinal cord injury, which meant that she would be paralysed from the neck down. Further, she would be unable to breathe for herself and would require support for her breathing with a ventilator for the rest of her life. There was one further issue to be resolved. It was not clear whether M had suffered any brain damage from a lack of oxygen around the time of her injury. This would become clearer as her sedation was stopped. M's parents, who were being kept informed of the situation, were clearly devastated at the news.

After 48 hours the sedation was stopped and it became clear over subsequent days that M had suffered significant brain damage. An MRI was performed that confirmed this. M would never be able to live a normal life even if she were not paralysed, although the final extent of the damage could not yet be determined. Further discussions took place between the intensivists, other medical teams and M's parents. A number of these discussions concentrated on the level of care that M would require and the package of care that could be put in place to help them. M would require a tracheostomy – a tube placed directly into the windpipe from the front of her neck – and would be permanently connected to a ventilator. She would require regular suction down the tracheostomy tube but even with this she was likely to have numerous chest infections. At home she would require 24-hour care by a team of carers in the house. It would take at least six months for her to have a package in place to go home, more if significant modifications were required to the family home. During these discussions M's parents were adamant that this is what they wanted as long as M would benefit from it. It was agreed that any firm decision be put on hold for a time to enable the extent of M's brain damage to be further assessed.

Over the subsequent few weeks M continued to be ventilated on the PICU. During this time the level of her brain damage became clear. She could not interact with her parents, siblings or her environment. By the time of their last discussion with the team caring for M, her parents had made their decision that intensive care should be withdrawn. They decided that this should take place on the PICU where she had spent the last few weeks of her life. They spent a final day with her before ventilation was withdrawn and she died peacefully in their arms.

Discussion

These case studies of H and M illustrate end of life decision-making within PICUs and some of the consequences of the decisions. In the first case study, no definitive decision was made at the time of discharge as to whether intensive or palliative care would be offered in the future but rather it was expected that the decision be made outside of the acute environment. Indeed, this did happen: the decision was made between H's parents and their own doctor away from hospital so that when she became ill again intensive care was not offered but rather she received symptomatic relief and support. This is not always so. Discussions may not take place or become so protracted that the child requires a further episode of intensive care before the decision is made.

In the second case study, a decision to continue treating M would have triggered a pathway of care that would have continued for many years. However, time was available to give due consideration to the decision being made. There did not have to be a once and for all decision during the early part of her admission but rather care could be continued allowing time for more information regarding her prognosis to become available. Over time the level of M's future disability became apparent enabling her parents alongside the team caring for her to make their decision based on a much clearer understanding of her prognosis. The decision was made that it was inappropriate to continue treatment, intensive care was withdrawn and symptomatic relief was given until M died.

The discussions held with the parents of both H and M have become almost routine within PICUs where modern technology is able to keep children alive but not necessarily able to cure them of their underlying disease. As a result, death usually occurs when life-sustaining treatment is withheld or withdrawn rather than through failure of immediate therapy or cardiac arrest.[3]

---

3   Withdrawal of sustaining therapy was the mode of death in 55 per cent of 204 deaths described in a single PICU over a 10-year period: Sands, R., Manning, J.C., Vyas, H. and Rashid, A. 2009. Characteristics of deaths in paediatric intensive care: a 10-year study.

Before exploring the discussions relating to H and M further it is worth us considering the basis upon which these types of decision about children are made.

Clinical Guidance

The primary clinical, as opposed to legal, guidance relating to withholding and withdrawing life-sustaining treatment in children has come from the Royal College of Paediatrics and Child Health (RCPCH),[4] which can be read alongside the framework provided by the General Medical Council (GMC).[5] Under this guidance, the decision to withhold or withdraw therapy is usually made in consultation between the medical team, the patient (if possible) and the family; the decision is made in the 'best interests' of the child.

The concept of best interests causes some difficulty. What is meant by the concept of best interests and how can anyone decide that it is in the best interests of another to die? As Chapter 8 indicates, legally competent individuals may decide for themselves that their life is no longer worth living and that they want to die. However, the vast majority of infants and children are not able to make this decision. The decision has to be made for them, and, in doing so, those making the decision are affirming that it is in the best interests of the children to die; to end the one life that they have.

We can discuss the academic, ethical and legal considerations about the concept of best interests and whether other principles such as substituted judgment are preferable,[6] but the reality is that decisions relating to end of life care have to be made and a practical approach to making them is needed. Whilst both legal and professional standards hold to the best interests principle, a practical approach to determining these is required in day-to-day practice. So we must have a useable definition of best interests and specific parameters in which the concept of best interests can be used in end of life care. The definition as used by the GMC involves:

Nursing Critical Care, 14(5), 235–40. This is in keeping with the Ethicus study of patients on adult ICUs where the mode of death for 1,505 patients in Northern European ICUs was found to be 38.2 per cent and 47.4 per cent for withholding and withdrawing treatment respectively: The Ethicus Study. 2003. End of life practices in European intensive care units. *Journal of the American Medical Association*, 290(6), 790–97.

4   Royal College of Paediatrics and Child Health. 2004. *Witholding or Withdrawing Life Sustaining Treatment in Children: A Framework for Practice*. 2nd edn. London: Royal College of Paediatrics and Child Health.

5   GMC. 2010. *Treatment and Care Towards the End of Life: Good Practice in Decision-making*. London: General Medical Council.

6   Birchley, G. 2010. What limits, if any, should be placed on a parent's right to consent and/or refuse to consent to medical treatment for their child? *Nursing Philosophy*, 11, 280–85.

weighing the benefits, burdens and risks of treatment for the individual child. In addition a child's best interests are not always limited to clinical considerations and, as the treating doctor, you should be careful to take account of any other factors relevant to the circumstances of each child.[7]

This can then be put into the context of the five parameters put forward by the RCPCH under which life-sustaining treatment can either be withheld or withdrawn. These parameters are:

1. The 'Brain Dead' Child.
2. The 'Permanent Vegetative State'.
3. The 'No Chance' Situation. *The child has such severe disease that life-sustaining treatment simply delays death without significant alleviation of suffering. Treatment to sustain life is inappropriate.*
4. The 'No Purpose' Situation. *Although the patient may be able to survive with treatment, the degree of physical or mental impairment will be so great that it is unreasonable to expect them to bear it.*
5. The 'Unbearable' Situation. *The child and/or family feel that in the face of progressive and irreversible illness further treatment is more than can be borne. They wish to have a particular treatment withdrawn or to refuse further treatment irrespective of the medical opinion that it may be of some benefit.*[8]

Few would argue that if a child was 'brain dead', or in a 'permanent vegetative state', it would be unreasonable to withhold or withdraw life-sustaining treatment provided there was certainty in the diagnosis. It is unlikely that a close consideration of best interests would be undertaken in these types of cases because in both states the individuals affected have already been lost to those around them: they have no awareness of their surroundings and no prospect of recovery; all that is left is an empty shell. Rather than considering best interests these children may be regarded as having 'no best interests of any kind'.[9]

The judgment of best interests becomes more difficult when the other three criteria of the RCPCH guidelines are considered. These parameters were the focus in our two case studies and will therefore be examined in more detail.

The first of these parameters to consider is the 'no chance' situation whereby treatment would only delay death without significantly alleviating suffering. Within the context of a PICU the question immediately arises: how can anyone be certain that there is no chance of the child surviving? It is an all or nothing question that is difficult for the medical team, who work more often in terms of probabilities, to answer. There are, however, situations where it is very clear that there is no chance

---

7   GMC, *supra* n. 5, at para. 92.
8   RCPCH, s*upra* n. 4, at pp. 10–11.
9   Lord Mustill in *Airdale NHS Trust v Bland* [1993] 1All ER 821, at 897.

of the child living and that treatment is just delaying the inevitable, often because the disease process has caused such devastating injury, particularly to the brain, that survival is impossible. The child may not be brain dead but they cannot live with the brain injuries they have suffered.

For both children in our case studies there was no chance that they would live normal lives and most probably would both have had shortened lives but they had survived their immediate conditions and may have continued to do so. It was fully expected that, having been discharged from PICU, H would suffer from further infections and that if no decision were made otherwise, would require further intensive care but there was no certainty that her next infection would cause her death, or indeed the one after that. She may have lived for a few months or many years between episodes. For M there was no chance that she would be able to live without the constant aid of a ventilator but that did not mean that she had no chance of living albeit with the additional disability brought about by the brain damage she received. It was the quality of her life that was at question.

There is good evidence that the number of children dying in PICUs has decreased over the last 20 years but this has been at the expense of an increase in the number of children surviving with moderate or severe disability.[10] For these children any thought of withholding or withdrawing life-sustaining treatment is not about whether there is a chance of survival but rather whether there is any purpose in them surviving. Death is an all or nothing situation: the child either dies or survives but at what price does survival come? Survival with disability adds both unknown factors, such as the level of disability the child will have, and value judgments, such as the acceptable level of disability, to the decision-making process.

The 'no purpose' guidelines from the RCPCH describe the situation in which '[t]he degree of physical or mental impairment will be so great that it is unreasonable to expect [the child] to bear it'.[11] For this reasoning to be valid the level of impairment must be 'so great' that it is not in the child's best interests to continue to live: the burdens and risks of treatment outweigh any benefits that may be gained from it. An adult who suffers a significant spinal injury resulting in paralysis or who develops a progressive neurodegenerative illness usually has the ability to make this judgment for themselves although they may not have the physical ability to act upon their decision if such a decision is to end their own life. This decision may be based not only on the physical limitations and burdens

---

10   A recent study from Melbourne showed that between 1982 and 2005–06 deaths in PICU fell from 11.0 per cent to 4.8 per cent whilst those surviving PICU with moderate or severe disability increased from 8.4 per cent to 17.9 per cent: Namachivayam, P., Shann, F., Shekerdemian, L., van Sloten, I., Delzoppo, C., Daffey, C. and Butt, W. 2010. Three decades of pediatric intensive care: Who was admitted, what happened in intensive care, and what happened afterward. *Pediatric Critical Care Medicine*, 11, 549–55.

11   RCPCH, *supra* n. 4.

they find themselves with but also on the loss that they have suffered; the loss of the life they were living before.

The situation differs with infants and children, many of whom have never known a life other than that which they are experiencing. They have not suffered loss in the same way as adults in the same situation. H was born prematurely and was neuro-developmentally delayed but she had never known anything different and therefore had not suffered any loss. This was her one life that she was living. It may not have been the same life as other children and it was unlikely to be as outwardly productive, but it was her life and would have brought its own rewards to her and to the family who cared for her. M was in a slightly different position in that she was living a normal life before the accident and would have had a very different life afterwards should the decision have been made to continue treatment. She had suffered a significant loss but because of her age and the nature of her brain damage was unlikely to be aware of this loss.

In both cases, the parents and family would have suffered loss. For the family of H it would have been the loss of the normal child they were expecting with all their associated hopes and aspirations. M's family not only saw her suddenly lose her physical ability but also the character and personality she had developed over the two years of her life. For many, it could be considered that the family had lost the child that they knew and loved to be replaced by another with the same outward appearance but vastly different needs and expectations.

Similar feelings were likely to have been present within the multidisciplinary teams caring for these children. Members of the teams would not have suffered any personal loss but may still have viewed these children in terms of loss for the family and distance from an expected social norm. In the case of H, these feelings were likely to be exacerbated by meeting her at the time of medical crisis when her level of activity and interaction was at its lowest and therefore her disability appeared to be greater than it was in reality.

Under these circumstances, what approach should be used in describing the 'no purpose' situation? One way would be to ask what makes the life of a child with severe physical or mental impairment worth living? I would suggest, however, that this is the wrong question. As each of us has a single life and, as we have seen, many children with physical or mental impairment know of no other life, we should reverse the question: what makes the life of a child with severe physical or mental impairment no longer worth living?

The simple answer to this question is when the burdens of any treatment outweigh the benefits of that treatment to the child. That is, when it is no longer in the best interests of the child to continue to treat her. Although this seems obvious for many, the question equates not only to health needs but also to other aspects of her life. In this context the definition of best interests may be considered too narrow and the wider legal definition that 'encompasses medical, emotional and all other welfare issues'[12] may be considered more appropriate. Whichever definition is used, the child's disability is a core aspect for consideration. Does the child have such a level of disability that we should not be treating her? What level of disability is this and, indeed, should disability per se form part of the consideration? To look at this further we need to go back to infancy.

The needs of an infant may be regarded as basic with feeding, changing of nappies and comforting central to their care. It is not, however, expected that this existence will continue. The infant will develop over time becoming more interactive, smiling, socializing and developing a personality. There is an inherent individual potential. When H first went home she would have been like other infants albeit with a number of additional needs such as home oxygen and the requirement to tube feed. As time passed, her level of physical and mental impairment would have become more obvious as her development failed to keep pace with other infants of her age. She was not realizing the inherent potential normally present within an infant. Her parents described her ongoing needs but also a personality of her own that was apparent to them, although it may have objectively been regarded as rudimentary. Her parents, as with other parents of disabled children, '[w]ill often have a detailed knowledge of that child's habits, likes, and dislikes, e.g. knowing they find wet nappies intolerable, blowing raspberries funny, or hate their feet being touched'.[13] H was spending more time in hospital than other children and her underlying health problems were such that they would limit her life expectancy. It was a matter of knowing when this limitation had been reached.

This brings us to another aspect of end of life decisions and the last of the parameters described by the RCPCH, the 'unbearable' situation when the child or family decide that '[i]n the face of progressive and irreversible illness further treatment is more than can be borne'.[14] In our case studies, the parents of H made their decision at a time when they felt that H's general health and well-being had deteriorated so far over time, leaving her so prone to multiple infections and hospital admissions that the burdens of treatment, including the time between them, were outweighing the benefits of that treatment, such as time at home in relatively good health. Many parents do not describe an objective weighing up of these factors but rather an instinctive knowledge of when the time to stop would be. As will be seen, this time may be different from that of the health care professionals caring for the child.

The situation was different for the parents of M. She had suddenly developed an irreversible condition having been paralysed and brain damaged. Her parents did not have months or years to make a decision, as had the parents of H. M's parents were participating in a decision with long-term consequences at a time when they were still suffering the loss associated with M's original injury. They were also

---

12   *Re A (medical treatment: male sterilization)* [2000] 1 FLR 549 at 555 per Butler-Sloss P.

13   Birchley, *supra* n. 6, at p. 283.

14   RCPCH, *supra* n. 4.

without the understanding of the reality of caring for a disabled child. Under these circumstances were M's parents the right people to make any decisions?

Who Should Decide?

Having discussed the five parameters by which life-sustaining treatment can be withheld or withdrawn we can now move on to the practical realities of who should make the decision. Should it be the parents alone who make any decisions, the health care professionals or, pragmatically, a combination of the two?

If we consider the parents of H, allowing them to make the decision was quite compelling. They knew their child, her life out of hospital as part of their family. They understood her likes and dislikes and how her health had changed over time. They knew that the burdens of treatment were starting to outweigh the benefits for her. For these children it makes sense that parents should be the key decision-makers on their behalf. A recent American study has suggested that this is the overwhelming view of parents with children in PICU.[15] What factors do parents use to make decisions relating to end of life care? This same study[16] noted that most parents would make decisions based upon parameters such as quality of life, suffering and the presence or not of effective treatments. Faith would also play a role, as would the passage of time. A few parents described intuition, that they would instinctively know that the time was right, whilst others mentioned lack of resources, but this was within the climate of the US health care system rather than the NHS, although other areas of support, both practical and financial, need to be taken into account. A small but significant number of parents stated that they would never consider withdrawal of care, some citing their faith as the reason for this decision.

It is clear that parents should act as advocates for their child but should they be alone in this? It is hard to conceive that parents will look at the best interests of their child in isolation; rather they will look at these best interests within the context of the family and with all the emotions associated with the life of their child. This is all the more so when the child in question has such disability that they may be described as having '[v]ery marginal autonomous interests, instead having interests that are intimately bound to the interests of their parents'.[17] Under these circumstances, it is about weighing up not just the benefits and burdens of treatment but also all the love, emotion and hope that the life of their child brings to the family. She will also have an impact on family life, not least on her siblings whose childhood will be so closely linked to hers. Parents cannot reasonably be

---

15   Michelson, K.N., Koogler, T., Sullivan, C., Ortega, M., Hall, E. and Frader, J. 2009. Parental views on withdrawing life-sustaining therapies in critically ill children. *Archives of Pediatric and Adolescent Medicine*, 163, 986–92.

16   *Ibid.*

17   Birchley, *supra* n. 6, at p. 282.

seen to be objective, nor should they be. Part of life within a family is that the overall benefits substantially outweigh the loss of some elements of best interests. Thus, for a child with a severe learning disability their best interests lie within overall family life.

Parents may consider themselves the main decision-makers but this does come at a cost. There is evidence that predisposition to post-traumatic stress is higher in those family members whose relative died after an end of life decision was made and even more so if they shared in the end of life decision.[18]

The alternative to parents being the main decision-makers is that this role should fall to the medical professionals caring for the child. Interestingly in the American study noted above, only half of parents identified physicians as key decision-makers. One of the reasons put forward for this was a 'suggested mistrust or doubt of physicians'[19] whose prognosis may be incorrect. This mistrust of professionals is well recognized[20] and for many parents has a firm foundation. Medicine is not an exact science and a prognosis is often couched in percentages or with caveats. For parents like those of H, this is often borne out by their own experience with their children overcoming acute illnesses when physicians have told them to expect the worse. These parents will describe their children as 'fighters' who have 'proved doctors wrong' before and are likely to do so again. They may ask: how can the physician 'be certain' this time? After all, even when life-sustaining treatment is withheld or withdrawn a proportion of children will continue to survive.[21]

Under these circumstances, a mistrust of doctors, or more specifically their prognosis, becomes understandable and parents come to rely more upon themselves and their own decision-making processes. The parents of H would have been through many difficult discussions, usually at the point where their child was at her most poorly, with doctors they had barely met and who had only a passing knowledge of their child, their child's condition and her long-term prognosis. In some meetings they may not have been given all the information they needed or

---

18   Azoulay, E., Pochard, F., Kentish-Barnes, N., Chevret, S., Aboab, J., Adrie, C., Annane, D., Bleichner, G., Bollaert, P.E., Darmon, M., Fassier, T., Galliot, R., Garrouste-Orgeas, M., Goulenok, C., Goldgran-Toledano, D., Hayon, J., Jourdain, M., Kaidomar, M., Laplace, C., Larche, J., Liotier, J., Papazian, L., Poisson, P., Reignier, J., al Saidi, F. and Schlemmer, B. 2005. Risk of post-traumatic stress symptoms in family members of intensive care unit patients. *American Journal Respiratory and Critical Care Medicine*, 171, 987–94.

19   Michelson et al., *supra* n. 15.

20   Although doctors are trusted more than other professionals (Royal College of Physicians. 2009. *Trust in Doctors 2009*. London: Royal College of Physicians) there appears to be a differentiation within health care professionals with nurses and GPs more trusted than hospital consultants: O'Neill, O. 2002. A Question of Trust. BBC Reith Lectures. Available at: http://www.bbc.co.uk/radio4/reith2002/lecture1.shtml [accessed 6 August 2011].

21   The Ethicus Study found that 11 per cent of patients for whom intensive care was withheld survived to leave hospital: *supra* n. 3.

wanted whilst in others they may not have been given the time they required. Her parents may have been left feeling that these discussions were part of an ongoing fight to obtain the best for their child against both the health care system and social services. Further, the parents of H may have seen the medical team as too objective, cold and calculating in their consideration of the life of their child. If the medical team had never met the child before, they would have had little or no understanding of the life of H within the context of her family. They only knew her in the impersonal, artificial surroundings of a hospital and, in particular, whilst severely ill in an intensive care unit. For a child like H this would naturally have led the medical team to overestimate the degree of her disability and underestimate her level of interaction and personality. This would have made it much easier to ask if it was in H's best interests to continue to be actively treated. In addition, the decision is much less difficult to make if the individual making that decision does not have to live with the consequences, the everyday reminders and the 'what ifs?' that parents would have. How can the parents' memory of a few extra weeks or months at home with their child be calculated objectively?

Should the medical team always acquiesce to parental decision-making? After all, the team looking after a child in a PICU collectively has a wealth of understanding and experience that gives them a far better insight than parents into the long-term outcome of such a child. Further, parental decision-making is not the basis of care within a PICU. For example, in the first few hours of admission a child in septic shock may require intubation and ventilation and an intra-osseous or bone needle into their tibia to provide fluid before a central line is inserted. An arterial line would be required alongside the need for infusions of inotropic drugs to support the heart and circulation and blood transfusions. If renal support was also required, this would require a second central line. Each of these procedures carries risks and benefits both major and minor. It is not possible to describe in detail each of the procedures at such a time but rather an overall picture is given and assent obtained from the parents for 'intensive care'. This has led to PICUs being driven by high levels of discussion and lower levels of formal consent than would be seen in other areas of health care. There is a strong argument that this process should continue through all aspects of PICU care including the withholding and withdrawing of life-sustaining treatment.

If the medical team always acquiesces to parental wishes there will be a cost to the professionals involved who may be asked to provide care that they consider futile and therefore not in the child's best interests to provide: their clinical judgment will be undermined. This is not an unusual situation within a PICU. In one 2001 study of a 20-bedded PICU, Goh[22] found that the care of 34 of 662 patients (5 per cent) could be considered futile either through the risk of death, an underlying lethal condition or through a qualitative measure. It should be noted that, of 34 children, only 19 died, 15 from the withdrawal of intensive

---

22   Goh, A.H. and Mok, Q. 2001. Identifying futility in a paediatric critical care setting: A prospective observational study. *Archives of Diseases in Childhood*, 84, 265–8.

care. In another study of 111 PICU patients[23] the care of 21 per cent of patients was considered to be either 'futile' (8 per cent) or 'inappropriate' (13 per cent). Staff are used to looking after patients whose reason to receive intensive care may be described as marginal; indeed it may be regarded as integral to the care that is given. Although commonplace, it is likely to give rise to additional stressors within an already stressful environment for staff to work.

Another key difficulty lies in the definition of 'futility' even if, within everyday practice, it is couched in terms such as not being in a child's best interests to continue to receive treatment. Studies such as the ones described above would suggest that there is a clear line between futile and non-futile care but this is not the case, as can be seen from both our case studies. With the exceptions of brain death and persistent vegetative state, which have clear diagnostic criteria, the principles put forward by the RCPCH are open to interpretation. Under these circumstances non-futile and futile care may be considered two extremes of a spectrum with no clear boundary between the two. Most members of the multidisciplinary team will at one time or another have felt that the care they were giving was futile but it would often be difficult for them to describe precisely why this was so. There is often a nagging doubt that becomes stronger over time, especially when there is little or no prospect of resolution, and may relate to previous experience of other patients. Rarely does this prevent the health care worker from participating in the day-to-day care of the patient, but a pragmatic approach is taken with the best interests of the child on that day rather than the overall best interests of the child being made the focus. Where conflict can arise is in the nature of the intensive care given and the specific procedures that are required to provide that care.

There are certain escalation points within intensive care that can be used to reassess the care given such as the use of inotropic drugs like adrenaline to support the heart and circulation and the need for renal replacement therapy. For children in whom there is concern regarding futility, these points may be used to have further discussions with the parents. Extraneous to these escalation points, it becomes very difficult to reconcile specific parental decision-making to the requirement for intensive care. If intensive care is regarded as a package, then for a parent to want one part but not another puts the multidisciplinary team into a very difficult position. Each aspect of care, each procedure undertaken, is done to provide the team with the best conditions to look after the child and therefore to provide the best opportunity for that child to recover. To limit these activities compromises the team in the care that they can give. It will also leave members of the team feeling compromised in that they have not been able to fulfil their professional obligations to the child by acting in the child's best interests.

Thus, if we return to whom should make the decision, the practical approach is again to consider a continuum with parental decision-making at one end and medical decision-making at the other. Under these circumstances, the best approach

23 Vemuri, G. and Playfor, S.D. 2006. Futility and inappropriate care in pediatric intensive care: a cross-sectional survey. *Pediatric Anesthesia*, 16, 309–13.

is likely to be in the middle with health care workers and parents developing a partnership in which the decision can be made.[24] This means that we now have two parallel continuums, those of futility versus non-futility and parental versus medical decision-making. How can these be practically reconciled within a PICU? The most appropriate description of this reconciliation is that of a narrative or journey. For any child who is admitted to a PICU there is a journey that is embarked upon by all involved, the child, her family and the multidisciplinary team looking after them. This journey may be short or long, and may end with the child living or dying, but it is nonetheless a journey that will form a major event in the life of the child and mould the way in which the family relates to her. In considering an admission in this way, it becomes clear that there will be certain junctions in the road where decisions can and need to be made. Further, these junctions can be predicted in advance so that both family and professionals know and accept that questions will need to be asked and decisions made at certain points. It can also be made clear at each juncture what progression involves in terms of procedures and their overall risks and benefits for the child. There is no single, once and for all decision but rather decisions that can be made at various points along the path such as when there is a need for further escalation of care. This has a further advantage in that it allows time for staff and parents to get to know each other so that the partnership can develop, reducing tension between discussions and allowing time for other health care professionals such as the long-term consultant caring for the child to become involved in the decision-making process.

It may be that one party is further along the path in terms of eventual outcome than the other but this is less likely to cause conflict if all parties are seen to be travelling along the same path. It is much easier to wait for someone following along the same path than to find them along another path that occasionally intersects. In addition, excess pressure on parents at one point along the path may push them off course and make it more difficult to establish a consensual decision later in the journey. If a decision is made to withhold or withdraw intensive care then there is a change in direction but this still remains part of the same journey. It may be that withdrawal occurs within the PICU or that the child moves into a more defined palliative care route, but in either case there is an imperative placed upon the health care team to prevent suffering through the treatment of symptoms such as nausea and pain even if these treatments in themselves require further intervention or result in a shortening of the child's life. Following the decision parents continue to have input into the care of their child, giving them some element of control. For the parents, the place and mode of death is a defining point in the narrative of their child's life and every effort should be made to fulfil their wishes at this time.

For the parents of H, the decision was made outside of the confines of the PICU with their own doctor who knew her well and understood her developing health problems, and with whom the parents had built up a significant level of trust. This decision enabled advanced care planning to be initiated using an integrated

---

24   GMC, *supra* n. 5, at para. 95.

multi-agency care pathway that was used to take her through the rest of her life, including the levels of care that she was to receive with future infections and decisions relating to resuscitation.[25] Even if no decision had been made and she had a further admission to PICU, a decision to move towards palliative care whilst in PICU would have given H and her parents a greater opportunity for her final care to be given in the community, either at home or in a hospice.[26]

The decision relating to M was, in many ways, more difficult than that relating to H but it still had to be made. In postponing a decision the medical team gave her parents time to spend with her. This time also enabled them to build up a level of trust with the medical team and for the team to gain a greater understanding of her prognosis, which could be used to inform further discussions.

Had a mutually agreed decision not been made between M's parents and the medical team a further avenue of resolution could have been employed; the hospital's clinical ethics committee. Clinical ethics committees are made up of both professional and lay members who have an interest and developing skill in medical ethics. The committee will not make a binding decision but rather provide both an ethical framework in which factors relating to a decision can be discussed and support for those making the decision, including members of the multi-professional team, the patient and their family.[27] A further aspect of such a referral is that it provides another means by which a natural break in discussions can be created, enabling all those involved to step back, to work together in caring for the child and to strengthen their partnership of care.

An outsider may have considered that M was suffering unnecessary harm whilst waiting for a decision to be made, particularly as the final decision was to withdraw care. She gained nothing from this time other than to receive an additional period of intensive care. How could this be acting in M's best interests? This question can be considered in a number ways: first, that it was in M's best interests that the correct decision was made for her; second, her best interests continued to be intimately intertwined with that of the family and therefore had to

---

25 There is considerable development in palliative care for children including personal resuscitation plans (Wolff, A., Browne, J. and Whitehouse, W.P. 2011. Personal resuscitation plans and end of life planning for children with disability and life-limiting/life-threatening conditions. *Archives of Diseases in Childhood*, 96, 42–8) and the development of end of life care pathways (Fraser, J., Harris, N., Berringer, A.J., Prescott, H. and Finlay, F. 2010. Advanced care planning in children with life-limiting conditions: the Wishes Document. *Archives of Diseases in Childhood*, 95, 79–82; and Johnson, M. (ed.). 2011. *A Care Pathway to Support Extubation within a Children's Palliative Care Framework*. Bristol: Association for Children's Palliative Care.

26 Fraser, L.K., Miller, M., Draper, E.S., McKinney, P.A. and Parslow, R.C. 2010. Place of death and palliative care following discharge from paediatric intensive care units. *British Medical Journal* [Online]. Available at: adc.bmj.com. 1136/adc.2009.178269 [accessed 31 March, 2011].

27 Further information can be obtained from the UK Clinical Ethics Network at www.ethics-network.org.uk.

be considered together with her family; and third, that high-quality intensive care and the best interests of the child are such that M should not have been suffering pain or significant discomfort. It is more likely that M's family, watching on as she received intensive care, were suffering more than her.

Conclusion

It is very easy with hindsight to look critically at decisions made on a PICU but it is rare that a decision is right or wrong in absolute terms. More often a decision is the best available for the child in the context of her health and well-being at that particular point in time. At another time, or in a slightly different context, another decision may be more appropriate, but that is in the realm of speculation and not practical decision-making.

Even as we look back on the case studies of H and M, we may wonder if we could have made different decisions or the same decision earlier. The families of patients such as H and M will be looking back at the same narrative from another perspective and maybe asking if they should have made the same decision or deferred the decision to give their child more of a chance. The finality of end of life decision-making makes 'what if?' questions all the more poignant, more likely to be considered and difficult to reconcile. No wonder that families who participate in these decisions suffer as a result. This does not mean that they should not be involved but rather that support should be put in place for them once the decision is made and in the months and years thereafter.

The work of a PICU continues. There will be more children like H and M to care for and decisions such as the ones described in this chapter will remain an everyday reality. These decisions will never be easy, they will have profound consequences and there will be disagreements between parents who want their child to receive ongoing medical interventions and medical teams who believe these interventions would fulfil no purpose. As time passes advances in health care will change the parameters in which decisions are made but not their nature.

This chapter has provided a framework within which end of life discussions can be held. There is a narrative of care in a PICU with families and staff moving forward together to provide the best possible care for each child. For some, discussions relating to end of life decisions form an important part of this narrative and should be seen within this context.

Chapter 10

The Story of Isabel

Sabine Vanacker

Introduction

Our daughter Isabel died at the age of four and a half as a result of Tay-Sachs disease. Tay-Sachs is an extremely rare, degenerative and terminal illness arising from a genetic mutation in both carrier parents. It is one of a range of lysosomal storage diseases with similarly devastating effects, resulting from 'a common biochemical defect: the inability of the body cells to dispose of certain metabolic waste products'.[1] As the child grows older, these 'waste products' build up in the cells to disastrous effects: it causes a variety of symptoms and, in the case of Tay-Sachs disease, mainly affects the nerve cells. Gradually the child loses all motor and cognitive skills until they die, generally between the ages of two and five, and often from respiratory infections or epilepsy. All through Isabel's illness, we were under the care of the Sheffield Children's Hospital, now the Sheffield Children's NHS Foundation Trust. Organized by our consultant and our specialist nurse, this care was very extensive. It involved at any one time a social worker, physiotherapists, occupational therapists, play specialists and a team of overnight nurses. Initially Sheffield Social Services organized this team. Later, their role was taken over by a much-loved and dedicated neurological home nursing team. We were also supported by many doctors and other specialists at the Children's Hospital; these included the mortuary staff and the bereavement counsellor who helped us during the difficult years after Isabel died.

Isabel's was a 'normal' birth. She was a breech baby, born by Caesarean section in February 2000. A lovely, black-haired baby, she came home equipped with a frighteningly healthy pair of lungs. She reached her milestones normally until the age of about ten months. At a less conscious level, however, we had started to notice small differences in her responses and reactions from children of the same age. At about ten months, she did not sit up confidently but used her arms to steady herself. Her nursery also reported that she did not appear to 'track' people and there was developmental delay of her fine motor skills. A few months earlier, we had noticed that at times she became distressed when we put her on her changing mat. This was initially put down to a cold and possible ear pain, but we

---

1   Borfitz, J.M. and Margolis, M. (no publication date given). *The Home Care Book: A Parent's Guide to Caring for Children with Progressive Neurological Diseases*. Brookline, MA: National Tay-Sachs and Allied Diseases Association, at p. 38.

now know this to be the typical 'startle' reflex in Tay-Sachs children, who have a sensitivity to movement that increases over time. Alarmed over the Christmas period, we saw a Belgian paediatrician for an assessment while over for a family visit. We also received a referral to a paediatrician in Sheffield. Just past her first birthday, Isabel was diagnosed in the Sheffield Children's Hospital with Tay-Sachs disease. Isabel was very, very unlucky. We were relatively lucky that we received a diagnosis so quickly.

When Isabel was diagnosed with her illness (and indeed now), we felt that it was an outrageous trick of fate, offensive in the casual genetic elimination of our daughter, a response undoubtedly shared by all parents of children who have died. It was the 'insidious, implacable theft of a life', as Susan Sontag phrases it in connection with the young TB victims of the nineteenth century.[2] The consultants at the hospital who had diagnosed Isabel's condition rang my husband David for a meeting at our GP's surgery. Unluckily I was away for the week but David preferred not to postpone the meeting. When I got home from my trip, David first let me recover and then told me at the breakfast table, Isabel on our lap. The doctors had given him as much information as he wanted. They had explained and re-explained Isabel's diagnosis and prognosis, and then had given him the time to ask questions, letting him steer the conversation. Our unstable, fragile little family went to ground for the next week, both of us taking time off work and spending it with Isabel. Undoubtedly, there was shock but, apart from a number of crying sessions, we soon developed a ritual during those days, going out to lunch, listening to the radio and playing with Isabel. One-year-olds demand attention and Isabel was still as lovely and delightful: we felt at the time that she helped us through this period. She was a very smiley little girl and still wanted entertaining, cuddles, nappy changes and food.

David (and most of our friends) researched the Internet and contacted organizations such as Climb UK (Children Living with Inherited Metabolic Diseases) and a specialist organization in the US, the National Association for Tay-Sachs and Allied Diseases (NTSAD).[3] Via the NTSAD website, he found DJ's Website, a site written by Davis Yang and Akari Yamada, the Chicago parents of four-year-old DJ.[4] Written with acceptance, serenity and a positive outlook, this site provided the most useful information delineating the possible progress of Tay-Sachs disease. It offered practical care advice as well as many suggestions for creating good, happy memories. It was shocking reading nevertheless. Using this

---

2   Sontag, S. 1991. *Illness as Metaphor and Aids and Its Metaphors*. London: Penguin, p. 4.

3   *The National Information Centre for Metabolic Diseases: A resource for young people, adults, families and professionals*. 2011. Available at: http://www.climb.org.uk/, last update 19/04/2011 [accessed 19 April 2011]; and National Tay-Sachs and Allied Diseases Association, Inc. 2011. Available at: http://www.ntsad.org/ [accessed 19 April 2011].

4   Yang, D. and Yamada, A. 2003. *D.J.'s Home Page*. Available at: http://www. djhomepage.com/ [accessed 19 April 2011].

site, and a number of parents' articles, David devised a timeline of what we could expect to happen to Isabel: the arrival of epileptic fits, an increased loss of control over her muscles until she could no longer swallow or cough, the feeding tubes, the bowel problems, the danger of chest infections, the gradual loss of sight and her ability to react to us, the loss of her smile and, in the end, perhaps her ability to recognize us. At the same time, it all remained theoretical and there was a sense of phoney war as we settled in on a schedule of doctors' appointments and visits by nurses, social workers, play specialists and occupational therapists.

It is impossible to decide when we 'accepted' Isabel's future death or, for that matter, whether we accept it now. Even now, it is almost unbelievable that we had Isabel and that she died. In fact, we feel that, on her behalf, we should refuse to accept that she had such a short, difficult and often painful life. Moreover, we have learnt, also from other bereaved parents, that it is impossible to come to a standstill on how we feel about her death. While we undoubtedly have come through the worst of the bereavement process, because we are much stronger than in those terrible early years, we both feel that our relationship with Isabel is ongoing and that our feelings about her illness and death too are ever changeable. These feelings will never come to an end, to a point from which we can consider her death objectively and at a distance. Moreover, this is only the experience of one child and one set of parents. The NTSAD Home Care Book takes care to point out: '[e]ach individual handles his or her situation in a unique and personal way',[5] and there are many more valid responses than ours. As a result, this is only a temporary, provisional and incomplete set of ideas and responses about Isabel's disease, her death and those periods when she became very ill and we had to consider end of life questions and decisions.

Isabel's Illness

In our early conversations with medical staff, the language that dominated was often a language of acceptance, of preparedness, a language of the present strangely reaching towards the future. In the beginning the nurses, doctors and occupational therapists emphasized that we had to learn now what Isabel liked and enjoyed, since she would be less and less able to indicate it. It was suggested to us regularly by the staff that we should not delay in taking pictures and videotapes to create memories of ourselves with Isabel. It is a strange feeling to be living at once on the surface of an ephemeral present, while trying to create deep and lasting memories for the future, an odd sense of future belatedness.

Illnesses occur in a context, as Susan Sontag has described so eloquently in the case of TB sufferers and those living with Aids.[6] Isabel's first big crisis, too, is coloured by the context. In September 2001, we went on a brief family holiday

---

5   Borfitz and Margolis, *supra* n. 1, at p. iv.
6   Sontag, *supra* n. 2.

to Paris, a bit foolhardy given that many Tay-Sachs children develop epilepsy around this age. A few days before we left Isabel suffered a few small epileptic fits, small 'absences', and we duly set off to Paris with precautionary prescriptions of Epilim and Midazolam. However, after a few days, Isabel's absences became more frequent and we became increasingly worried. Then, one afternoon in a French café, we heard planes had crashed into the twin towers of the World Trade Centre. We spent the last two days of our time in Paris watching television, ringing the Children's Hospital in Sheffield and monitoring Isabel. It was a strange alignment of experiences: Isabel showing the first frightening symptoms of her illness and the shocking images of outrageous death and chaos in New York. On the day of our return to England, Isabel stopped being able to swallow and we had to take her from the airport straight to the hospital, which had prepared a bed for her. It took four months to get Isabel's epilepsy under control, when we were delighted to discover that her smile returned. When we finally got her home, walking up the path to our house after her long stay in hospital, she suddenly realized she was home and was clearly so happy.

Isabel's situation was full of contradiction, irony and paradox. We enjoyed our life with her; she was lovely and loving; she allowed us to meet so many great people, nurses, doctors and the parents of other 'poorly' children. The contradiction was that we experienced, at the same time, feelings of loss and grief and constant thoughts about a death foretold. As parents, we settled into a pattern that we started to recognize. As we noticed small changes and deteriorations in Isabel's condition, we would experience a period of bereavement. Then we would note to each other that Isabel's condition had worsened a little, she would have lost the ability to do something for instance, and then we would get used to the new situation and settle in as if this was how things would be from now on.

Just as paradoxically, Isabel's relationship to her body changed and developed: as she grew into a young child, she seemed to become more comfortable in a body that was also failing her. As she became older, she would simultaneously both lose existing skills and learn new abilities. On the one hand, Isabel developed 'normally', from an infant to a more confident and self-contained toddler, from a toddler to a wiser, more experienced, emotionally balanced little girl. At the same time, she would lose skills and abilities, the ability to sit unaided, to use her hands, to turn her head, to see things. Yet she also 'grew' into her illness, learning new tricks to cope with the excess of saliva in her mouth for instance and learning to cough better. Even though she was less able to move and do things, her personality would come out more clearly, a charismatic little girl, a wise little girl who often appeared to us so admirable, so tolerant, so accepting, so loving, so able to tie people to her and make new friends. Most of all, even though she could do very little independently, we loved her body, the tiny little birthmark on her hand, the rounded, portable lovely package she was as a toddler, the tall child she became and always the imprint of her head on our shoulder as we sat with her in the rocking chair for cuddles. Although she could do increasingly little, sometimes, as if by chance, her hand would wind up on ours as if she was making opportunistic use of gravity.

When Isabel was older and more advanced in her illness, it became increasingly difficult to describe her life to work colleagues and to friends who did not know her. You would explain that she could not do much at all by herself but people would ask you what toys she liked to play with. Then you would start again and explain to a shocked colleague or friend that she could not really swallow, so handling dolls was out of the question (even though she liked the touch of dolls or having her arms and legs moved or having her hand put against your or her own face). People removed from the situation had, we felt, an image of Isabel's illness that both over- and underestimated the situation. They would picture a small patient, like saintly little Eve in *Uncle Tom's Cabin*, a beautiful and tragic child. They would mistakenly picture us continuously steeped in grief, when really her illness, her disability, the continuous presence of nurses and health staff, was normality for Isabel and us, a medical bubble at some remove from the rest of the world. We would try to do our jobs, we would enjoy talking to the nurses and hearing about their families and boyfriends, enjoy sitting with Isabel on our lap, having her snoozing or we would feel frustrated during those months that she was (still) coughing or if she were breathing fast. At the same time, people underestimated the situation. They were unable to comprehend how busy we were, how little time we had to play with Isabel or be with her in the daily race to give her medicines, to do chest physiotherapy, to ensure she had her milk, to keep an eye on the colour of her secretions and to make sure that the whole, intricate timetable did not collapse around our ears.

In the final year of her life, we realized that more and more our days were about failure, failing to do all the things in her daily schedule. We had a lovely fourth birthday party but I had been too busy to wash her hair (still such a cause for shame). Enjoying some time in the garden sometimes meant not quite doing her physiotherapy early enough; spending more time on physiotherapy meant not giving her a nice time in the garden or being late with medications and milk. We slowly realized that, as time went on, these failures inevitably would mount up, that someone would make a mistake. At our most negative, we felt like fake parents, parents with no future, two people merely pretending to be parents.

As David had found in his investigations early on and from the documentation sent to us by Climb and especially the NTSAD, there was a certain expected progression for Isabel's illness and there was the constant anticipation of her death, a certainty, however notional and theoretical. We 'beat ourselves up' with very negative feelings. There were shameful projections of failure. I felt I would really have failed if Isabel died before a certain age, for instance, however much the doctors and nurses emphasized that a lot depended on chance: how many viruses she encountered and how her body responded. In part, Isabel's illness was an experience of constantly failing and constant neediness: wanting to sit down, wanting to escape, anxious about things happening to her and relieved when a nurse came to take over and to buffer us a bit from the anxiety. Our feelings changed continuously, from self-pitying crying during quiet Saturday mornings, to a belief that we wanted to stretch out this time forever, to the awareness that we might not manage it and the realization, after her death, that we missed the Isabel we knew but not the illness that was part of her. However, we also know that we were very lucky, very much cushioned by all the nurses, our lovely respite carer Cathy, the wonderful NHS and the many people looking after us.

'Little Chats' and Quality of Life

'Illness is the night-side of life, a more onerous citizenship. Everyone who is born holds dual citizenship, in the kingdom of the well and in the kingdom of the sick': Susan Sontag's words seem so apt for Isabel, for whom qualities of 'wellness' and 'sickness' interflowed and existed simultaneously.[7] 'Normality' for Isabel was radically different from the everyday lives of other children. As an increasingly disabled little girl, Isabel also made us think differently about the essence of human beings. Our society favours certain qualities in its perception of the individual: autonomy, rationality, a capacity for independent action and agency, the ability to communicate and express a self, all qualities that we try to nurture even in very little children. Increasingly, Isabel's life set limits to these qualities, to her autonomy, to her agency and to her self-expression. Isabel's existence was neither autonomous nor independent and yet in a very effective way she continued to influence us and act upon us. The expression of her emotions and feelings occurred through smaller and smaller signals and yet they were still there. Sometimes it was hard to assess how she felt, most worryingly whether she was uncomfortable or in pain. However, when we were all alert, we would sense her signal ('pick me up') from her bed and somehow she would get across that she was happy to see us. We knew what she liked and disliked because we remembered it. Sometimes we may not have known what she thought about us, although sometimes we did, but we knew that, as a little girl, she wanted to stay with us, her parents. Despite her ability to do very little, there was a charisma there, a sense of identity and the expression of a sense of self.

Knowing Isabel, our perception of that abstract concept 'quality of life' has changed and become more fluid. In our conversations with nurses and doctors they frequently pointed out that we, the nurses and carers who knew her well, were the specialists in Isabel's case and that we knew what normality was for her. For the average healthy child, admission to hospital and intensive care is often the result of a catastrophic, perhaps unacceptable decline in health. For a child as naturally frail as Isabel was in the last two years of her life, quality of life did not mean independent play, self-determined activity or agency. Normality for Isabel meant enjoying cuddles, sitting on someone's lap, perhaps snoozing, looking at her coloured lights, enjoying a massage, listening to music and sounds, enjoying

---

7   Sontag, *supra* n. 2, at p. 3.

a bath, having her hand made to touch interesting textures, perhaps seeing her favourite dolls and definitely having her favourite nurses and carers talking to her, singing to her and telling her stories.

Throughout her illness, our doctors and nurses would undertake what we all eventually called 'little chats', those difficult conversations about Isabel's future, taking place in small side rooms off wards and clinics, an unthreatening, intimate, chintzy environment with hankies, a big comfy sofa for the parents and a hard chair for the professionals. Early on in her illness, they would try to get us thinking about the end of her life, about what the circumstances might be and how we might feel and respond. So many of the medical staff, all specialist doctors and nurses in neurology or terminal care, were so genuinely gifted in talking about this hard topic, allowing themselves to be emotional and yet professional and authoritative. Early on, we discussed the end of Isabel's life in our consultant's office, with Isabel still sitting upright in her buggy. The consultant sought to make this future a little real for us by investigating the possibilities: Isabel might die in her sleep, she might have a terminal epileptic fit, or, most likely, she would die of a chest infection. Inexperienced, we were shocked to hear that we might have to make the decision not to prolong her life while she was alert and awake and struggling to breathe. If we felt we could not make this decision at any stage, the consultant reassured us, the doctors were there to take the responsibility but it was important that we thought about these scenarios. Hard as it was, we did and we do appreciate the doctors, nurses and carers who undertook these conversations with us. It was something we needed to hear and hear several times, something we needed to think about for a longer time and it did help to prepare us. I had a similar conversation with our respite care lady in a quiet corner of a department store restaurant. Very carefully and sensitively, Cathy brought up the question of what we wanted to happen if Isabel were to die in her care. Did we want to come and pick her up? Did we want Cathy and her husband to bring Isabel home to us? We discussed where Isabel would die: would we stay in hospital or bring her home?

In her short life, Isabel had several intensive care unit (ICU) admissions when these decisions came closer. Perhaps because we had explored these issues in many conversations before, we always felt there was full consultation from our doctors. We felt they listened to us and that the decisions about Isabel were collaborative, even if we needed to debate and disagree. Inevitably, looking around an ICU, for instance, you became aware that there was a limited number of beds, that there would be quiet periods with lots of free beds and very busy periods when the unit was full. Although no doctor or nurse ever raised the issue at all, we would be aware of the quandary we presented to the doctors and nurses in ICU, of the unspoken anxiety that we might be in denial and that we might never agree to let Isabel go. One nurse described being ventilated after an operation, being half awake and hearing the incessant, frightening noise of an ICU unit, which also brought home to us that it was not a decision to undertake lightly.

Two Decisions about Quality of Life

Just before her third birthday, we had to consider these issues. Isabel wound up in Intensive Care and needed intubation because of breathing problems. After a few days on ventilation, the day before her birthday, the doctors decided to extubate to avoid damage to her lungs. However, once the ventilation tube was removed, she coped very badly: she spent her third birthday struggling for breath while we hastily scaled down the birthday party that our nurses had organized for her. In the middle of the night, we had a discussion with the consultant on-call who did not really know Isabel. This consultant felt re-intubation was no longer appropriate and asked us to consider letting Isabel go. Isabel would get some morphine to ease her and this would probably result in her eventually stopping breathing. At this stage and based on our experience of how well Isabel had been just before her illness, we felt she might recover a good quality of life. She was clearly alert and in distress but she had, only a few days before, been quite well, enjoyed cuddles, enjoyed her massages at the carer's, enjoyed looking at her lights, and we felt it would be too soon and anomalous to let her go. Together with her carer and other medical staff we felt that Isabel's illness meant that, in comparison to other children, she needed to do everything more slowly and could not be rushed. We felt we needed to discuss Isabel's situation with the consultant who knew her best and, in the middle of the night, he got into his car to come and see us in the hospital. We discussed the situation with him and, when he went to see Isabel, she gave him a long, hard stare. He agreed with us and re-intubated her for a few more days.

While we waited to try to take her off the ventilator again, the nurses started to prepare us for the likelihood that she would not manage to breathe independently and that this might mean making the decision to let her die. On the Sunday, Isabel's nurse insisted that we change her bed for a larger bed, allowing one of us to sleep next to Isabel. It seemed strange at the time but now we realize what a good idea it was, considered from the perspective of a little girl alone in a bed. Over that Sunday, this nurse managed to calm us down and to start accepting that Isabel might not make it and that we had to start thinking about making her last hours as comfortable as possible. The next day, the ventilator was withdrawn while Isabel was on my lap. Like the trooper she was, she did fine and breathed by herself without any problems. After a few days, she went to a ward. Isabel had lost a lot of weight, she seemed drawn but she had an ecstatic hour in her ward room one day, when she clearly felt suddenly so much better and smiled and crowed with delight. I ran into the corridor and dragged a doctor in to make him see 'quality of life', how she could be when she felt well, how she loved to be with us and around us.

Isabel went home and lived for another year and a half. Both then, and later, we thought frequently about our decision and about this extra year. Before and after she died, we weighed up our decision, we tried to estimate whether it had been right for Isabel, whether we had made her suffer too much for an extra year. On balance, we still feel it was the right decision. After we returned home, Isabel had a good summer. Thanks to the new home nursing team, she had fewer serious infections and managed to stay out of hospital for most of this year. We actually started to feel she could just go on. She had a magnificent fourth birthday, clearly sensing that we were proud of her, that she had done something very special. She enjoyed her day, being held by her favourite carers and nurses: Cathy put on the blue check shirt that Isabel liked so much and at the end of the day she was tired and snoozed a little while being held.

In the few months before her death, however, Isabel's health declined yet again. Occasionally, she would pause between breaths and it would take a little nudge or a touch to remind her to breathe again. More importantly, we all noted that she started to sleep more often and for longer, that the chest physiotherapy would tire her out and that her moments awake became shorter and rarer. When we talked about this, we felt the balance had shifted. The issue of having a Do Not Resuscitate Order was raised with us. Part of the reason for this was to give the night nurses, alone with Isabel without colleagues or doctors, clear guidance. We decided that, if Isabel 'forgot' to breathe or had a terminal epileptic fit, the nurse would not resuscitate her but let her quietly go: it was made clear that this did not mean that Isabel would not continue to receive care, treatment and medication but that, in a catastrophic event, we would not revive her. Eventually in June, Isabel became seriously ill as the result of a totally unexpected problem: peritonitis owing to the inevitable deterioration of her stomach lining. It took a few days, while we were in hospital, for the doctors and surgeons to identify the problem, but on the Sunday they told us that they really had no further options and that there was nothing they could do. We went to bed in the parents' room distraught, but also feeling rather numb.

The next morning I got up early to go downstairs and see Isabel. While I was there, one of her doctors came in. She had been on duty all night and must have been tired but came and sat with us. It felt like she was taking the conversation very slowly. There were long gaps in our conversation and I remember she waited very patiently for me to give my responses, giving me time to let me think. Suddenly I clearly realized that we should take Isabel home and that, rather than suggesting this to me, she had really helped me to come to this conclusion myself. I asked 'Should we go home?' and whether there was enough time to go home. She said yes, she thought there was. When David came downstairs soon after, we decided to go. A few hours later, we went home by ambulance with several members of our nursing team. When we got home, two of the nurses went shopping for food, wine, cheeses, bread, comfort food and cakes. The next day Isabel's temperature kept mounting. I suggested that we give her something to get her temperature down and again realized with a small shock that we were no longer about this. This was no longer about curing but about palliative care, about keeping her as comfortable and pain-free as possible. Isabel spent her last day on our laps on the sofa where we had always held her, while some of her nurses and her doctor came by. Isabel even recognized their voices. We felt that the day stretched endlessly. With hindsight, we realize that we were, in reality, unable to take it all in, we felt 'in a zone'. Strangely, it felt as if this, too, was yet another 'dip' in Isabel's health, just another phase in her illness that we would get used to in a day that would last forever. Towards six o'clock, just after we had moved Isabel from my arms to David's, she died. Strangely, it felt like an independent action: not that Isabel was taken but that she left. It seemed as if this little girl, who could do so little for herself, had decided and her decision was to go.

After her death, we moved Isabel to the Children's Hospital where we could go and see her in the mortuary. Surprisingly, to us, in the week before the funeral we settled into an old and very similar pattern. A member of our nursing team would pick us up in her car and we would go and visit our daughter in hospital, in a small cosy children's bedroom, surrounded with toys and child-friendly pictures, while the nurse waited with the lovely women who looked after the children in the mortuary and the bereavement counsellor. We would be left with Isabel for as long as we liked, holding her, having a cry and then we would leave her, knowing that we would see her the next day. On the way out of the hospital, David would buy a Tunnock's tea cake each for all three of us and the nurse would drive us home to the organizing, planning and decision-making. It was a restful moment every day and something we looked forward to and needed to have. It really helped during those few days to still have her body, to be able to hold her and look after her a little. We would note the small daily changes and we would realize slowly, every day more, that she was gone. Visiting Isabel after her death was important and part of a continuous leave-taking that only started on the day she died. For weeks and months afterwards, we would still feel an urge to report on Isabel and it felt odd that people no longer asked us how she was.

Isabel's death is now almost seven years ago and, in common with other bereaved parents, we realize now more than ever how important it is to keep our bond with Isabel, to keep her memory alive and strong, and to keep reminding others of her life, her character, her charisma and her presence in the world.

Acknowledgements

With thanks to the amazing staff of the Sheffield Children's Hospital and, as always, to wonderful Cathy Edwards.

Index